Confessions of
a Literary
Archaeologist

ALSO BY CARLTON LAKE

A Dictionary of Modern Painting (editor)

Life with Picasso (with Françoise Gilot)

In Quest of Dali

Baudelaire to Beckett:
A Century of French Art & Literature

No Symbols Where None Intended:
Samuel Beckett at the
Humanities Research Center

Carlton Lake

Confessions of a Literary Archaeologist

A NEW DIRECTIONS BOOK

Grateful acknowledgment is given for permission to quote from *The Autobiography of Alice B. Toklas* by Gertrude Stein. Copyright 1933 and renewed 1961 by Alice B. Toklas. Reprinted by permission of Random House, Inc.

Manufactured in the United States of America
New Directions books are printed on acid-free paper
First published clothbound by New Directions in 1990
Published simultaneously in Canada by Penguin Books Canada Limited

Library of Congress Cataloging-in-Publication Data

Lake, Carlton.
    Confessions of a literary archaeologist / Carlton Lake.
       p.   cm.
    ISBN 0-8112-1130-4 (alk. paper)
    1. Lake, Carlton—Library.   2. Book collecting—France—History—20th century.   3. Manuscripts—Collectors and collecting—France—History—20th century.   4. French literature—Bibliography—Methodology—History—20th century.   5. Arts, French—Bibliography—Methodology—History—20th century.   6. French literature—Manuscripts—Collectors and collecting—History—20th century.   7. Arts, French—Manuscripts—Collectors and collecting—History—20th century.   8. University of Texas at Austin. Humanities Research Center—History.   I. Title.
Z997.L189   1990
018'.2'0976431—dc20
                                                  89-13707
                                                 CIP

New Directions Books are published for James Laughlin
by New Directions Publishing Corporation,
80 Eighth Avenue, New York 10011

To the like-minded reader
for whom this book was written

———————

ACKNOWLEDGMENTS

Most of the books, letters, manuscripts, and drawings discussed in these pages, as well as the majority of the photographs used as illustrations, are in the French collections at the Harry Ransom Humanities Research Center of the University of Texas at Austin. I am grateful to the Center and to its Director, Thomas F. Staley, for making them available for the purposes of this book and for allowing me to use those passages which I have adapted from HRHRC documents and publications. My thanks go also to the private owners who loaned photographs not available in the Center's collections and to estate representatives who granted permission to quote from material under copyright. Translations are my own.

C.L.

Contents

Foreword

For years now, people who know something about what I've been doing as both a private and an institutional collector have suggested I write a book about some of my adventures. I've always said, "Yes, one day," and then let the idea fade away until the next time somebody brought it up. Eventually I came to realize that writing about those adventures would be a means of renewing the pleasure and reliving the excitement they had brought me.

But how could I tell about the ways of a literary archaeologist whose life, across half a century, has involved digging up and bringing back so many hundreds of thousands of books and papers and not bury the reader alive? Arbitrarily I decided I would write ten chapters, each of which would tell a story in its own fashion and, finally, come together with the other nine to paint a picture. Episodes crowded into my mind. I listed them all and made my first brief notes for each one. When I began to write, I found that the choice and the order were determined by an indefinable yet irresistible pull on the Ouija board of the heart.

En route to ten, my plan broke down—not in spirit but in number—when one of the chapters, through what the insurance companies call "inherent vice," proved to be not one but really two. So ten became eleven, which pleased me: I've always liked that number. But whether ten or eleven, these chapters must in the end let you understand what there is about a book or a manuscript or an archive that will make a collector lust after it, often complicate his life endlessly in the process of tracking it down and hauling it in, and even sometimes—when it's just about ready to fall into his lap—get up and walk away without it. Have they done the job? I'll leave that for you to decide.

C. L.

Chapter 1

The late Dr. A. S. W. Rosenbach, a scholarly and imaginative Philadelphia bookseller who helped form many of the great American rare-book collections and accumulated a moderate-sized fortune in the process, once made the claim that "after love, book collecting is the most exhilarating sport of all." In more than a half-century of rubbing elbows and knocking heads with book collectors, book dealers, book scouts, and their by-blows in various corners of the rare-book world, I have yet to find a single *true* bookman who would agree with the Doctor on that point: they would all, I think, insist he had the order reversed.

I say "true" in the theological sense of having the vocation—not just being in the book business as a way of making a living, or having more money than one needs and finding the collecting of rare books of one type or another a creditable way of displaying it (a motivation that could fairly be applied to the formation of many art collections, for example). No, when books are in one's blood—the searching, tracing, digging, collating, the whole archaeological range of gathering them together and preserving them, in response to whatever compulsive demand—love (at least the sporting variety to which Dr. R. was referring) can be counted on to start only a relatively small number of fires.

In my own case, the affliction took root early, triggered by two practices: (1) reading, non-stop, everything I could lay my hands on at home—*Don Quixote* and *The Pilgrim's Progress*, the Complete Works of Shakespeare, Dickens, and Balzac—and (2) browsing in secondhand bookstores and when I ran out of those, in plain old secondhand stores that had a few shelves filled with books that sold for ten or fifteen cents apiece. By the time I reached the university, at the age of sixteen, and broadened my base of operations to Boston and Cambridge, I was

1

gobbling up great chunks of "new" authors—including Voltaire, Rabelais, Montaigne, and Molière, in that order.

There had been great indecision in my family about where I should go to college. I leaned, a bit too passively, toward Harvard and, in the end, missed the deadline. I enrolled at Boston University, a sobersided Methodist institution where some of my elders had gone, and told myself I would transfer to Harvard later on. I put down roots in the Back Bay and soon became addicted to the nearby Exeter Theater, which showed most of the foreign films and art films that came to Boston. I spent many class hours in that noble, quasi-Romanesque pile and became convinced I was getting a good education. But I commuted often to Harvard Square, where I ushered at Mrs. E. K. Rand's French movies over on Divinity Avenue, attended lectures by Professor André Morize, and—above all—hung out in the bookshops that have always been one of Cambridge's special treats. Within a year or two, abetted by an indulgent grandmother, I was energetically collecting the modern poets, essayists, and novelists that I was now beginning to read: Ezra Pound, Norman Douglas, James Joyce, D. H. Lawrence, Aldous Huxley, T. S. Eliot, and many more. Soon I began to be chiefly interested in the great nineteenth-century French poets: Baudelaire, Verlaine, Rimbaud, Mallarmé.

One day in the spring of 1936, at the Dunster House Bookshop opposite the Lampoon in Plympton Street, off Harvard Square, I came across the catalogue of the sale at auction of the library of the late Harry B. Smith, scheduled to take place five days from then at the American Art Association Anderson Galleries in New York City. Smith was probably the most prolific and most successful of all the writers of musical comedies for the American stage. He had collaborated with Jerome Kern, Irving Berlin, Franz Lehar, Sigmund Romberg, Victor Herbert, and Florenz Ziegfield and, obviously, had made a good deal of money—enough, in fact, to attract the interest of Dr. Rosenbach, who sold him first editions and letters of the Brontës, the Brownings, Byron, Shelley, Coleridge, and Dickens, among other nineteenth-century stalwarts. I flipped through the catalogue with curiosity but no great enthusiasm until I came to a little section headed "French Literature," with an alphabet of its own, and then my heart began to beat faster. Almost immediately one book had caught my eye and held it. It was a first edition—1857—of Baudelaire's *Les Fleurs du mal*, certainly the greatest book of poetry published in France in the nineteenth century (and many people would delete the phrase "in France" from that sentence). It was an exceptionally desirable copy in that it had a presentation inscription from Baudelaire to Nadar, the pioneer photographer, balloonist, caricaturist, and writer who was one of Baudelaire's three or four closest friends. Nothing gives a book more savor than to have an association *that* intimate made a part of it. There were, in addition, several markings in Baudelaire's hand correcting textual errors, and among a group of autograph letters tipped in was one addressed by Baudelaire to the book's publisher, Auguste Poulet-Malassis, at that time confined in Clichy prison. Two lots further along was the description of something listed as "Works": the 1868 edition of Baudelaire's *Oeuvres Complètes*, but here rather *incomplètes*, with only four of the required seven volumes. A copy of the Collected Works has moderate interest when complete, but almost none incomplete. However, someone along the route of ownership had inserted the corrected proof sheets, from the first edition, of *Les Fleurs du mal*, of one of the longer and more celebrated poems in the book, "Les Litanies de Satan." Obviously those proofs didn't belong in an incomplete set of the Collected Works, but they *did* belong with that exceptional copy of the first edition.

I had never been to a book auction and the fact that it was in New York didn't simplify matters. The owner of the Dunster House Bookshop, a gentle, bibulous bookman named Al Delacey, arranged for a New York colleague to accompany me to the sale. I had to have that copy of *Les Fleurs du mal* and I intended to get all of the Baudelaire lots while I was at it.

At the sale, the New York dealer, for whom this was routine, sat beside me and did the bidding. I didn't see him bid, but when the auctioneer's gavel fell after his chant for *Les Fleurs du mal* had stopped, I whispered nervously, "Who bought it?"

"You did," he said and continued to fix his attention on the auctioneer, already working on the next lot. He bought all the books I wanted and after the sale—it was an evening session—we went to a Longchamps restaurant nearby and toasted the occasion.

When I got back to Boston, I learned that the corrected proof sheets of "Les Litanies de Satan" were a real treasure. When I first examined them before the sale, I had seen that there were autograph changes of some kind on almost every line on both sheets of proof. What I had not known until after returning home and digging a little deeper was that the original typeset version shown on the proof sheets differed from the published text and had never appeared in that form. Beyond that, the version as corrected by Baudelaire differed from the one in the first edition and it had never been published, either. Now, thanks to those proof sheets, I knew that there were at least three versions of that poem rather than just one.

Everybody needs some kind of revelation—illumination—to set his feet in the right path. Saul of Tarsus had his on the road to Damascus; Paul Valéry had his one stormy night in Genoa in 1892, and Samuel Beckett, his, as he wandered about the Dublin harbor district on an equally stormy night after the war. (He hints at it, in disguised form, in *Krapp's Last Tape*.) At a less cosmic level, mine came at that Harry B. Smith sale in New York and was reinforced by my study of those proof sheets from *Les Fleurs du mal*. After a few years of amiable but aimless collecting, I had bought an exceptional copy of a truly great book and in doing so—with help from those corrected proof sheets—I had learned something about a great poem by a very great poet that no one had ever known before; or if they had known, had left no record of it. At that time I could quote Baudelaire's poetry—French and Latin—by the yard and become high in the process. Now I had a taste of another high: the joy that comes from finding a rare book, a unique document, a beautiful object that, along with the pleasure it gives, teaches us something entirely new. In the fifty-odd years that have passed since that sale in New York, I have experienced that high hundreds of times. It has never lost its freshness for me.

* * * * *

I had majored in Romance Languages and Literatures at Boston University and was planning to do graduate study and then teach at some small, quiet, but academically respectable college. I had graduated with highest honors and the Italian government selected me to represent the New England consular district on a summer tour (for a dozen North American graduates similarly chosen) of Italian cultural monuments, from south to north and then back south again. Our schedule allowed only one day for Bologna but we were all eager to see what we could of the University—Europe's oldest—where Dante and Petrarch and, nearly three hundred years later, Tasso had studied. And for me there was an added incentive. Just before leaving home I had received word of my appointment as Giosuè Carducci Fellow at Columbia for the following year. Carducci had lived and worked in Bologna and lectured at the University for more than forty years and had died there in 1907. The least I could do, it seemed to me, was look over the landmarks.

We had got an early start, done the sixty-three miles up from Florence in less than an hour and a half, made the most of a long morning, and then settled down to our *tagliatelle alla bolognese* at the Pappagallo in the Piazza Mercanzia. After lunch we felt decidedly less ambitious and our stroll along the arcades led to no cathedrals, no museums; only that shaded café and somnolence. We hadn't been there long, though, before I began to be troubled by the realization that I had been in Bologna for the better part of the one day we had there without having entered a single bookshop. Thoughts of what might be lying in wait for me just around the corner in this city that had been harboring poets and scholars for nearly a thousand years began to buzz around me like so many hungry mosquitoes. Only an indulgent masochist could have sat on. Pretexting a need for exercise that could have seemed plausible to no one (with the thermometer bubbling into the mid-nineties), I got up and walked out into the Square, with no other compass than my nose.

Shutters were still down on a good many shops, their owners, presumably, finding the long native siesta more appealing than the tourist trade. I passed a few new-book shops that were open, and paused briefly to look at their window displays, but a new book—considered strictly as an object—has an unripe quality that is not very exciting to a book collector, and masses of new books—clean, unread, even unopened— are apt to be a bit depressing. As the afternoon wore on, though, I had not sniffed out any more stimulating possibilities and so I entered a new-book shop in a little street not far behind the Piazza Vittorio Emmanuele. It was a small, well-shaded shop, comfortably cool. The proprietor (as I then assumed and later confirmed) made no effort to sell me a book; in fact, he took no cognizance whatever of my presence—an ideal type of bookseller. I made the tour of his shelves and, finally, finding nothing more interesting to carry away, took down a copy of a book called *La Parabola dell'Eunuco* that was causing snickers all over northern Italy that summer. On my way over to the bookseller's desk, I passed a half-open door in the rear of the shop. I poked my head inside and saw that this was the back room without which no bookshop is a bookshop. It was a larger room than the shop itself, lined with wooden cases that served, apparently, for housing reserve stock. In one corner was a long table with the customary packing materials. In another—I could just see them by craning my neck—stood a few piles of very obviously secondhand books. I continued on to the bookseller's desk. He was still immersed in his reading—a Portuguese paperbound book entitled *O Beijo—The Kiss*. When I laid my book on his desk, he raised his head. I asked him if he had any old books I could look at. He smiled apologetically.

"There are a few things in the back room," he said. "Nothing of any great importance, I'm afraid." He led me into the storeroom and pointed to the piles of books I had just seen. "I don't know that there's anything there for you but you can take a look. They're the last remnants of the stock that was here when I took over this shop last year. As you see, I sell only new books, and I've pretty well liquidated the stock that came with the shop."

By this time I was well into the first pile. It consisted mainly of reading copies of early-twentieth-century French novels—Claude Farrère, the Comtesse de Noailles, and Paul Bourget were represented, I remember.

"What are you interested in, particularly?" the bookseller asked.

"First editions of nineteenth-century French poetry," I told him.

"Oh, you won't find anything like that there," he said. "What's there has been gone over pretty carefully. I have one book that might appeal to you, though." He walked over to a narrow table beside the door, opened a drawer, and took out a small, thin volume in a rather pleasing late-nineteenth-century binding of marbled boards with a pink-cloth back-strip. He handed it to me. It was a copy of the first edition of *Odes en son honneur* by Paul Verlaine, published by Vanier in Paris in 1893, just three years before Verlaine died. It is not a very rare book as Verlaine firsts go, but it contains some of his most appealing love lyrics. Finding it in a contemporary binding signed by Paul Vié—Anatole France's binder—gave it an added dimension of interest for me. I asked him how much he wanted for it. He quoted a very reasonable price and I told him I'd take it. Did he have any others?

"Nothing more of Verlaine," he said. "I have one first edition of Baudelaire, but it's a prose work." I told him I had no prejudice against prose, especially Baudelaire's. He turned again to the drawer in the little table and brought out a small book, a duodecimo—about seven by five inches and perhaps seven-eighths of an inch thick. It was bound in dark mottled-green boards with a shallow green-morocco back and tiny green-morocco corners—a binding that recalled, without quite duplicating, a type turned out by French binders of the Romantic period. Lettered in gold across the spine was the name Baudelaire and the title of the book: *Les Paradis artificiels*. There was something about the characters in the lettering, though, that was not quite French: they were a shade too tall and too narrow for that. The leather, too, had a faintly uncharacteristic finish and was more finely pebbled than the *petits maroquins* commonly in use in France at that period. I examined the edges and opened the front cover. Internally the book was as fresh as on the day of publication in 1860, and as I began to turn the first preliminary leaves, I could feel that tingle of anticipation, that shiver of delight—what Victor Hugo, on first reading Baudelaire's *Fleurs du mal* called a *frisson*—that comes to every collector when he picks up a book that for him exudes a very special kind of perfume, one that seems to attack directly his nerve ends and start the palpitations that let him know *this* is for him.

When I reached the half title—the page preceding the title page and bearing only the book's title—the quivers quickened. In the lower left-hand corner, stamped in dark-purple ink, was an oval mark that I recognized as the cachet of the Imperial Library at Tsarskoye Selo. When I saw that, everything fell into place.

Tsarskoye Selo (the name means the Tsar's Village and has been changed by the Soviets to Dyetskoye Selo—Children's Village) was about fifteen miles south of St. Petersburg, the present-day Leningrad. Originally it was a Finnish village called Saarimois that Peter the Great had taken over at the close of the Great Northern War and presented to his wife, Catherine I. The Tsaritzas Elizabeth and Catherine II subsequently developed it to the point of magnificence and from then on it was used as a vacation retreat by the Imperial family. Rastrelli and Cameron built the *grand château* on a scale of lavishness that sought to rival Versailles, and Catherine II—Catherine the Great—added a new palace, designed by Guarenghi, for her grandson Alexander I.

Each of the monarchs added substantially to its collections, as well. Catherine II, for example, had a special fondness for the work of the painter Greuze and by the middle 1760s had become his best customer. She wanted to bring him to St. Petersburg to lend a little tone to the second-rate court painters she had inherited from her predecessor, the Empress Elizabeth, but when she wrote of her plan to Diderot, he gave her such a bad report of Mme. Greuze's temper and reputation that she finally invited Hubert Robert instead. That didn't stop her from buying more Greuzes, however. Besides her pictures she accumulated bulging portfolios of prints and drawings, probably as many as ten thousand, by her favorite French artists.

Meanwhile the book collections were growing, also. All during the eighteenth century and on into the nineteenth, the finest French illustrated books and first editions of the works of the best contemporary French writers were finding their way into the Imperial libraries, through purchase or gift. The books were published in Paris in paper wrappers and many of them—except for certain sumptuously bound presentation volumes—were sent to Russia in that form.

By the time Baudelaire published *Les Paradis artificiels*, in 1860, the Russians had been luring French artists and craftsmen to St. Petersburg for nearly a century and a half: after the death of Louis XIV in 1715, work in Paris and Versailles for artists of all kinds had fallen off to a trickle. Frenchmen by the score signed lucrative contracts with the Tsar's recruiting agent in Paris, General François Lefort, and headed for St. Petersburg to help Peter build and decorate his palaces, lay out his formal gardens and fountains, and make his "paradise," as he called it, another—and greater (as he hoped)—Versailles.

Bookbinders, too, were imported. Ateliers were set up under the direction of Paris *contre-maîtres* but staffed, in part, by Russian workers and utilizing local materials. As a result, bindings executed there followed—at a respectful distance in time—the general tradition of the French but never *were* quite French. And so here, on this copy of *Les Paradis artificiels*, were visible all the characteristic elements of the early-nineteenth-century French half binding—the glazed mottled paper used on the sides, the fine-grained morocco, the very shallow leather back (by comparison to later nineteenth-century French practice), the tiny leather corners—and yet the result was not French. It could hardly have been called Russian, either, but it was certainly a most attractive hybrid.

I remembered that in the fall of 1933, a miscellaneous grouping of books from various of the Imperial Russian libraries had been offered for sale in New York, and among them were a number from Tsarskoye Selo. They all had the benefit of their provenance and some of them had a particularly significant association interest or an especially handsome binding, but none of them had the combination of everything that this book had. Not for me, at any rate.

I sat down at the narrow table and set the book on it in order to be able to study it more carefully. I noted that its original yellow wrappers were not present. In a book published twenty-five years later than this one, their absence would be considered a defect, because by 1885 it was beginning to be pretty generally agreed that a book published unbound, in paper wrappers, should, when bound, have its wrappers bound in, untrimmed. But in 1860—since this binding was, quite clearly, strictly contemporary with the book—only a handful of amateurs had adopted the refinement of conserving the wrappers that is standard practice today. And they were not Russian monarchs; they were, in fact, Baudelaire and some of his friends, including the poet Théodore de Banville, the bibliographer Asselineau, and the publisher Poulet-Malassis—publisher of Baudelaire's masterpiece, *Les Fleurs du mal*, of *Les Paradis artificiels*, and of other books of Baudelaire's as well. Today, on the rare occasions when a book from the library of any one of them—in its delicately fashioned *demi-maroquin* by Lortic or Amand—shows up for sale, French collectors who have reached the higher levels of connoisseurship in such matters gladly pay from ten to twenty times the normal value of the book in order to have *that* copy of it.

The question of wrappers aside, then, this was undeniably a superlative copy of *Les Paradis artificiels*; the pages, as I turned them, had almost the crispness of new banknotes. I finished leafing through the book. Every page was there, in its proper order, and intact. The rare-bookman's highest praise is contained in the adjective "mint"—which conjures up the image of the newly minted coin. No purist in these matters would have termed this copy mint, since the fact of binding had changed its original condition. But in a loose-constructionist sense of the term, it would have been hard to imagine the existence of a minter one. I took another look at the binding. Apart from the faintly Gothic yet curiously appealing characters used in the lettering of Baudelaire's name and the title, a good part of the charm of the backstrip lay in the five parallel horizontal bands of glistening black calf, about a quarter of an inch wide and an inch apart, bounded by gilt fillets, that formed the basic decorative motif. When a book is handbound, the sheets are first assembled and sewn together, generally at five equidistant points across the back. Very frequently these points are indicated, in the case of a leather binding (or half binding), by the presence of five parallel raised bands. The French term for those raised bands is the equivalent of our word "nerves." When the bands are not raised over the threads, but lie flat and are, nevertheless, clearly marked in the decoration of the leather, the French call them "false nerves." This copy of *Les Paradis artificiels* had five of those false nerves, and the contrasts they brought to the binding were enormously effective; first, the tone: the black set off against the dark green; then the texture: the smoothness of the calf against the fine pebbled graining of the morocco; and finally the luster: the flush of the calf, which had been laid on with a hot iron until it glistened, against the muted dullness of the unpolished morocco.

My hands were a bit moist as I walked out into the front of the shop, to which this ideal bookseller had discreetly returned after handing me the Baudelaire. I asked him the price. It was just half the limit I was hoping not to be forced to exceed. I tried to temper my enthusiasm with small talk, and as he wrapped my three books for me, I asked him why he had changed to new books rather than carrying on the antiquarian business he had taken over.

He smiled wryly. "My predecessor failed," he said. "He was always having books stolen. Even when his customers bought them, they often ran up bills they never paid. People don't seem to steal new books very much—not here, anyway—and for some reason or other they generally pay cash."

* * * * *

It is a well-established fact—in the minds of many noncollectors—that a person who buys a book because it is a first edition or because it is bound in a certain manner or because it has a particular provenance, doesn't read his books. Generous-minded noncollectors will sometimes concede that if a book is illustrated, a collector may, on occasion, go so far as to open it to look at the pictures. Although the first edition of *Les Paradis artificiels* has no pictures to look at—nor does any subsequent, illustrated edition have any *worth* looking at—its undecorated printed pages managed to hold my interest during most of the long train ride, a few weeks later, from Genoa to Naples. I had landed at Naples at the beginning of the summer, shed a wardrobe trunk and a suitcase or two at the hotel there before starting up the peninsula, and now, with the summer behind me, was heading back to Naples to pick up my surplus baggage and the ship for New York.

Not many present-day critics would deny that Baudelaire is nineteenth-century France's greatest poet: *Les Fleurs du mal* seems each year more worthy of a stronger statement than that. And his writings on

Charles Baudelaire. *Les Fleurs du mal.* First edition, 1857: title page and half-title showing Baudelaire's presentation inscription to his friend the photographer Nadar.

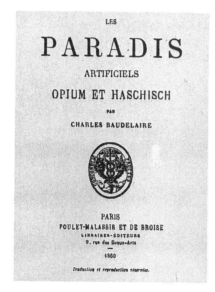

Charles Baudelaire. *Les Paradis artificiels. Opium et Haschisch.* First edition, 1860.

Charles Baudelaire by Carjat, *c.* 1862.

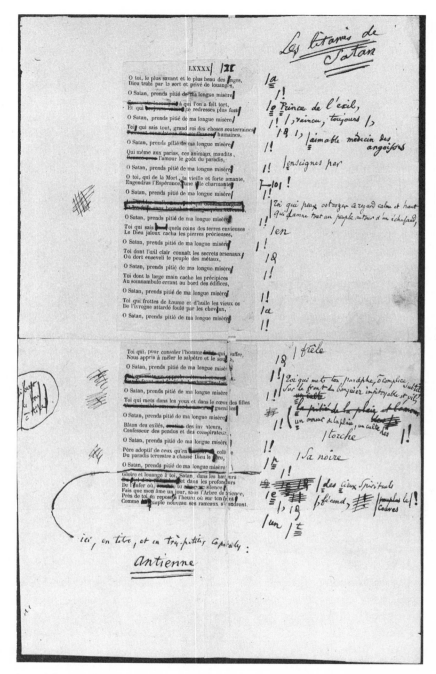

Proof sheets of Baudelaire's poem "Les Litanies de Satan," from the first edition, corrected by the author.

art, at least beginning with *Le Salon de 1846*, strike us today as incomparably the most clear-sighted criticism of his time and the first appearance of the modern mind in French critical writing. But Baudelaire is one of the most complete of French writers, and although it was neither the poet nor the art critic who wrote *Les Paradis artificiels*, the book has the lucidity and penetration of both. It is, in Baudelaire's own terms, a study of the immorality involved in the pursuit of a false ideal: man's attempt to create paradise through the use of drugs. And when he compared the addict to the "maniac who would replace solid furniture and a real garden by decorative canvas backdrops," he was speaking of something he knew. He had begun to use drugs in 1842—he had just come of age and had access to a modest inheritance. He had acquired a mistress, a quadroon named Jeanne Duval, an occasional actress of meager talent, distinguished chiefly for what one contemporary account calls her "exuberant and improbable pectoral development," and he was living on the Quai de Béthune on the Ile Saint-Louis. He moved away from the Ile briefly but soon returned to it, this time to a historic mansion then known as the Hôtel Pimodan, on the Quai d'Anjou, where he had two rooms and a small study on the top floor. Other writers and artists had lodgings there and it was in the third-floor *grand salon* that the meetings of Le Club des Haschischins took place.

The Club was a group of esthetes and literary dandies who were seeking to brighten their vision by experimenting with drugs. Out of their experiments came the idea for the first part of *Les Paradis artificiels*. Théophile Gautier, to whom Baudelaire was later to dedicate *Les Fleurs du mal*, was a member of the group and wrote about one of its séances in his story *Le Club des Hachichins* [sic], published in *La Revue des Deux Mondes* in 1846. His is a rather fanciful treatment, pale and studied beside the grave, implacable advance of the analysis Baudelaire gives us in *Les Paradis artificiels*. Baudelaire reports the clinical symptoms with a restraint and a credibility that end by creating hallucinations of their own. His picture of the "man who wants to play God and winds up as one of the lower animals, a soul selling itself off, piece by piece," is guaranteed to dampen the enthusiasm of anyone flirting with the idea of joining the ranks.

I had read *Les Paradis artificiels* two or three times prior to that summer, but it, like everything else Baudelaire wrote, is the kind of book that glows with greater intensity at each reading. I would insist, too, that reading it in the copy I have described so sharpened my senses and heightened my receptivity as to help make *that* reading the active, creative participation which, ideally, all reading should be. As a result, I think I must have been so imbued with that "grace" Baudelaire defines, in the section of the book he calls "The Taste for the Infinite," as a "kind of angelic excitation," that I was not quite ready to make the transition to the realities of Naples when we suddenly drew into the station shortly after midnight. There were no porters in sight. Leaving my luggage on the platform, where the conductor had piled it, I set off to find one. I returned, without a porter, just in time to see a man removing one of the smaller pieces from the pile. I shouted and started for him but I was neither near enough nor fast enough to reach him—or even to frighten him into dropping the bag. When he had disappeared into the night and I returned to the luggage that remained, I discovered that the piece that was gone was a small zippered case in which, as the train pulled into the station, I had stored the Baudelaire.

The next morning I was finishing a late and—in spite of the sunshine—gloomy breakfast in the garden of the hotel when the captain came over to tell me there was an inquiry for me at the desk. I went into the lobby and as I walked toward the desk, I could see only one man waiting near it and he was no one I recognized. He was dark, slightly built, about twenty-five perhaps, and neatly though poorly dressed. The desk clerk was holding animated telephone conversation with the linen room, but by pointing and shaking his head he made it clear that the man who was standing to the left of the desk, near the entrance, was the one who was waiting for me. I walked over to him and told him I was Signor Lake. He had been standing there a little nervously, I thought as I approached him, but as soon as I spoke, he began to smile and pump my hand and he unleashed a flood of Neapolitan of which I understood only the smaller half. Almost simultaneously he reached down behind him and came up with the zippered case I had last seen some ten hours earlier flying in the wake of one of the best sprints I had ever witnessed. He continued his explanation—at least I assumed it was one—and when he pointed to the tag I had fortunately attached to the case before leaving Genoa, with my name and the name of the Naples hotel I was headed for on it, I got at least the main idea—how he had found his way to me. I opened the case, saw that the Baudelaire was there, turned it over in my hands and thumbed through it quickly to reassure myself on its condition. It seemed intact. I set down the case, reached into my pocket, and found that I had just a hundred-*lira* note—then about eight dollars. I pressed it on him, with little resistance, along with numerous variations on the theme of gratitude—the latter in Italian, a language somewhat distantly related to the one he was continuing to speak all the while. The longer we talked at each other, the more overjoyed I became at my good fortune. I would have felt better to have given him another fifty *lira* but I had no other money on me. I decided to get the desk clerk to let me have fifty *lira* to save me the trouble of going upstairs for it, so I asked the man to wait while I spoke to the clerk. I didn't tell him why I wanted to speak to the clerk—it seemed more discreet not to—but I picked up the case and told him I'd be back directly. The clerk was just hanging up as I returned to the desk. I explained what I wanted and why, and he turned to look at the man. I did too. Something in our gazes must have communicated an idea—a wrong one—to him. Instantly he was gone. And there was something about those flying legs that was very familiar. Perhaps it was just as well that I was holding the case. The clerk started to laugh. "That's a fairly common routine," he said. "Often when they pick up something that turns out to have disappointing contents, they return it—if it has an address—gambling on the reward. I suppose that must have been the situation here." Up to now I had taken no thought of the contents—beyond the book. I removed it from the case and rummaged through the rest of the things—the laundry I had been accumulating over the past week.

"You see?" the clerk said triumphantly. "Who would want to bother with anyone's soiled linen?"

*   *   *   *   *

Over the next year my copy of *Les Paradis artificiels* made only one semipublic appearance. The late Paul Hazard, who had taken sabbatical leave from the Collège de France to come teach at Columbia, conducted a seminar in which, among other objectives, he sought to define Baudelaire's influence on later nineteenth-century French poets. Like most other cultivated Frenchmen Paul Hazard was something of a bibliophile. We had a number of chats about collecting Baudelaire and one day he asked me to show him some of my books. He exclaimed over several of them that were of substantially greater financial value than the Tsarskoye Selo copy of *Les Paradis artificiels*, but I noticed that that was the book to which he returned most often. He handled it not only with respect but with a good deal of patent affection—or as much as one so discreet would allow himself—and I saw that each time he set the book down, he did so with unmistakable reluctance. Observing that and recalling my own feelings when I first handled it in Bologna, I made a mental note not to have the book within easy reach: it seemed to have a way of sticking to one's fingers. Had *I* stuck to my resolution as well, what follows would be a considerably simpler story.

Soon after that, suffering from the confusion of values that often falls to the lot of the emotionally unwary, I added the book to a joint collection I had set up together with a young woman from Cambridge with whom I had become involved, chiefly, I imagine, because of our mutual interest in the same kinds of books—a dangerous basis for rapprochement as it turned out. She had a fine collection of Amy Lowell first editions and manuscript material. Often while I was at Columbia, when I went up to Cambridge for a weekend to see her and the books, she would get me to accompany her on a stroll through the grounds of Miss Lowell's old home off Heath Street in Brookline, during which she would chant interminably from *Pictures of the Floating World.* She had read every line ever written about Miss Lowell (including S. Foster Damon's greatly detailed biography three times) and under the influence of it all had just then taken up cigar smoking. At this point a curious psychic transference came about in which she ceased to identify with Miss Lowell and began to think of herself as George Sand, another cigar smoker. Two months later she had married her piano teacher, whom she saw as the twentieth-century Chopin and, with him, moved away to a small island off southeastern Massachusetts, taking the books—including *Les Paradis artificiels*—along with her.

* * * * *

I had some excellent teachers at Columbia—among them Dino Bigongiari, Federico de Onís, and Giuseppe Prezzolini—but eventually I developed an acute case of academic indigestion, brought on, at least in part, by lack of sleep and an unbalanced diet. And too many liquids, I expect. The family of the girl who had succeeded the cigar smoker in my affections was in the movie business. We had passes for all the Manhattan first-run houses, which we used often, and we never went home after a show without dropping by one of the clubs where Art Tatum or some other of my gods of the period was playing. Academe glowed dimly in the distance.

I stayed on at Columbia after the M.A., paying lip service to the idea of the doctorate, but attended no classes. Finally the charade became painful and I dropped out. My father thought I should return to Boston, and to hasten the process he cut off the money supply. I wanted to stay in New York, so I took a job—the only one I could find in that heart-of-the-Depression summer of 1937—as a trainee at a department store in Brooklyn. Assigned to the warehouse, I fell in with some of the most interesting co-workers I had ever encountered: unschooled Syrians, Greeks, Italians, Blacks, and a wide variety of East Europeans, all of whom contributed colorfully in one way or another to my education. However, nothing in my background had prepared me for the problems I had to handle on the job itself, and in eight or nine months, a harried but benevolent chief supervisor suggested I look for another job, perhaps back in Manhattan, but at least far away from Schermerhorn Street. It took a while but I did manage to find another job—another trainee, boot-camp arrangement—this time with a proprietary-drug manufacturer. I was somewhere in the coal-mining valleys of West Virginia learning how to sell when Orson Welles's historic radio broadcast, "The War of the Worlds," brought panic-stricken listeners out into the streets, in a race with imminent extinction. That set me to thinking seriously about the precariousness of the life I was leading, out in the boondocks, driving a truck full of cold salve and nose drops, putting up signs on barns and in pastures, occasionally antagonizing a nearby bull. Was it worth it? I went back to Manhattan and turned in my badge.

By the spring of 1939 I had eaten humble pie and was once more in Cambridge, not at school, not even in a bookshop, but doing market research for a giant-sized soap company. When the Personnel Department, seeking to fill a difficult spot on the organizational chart, discovered that I had some claim to literacy in four or five languages, I was made "Assistant Literary Counselor." It sounds silly—in fact it *was* silly—but it was certainly an improvement over peddling cold remedies to Greater Appalachian general storekeepers.

Pearl Harbor arrived and soon I was in uniform. For a number of months the closest I came to books in any form was a series of training manuals. Then, one Saturday, on leave in Boston, I dropped into a bookshop whose owner had sold me a fair number of books in previous years. That day he didn't even try; he was too busy with all the loose ends he needed to tie up before leaving for the Navy. I wandered around the shop a while, filling my lungs with that musty fragrance which is the bibliophile's catnip, and then, back in the bookseller's office, picked up a sale catalogue issued by the Parke-Bernet Galleries in New York. I had often bought books at their auctions, generally through an agent, the New York bookseller who had bought *Les Fleurs du mal* for me, but it had been months since I had seen one of their catalogues. I began to leaf through it casually and suddenly found myself reading the following description:

> BAUDELAIRE, CHARLES. Les Paradis artificiels.
> Opium et Haschisch. Paris, 1860.
>
> 12mo, contemporary half green morocco.
>
> FIRST EDITION, with the title page printed in
> red and black. From the library of the Palace
> of Tsarskoë Selo with the library stamp on the
> half title.

I turned back to the front cover to see when the sale was to take place. It had come and gone, three and a half months before. I looked quickly through the whole catalogue. It listed a number of other books I had last seen in company with the Tsarskoye Selo Baudelaire, including that presentation copy of the first edition of *Les Fleurs du mal*. The source of them all, therefore, was quite clear.

That evening I wrote to the New York dealer who had often executed my bids at Parke-Bernet. In view of the time that had elapsed since the sale, I couldn't feel very hopeful about recovering the Baudelaire material but I wanted to try, at least. I knew that if it had been purchased by a private buyer, the Galleries would not divulge his name. But if it had been sold to a dealer, they would. Of course, if it had gone to a dealer who was buying on order for a client, the trail would doubtless end there. My only chance, then, lay in its having been bought by a dealer for stock. And even that, after three and a half months, was not too reassuring a prospect.

I had a reply by return mail. "I thought I recognized those French books," the dealer wrote. "I wondered why you hadn't told me you were selling them." I had, of course, brought him up to date, in my letter, on their recent history. It turned out that he himself had bought one of them, a copy of the first edition of Baudelaire's translation of Poe's *Eureka*. He offered to let me have it at his cost. Most important of all, he arranged with the buyer of Nadar's copy of *Les Fleurs du mal* to return it to me. The buyer—a most unlikely one for that book—was Thomas W. Streeter, who had formed the great collection of Texana. He had bought *Les Fleurs du mal* for his son but generously relinquished it when he was told of the circumstances surrounding its sale. *Les Paradis artificiels*, the dealer learned, had been bought by a French dealer in New York. Did I want him to negotiate? I told him to go ahead. The Frenchman still had the book. His eloquent description of its virtues, forwarded to me by our go-between, was not far short of poetry. I didn't need his poetry to refresh my memory, but it had a very stirring effect all the same. In the end he made an extremely kind gesture. He turned over to me *Les Paradis artificiels* along with another purchase he had made at the same sale—the heavily corrected proof sheets of the poem "Les Litanies de Satan," now removed from the volume of Baudelaire's Collected Works into which they had been tipped, inappropriately, when I originally purchased them at the Harry B. Smith sale. He charged me his cost (which reflected the slump in the rare-book market at that period) plus a modest twenty-percent handling charge.

After the war I renewed my contact with him. He sent me his catalogues, came to see me in Cambridge where I had gone back to my job at the Soap Works, and on my trips to New York I often dropped by his shop. I bought things from him from time to time—he had a good stock and was exceedingly knowledgeable—and occasionally I swapped something I had for something he had that I wanted more. Ideally a swap presents, or seems to present, an advantage to both parties. One day I saw in his shop a very appealing book illustrated with original etchings by Chagall, bound in a meretriciously provocative full morocco binding. I let him talk me into thinking I wanted it. But I had difficulty digesting the price. Before the hypnosis wore off, we had made a swap: I took his Chagall book, with its whorish binding, and gave him, in exchange, *some* money and—God knows why!—the Tsarskoye Selo copy of *Les Paradis artificiels*. Back home, and very soon, the *post coitum triste* syndrome set in and I frequently upbraided myself for my fickleness. But a deal is a deal. For months to come I missed that book. I was constantly reminded of it, often in ways I could not easily escape.

Soon after that I gave up making soap literature and nostalgically returned to the Ph.D. trail, alternating between the Institute of Fine Arts at New York University and the Sorbonne. When I went to Paris in 1950, *The Christian Science Monitor*, which had always covered all the arts all over the world with exemplary thoroughness, was without a Paris art critic: an unthinkable situation at that time. So I signed on to do the job, taking leave a year later to return to NYU.

In the spring of 1952 I went back to Paris a little earlier than I had planned on doing, the *Monitor* having asked me to cover "Masterpieces of the Twentieth Century," a mammoth, month-long festival of the arts, sponsored by the Congress for Cultural Freedom. It included a major art exhibition mounted by an old New York friend of mine, James Johnson Sweeney, at the Musée National d'Art Moderne, as well as dance, music, theater, and a series of conferences and literary debates that featured André Malraux, William Faulkner, Katherine Anne Porter, Czeslaw Milosz, W. H. Auden, Allen Tate, and many others. The program was designed to prove to the world at large that the West was not the sinkhole of decadence portrayed in European Communist propaganda.

When the festival came to its end, I stayed on, still officially working on my dissertation and continuing to cover the Paris art and literary scene for the *Monitor*. I moved into an apartment in an early seventeenth-century house on the Ile Saint-Louis, next door to Baudelaire's Hôtel Pimodan, now magnificently refurbished, renamed Hôtel de Lauzun, and used by the City of Paris for entertaining visiting heads of state and other dignitaries.

The Hôtel de Lauzun has an unusually evocative past. It was built between 1650 and 1657 by Le Vau, one of the architects of the palace at Versailles, for a man named Gruyn, an innkeeper's son who had become *commissaire général des vivres de la cavalerie du roi* and had grown enormously rich, as quartermaster types sometimes will. Colbert's Chambre de Justice finally caught up with him, however, and he died in jail. The house passed through several other hands before becoming the property of the Duc de Lauzun, whose ill-fated affair with the Grande Mademoiselle—the Duchesse de Montpensier, Louis XIV's first cousin—caused him, also, to come a cropper. In 1842, considerably deteriorated, it belonged to Baron Pichon, a book collector of commendable taste, who undertook to restore it to its earlier dignity. At that time it was called the Hôtel Pimodan. The Baron rented parts of it to a few writers and artists—Théophile Gautier, the novelist Roger de Beauvoir, and the painter Fernand Boissard among them. It was somewhat later that Baudelaire, already an habitué of the house and the Club des Haschischins, joined the others there as a tenant. It was difficult to

pass the house several times a day, most days, without thinking of Baudelaire and *Les Paradis artificiels.*

Then, too, Baudelaire had dedicated *Les Paradis artificiels*, with some mysteriousness, to a "J. G. F."—a woman, as the text makes clear, but one whose positive identification has thus far eluded the Baudelairians. There are those who think, however, that she was a Mlle. Juliette Gex-Fagon, who had lived only a few yards from the apartment I had moved into. Those are not the only shadows Baudelaire's spirit cast about the island. As a sample, though, they will make it clear why the book kept obtruding itself, in spite of my attempts to set it aside.

Seven years later, the Paris bookseller Edouard Loewy was showing me, proudly, a new acquisition of his: the first edition, in twelve volumes, of Chateaubriand's *Mémoires d'outre-tombe.* As he took down the first volume and handed it to me, I had the feeling that I was in the presence of something very familiar. And then I realized what it was. Except for the fact that the tone of the boards and the leather was a warm reddish brown rather than dark green, the binding duplicated almost exactly that of the Tsarskoye Selo copy of *Les Paradis artificiels:* the same type of mottled paper on the sides, the finely pebbled grain of the morocco, the shallow backstrip and tiny corners, the attenuated gilt lettering, and the identical pattern of glistening flat bands—the "false nerves"—across the back. I opened the front cover. Inside was a small, nearly square bookplate with scalloped corners, bearing the entwined initials "AH," surmounted by what heraldists would do well to call a coronet effulgent. "Alexander Nicolayevitch," Loewy interpolated in his *Opéra Comique* Russian. I turned to the title page. In the lower right-hand corner was a small circular stamp in purple ink marking it as a discard of The Hermitage, the Leningrad museum and palace built by Catherine the Great and expanded by her grandson, Nicholas I, the father of the book's late owner. The *Mémoires d'outre-tombe* was published in Paris in 1849 and 1850, and this copy, quite clearly, had been bound in the same atelier as the Tsarskoye Selo copy of *Les Paradis artificiels*—perhaps, even, at the same time and by the same artisans; in any case, under the same bibliopegic regime.

About two months after that, I received a telephone call one morning from a Russian book scout named Roujitch, whom I had often seen at book sales at the Hôtel Drouot. He specialized in English-language books and occasionally brought me useful reference works—bibliographies, exhibition catalogues, and so on. An American print collector and art historian, Atherton Curtis, long resident in France, had died and his library had been sold privately. The best things had already been taken away by several dealers much higher than Roujitch in the local pecking order, but there remained a considerable bulk of material— "about six tons," he estimated—that was of no great interest to them and which he had somehow acquired. Knowing my fondness for handling old paper, he suggested I might like to look through what was left. "You won't find any treasures," he said, "but there may be a plaquette or two in all this that will be of help to you in your work."

The mass was piled up, in great disorder, in what had been, until recently, an empty shop in the Rue Jacob, not far from Saint-Germain-des-Prés. It was not the library of a bibliophile but that of a scholar, and although it had been "creamed," as Roujitch put it, it was unimaginable that I should not find something worth carrying away. I took off my jacket, rolled up my sleeves, and plunged in. The great bulk of the remaining material consisted of catalogues of collections and sales, notebooks of clippings, albums of reproductions cut from such magazines as the *Gazette des Beaux-Arts*, the *Burlington Magazine*, and so on. There were even *fichiers* of indexed notes for articles planned but never written. I had handled perhaps half of this bulk when suddenly I found myself staring at the cover of a large quarto catalogue bound in stiff wheat-colored wrappers headed *Bibliotheken der Russischen Zaren in Zarskoje-Selo*, issued by Gilhofer & Ranschburg in Lucerne for an auction on the 14th and 15th of June, 1932.

I turned to the title page. These were *Kostbare Bücher und Manuskripte*, it said, not only from the Libraries of the Russian Tsars in Tsarskoye Selo, but also from the Collections of the Herzog Albrecht von Sachsen-Teschen, the founder of the Albertina Museum, and of the eminent Viennese collector Dr. Albert Figdor. It listed such rarities as one of the four known copies of Mercator's *Nova et aucta orbis terrae descriptio ad usum navigantium emendate accommodata*—the first map on "Mercator's projection"—printed at Duisburg in 1569; a copy of the first dated edition of Thomas Aquinas's *Summa*, printed on vellum by Peter Schoeffer in Mainz in 1467; there were autograph letters of Raphael, Beethoven, and Goethe. I turned quickly to the section covering nineteenth-century first editions and illustrated books. There, under the number 463, I read the following description:

[BAUDELAIRE, CH.] Les Paradis artificiels.
Opiume [sic] et Haschisch, Paris, Poulet-
Mallis [sic] et de Broise. 1860. in-12.
D.-mar. (Rel. de l'ép.)
Carteret I, 126. Edition originale. Très
bel expl. Cachet sur le faux-titre.

When Edouard Loewy had shown me Alexander II's copy of Chateaubriand's *Mémoires d'outre-tombe,* with its binding so closely ap-
proximating the binding of that copy of *Les Paradis artificiels,* I had felt,
for a moment, as though I were very near to the Baudelaire. If he had
then handed me the Tsarskoye Selo copy of *Les Paradis artificiels,* I don't
think I would have been terribly shocked. It would have seemed an
entirely natural progression. Now, reading its description in the catalogue that had opened the door of its Sovietized Imperial cage and
liberated it to the world at large, I think I almost expected, once again,
the book itself to come to hand. I attacked the remaining half with
redoubled enthusiasm. I turned up many useful volumes, such as the
catalogues of the Impressionist and post-Impressionist collections of
Roger Marx and Henri Rouart, which went, along with the Tsarskoye
Selo catalogue, into forming the five-foot shelf of documentation I
carried away with me that day, but I came no closer to the book itself
than that almost tangible image of it that rose up before me as I read the
original catalogue description.

*   *   *   *   *

In New York, a collector who wishes to keep tabs on the movement of
books in the auction room has a fairly easy time of it. In Paris it is not
nearly so simple. With rare exceptions, all public sales of books (like
most sales of all other types of property except real estate) are held,
under Government supervision, at a building in the ninth *arrondissement* called the Hôtel des Commissaires-Priseurs, but generally referred to as the Hôtel Drouot, after the name of its street. The legal and
fiscal responsibility for each sale is the concern of a *commissaire-
priseur*—half lawyer, half auctioneer—but the actual direction of a book
sale rests with a State-approved *expert*—a book dealer. There are many
experts, of varying shades of expertise. For some sales no catalogues are
issued, only a printed postcard or a mimeographed sheet giving the date
and the highlights.

Sales at the Hôtel Drouot are held, as a rule, at 2:00 or 2:15 P.M., and since in general whatever is to be sold of an afternoon is displayed that morning, the only almost-foolproof method of keeping in touch with the smaller sales is to spend one's morning at the Hôtel, prowling among the baskets. And that is what the shrewd professional Paris *bouquiniste* does. Few others, though, have the time, the patience, or the inclination to carry things that far.

One sultry July morning I read a newspaper announcement by one of the more enterprising of the Paris *commissaires-priseurs* covering the exhibition and sale of a large group of Oriental rugs. The sale was scheduled for the next day. Because of their importance the rugs were to be exhibited that afternoon as well as the following morning. Since I needed a small rug, I decided to drop in at the Hôtel that afternoon. I arrived just at two o'clock. I saw that none of the rugs answered my need and then, on my way out, hearing the *crieurs* beginning to call out bids in some of the other second-floor rooms, I poked my head into several of them as I made my way along the corridor. As I stepped into the last room before the central staircase—my exit route—I saw that books were being sold there. The *expert*, seated at a table beside and beneath the elevated tribune of the *commissaire-priseur*, was one of the less active of the book *experts* and not one whose sales would normally come to my attention. But when I saw that a uniformed *commissionnaire* was handing out catalogues to two men who had entered just in front of me, I took one from him, too. It is too much to call it a catalogue; it was a printed list that gave, for each lot number, only the author's last name, the short title of the book, date of publication, and an abbreviated symbol for the type of binding. The sale, I assumed, had been going on for just a few minutes because I heard the *expert* announce *"numéro huit."* He began to read the abbreviated description, my eyes found the catalogue number, and I read the full entry for number 8:

Baudelaire: *Paradis artificiels.* 1860. D.-chag. E.O.

In other words, a copy of the first edition of *Les Paradis artificiels* in a half binding. As the *expert* finished reading, a *commissionnaire* took the book from him, held it up for the *commissaire-priseur*'s token nod of approval, and then began to parade it along the front bench. Every few feet, one of the *bouquinistes* who make a career of the Hôtel Drouot would reach out for the book, flip it over in his hands, thumb through it quickly, and then toss it onto the sleazy red cloth on the table in front of him, raising a little puff of dust in the process. The *commissionnaire* would pick it up each time and continue on his way. As he drew nearer to where I was standing, the bidding died down—still too low for a copy of the book— and the *commissaire-priseur* lifted his ivory-headed hammer. *"Je vais adjuger,"* he called out threateningly. Something—sentiment, the lure of a bargain, intuition—jabbed at me. I called out *"Cinquante, pour voir"* to stop his hammer and held out my hand for the book. *"Montrez à Monsieur,"* he ordered, and the *commissionnaire* brought me the book. It was still in his hand, reaching out toward me over the heads of three rows of bench occupants, when I saw *exactly* what it was. Hot as that airless room was, the sun beating down on its broad skylight, I felt a chill as I took the book into my hand and realized by what a slender strand it had been hanging, on its journey back to me, because there was no doubt in my mind—the binding was unmistakable—that this was the Tsarskoye Selo copy. I turned to the half title. The Tsarskoye Selo stamp was there. I then looked inside the back cover, where I mark in code a book's cost. There, in the lower corner next to the hinge, were my two sets of code letters, the lower set representing the price I had paid for the book in Bologna in 1936, the upper set New York 1942. The auctioneer thrust his hammer in the direction of the underbidder. *"C'est pas vous, Monsieur,"* he warned. The man shook his head. The hammer fell. I paid for the book, tipped the *crieur*, and blissfully left the room.

Chapter 2

It was not long after I had moved to the Ile Saint-Louis, in the shadow of the historic Hôtel de Lauzun and of Baudelaire, that another poet took over my attention. On November 18, 1952—a Tuesday—shortly after one o'clock in the afternoon, I was listening to the Paris radio and heard the news broadcast announce the death of Paul Eluard. He had been ill for several months, according to the announcer, and on his return from convalescence in Dordogne had caught cold and died suddenly that morning. He was in his fifty-seventh year.

By American standards it would be difficult to measure the full effect of that bulletin. First of all, we have no poet whose work can reasonably be compared to the work of Eluard—a great poet and a popular poet. Furthermore, he had become a political symbol: In a country where the Communist Party wields political power—although much less today than in 1952—Eluard's activism of his last ten years had brought him the lifetime canonization the Party has always accorded to those top-ranking poets and painters who figure among its chief propaganda weapons.

The first detailed account of Eluard's death reached newsstands that same Tuesday afternoon in the Wednesday edition of *Ce Soir*, the Communist daily paper edited, until it ceased publication about four months after Eluard's death, by Louis Aragon, at that time the intellectual wheelhorse of the French C. P. The first paragraph set the tone:

Paul Eluard died this morning as the first snow was beginning to fall. . . . He had just eaten his breakfast and finished reading the newspapers. . . . The last news story he read concerned the refusal of the petition of Ethel and Julius Rosenberg, that young American couple condemned to die in the electric chair. . . . From his sickroom he had insisted, only a few days ago, on launching a last appeal that their lives might be saved. And now death has struck him down on this evil day.

The headline, picture, and news story covered more than half of *Ce Soir*'s front page. Telephone and telegraph wires were humming that morning, *Ce Soir* said, "from capital to capital, from Moscow to Prague, from Berlin to Peking, from Rome to New York, to Santiago . . . wherever men and women love, love life and peace. . . ."

Eluard had been born Paul-Eugène Grindel in the outlying Paris suburb Saint-Denis. A dreary childhood in that grim little factory town, illness, then convalescence in Switzerland brought him to the threshold of war, and in 1915 he was called up. His first collections of poems, pacifist in tone, appeared while he was still in the Army. Walt Whitman's *Leaves of Grass* was an early influence and a lasting one.

At the end of the war Eluard joined forces with other young apostles of a new order—Aragon, Philippe Soupault, André Breton, and Tristan Tzara were in the group—to create poetry and history, "to sleep with the moon in one eye and the sun in the other."

Through Dada and Surrealism, manifestoes and manifestations, poetry ruled their world, and in that world Eluard remained truest to poetry. Others became politicians and propagandists; Eluard was always a poet. His work was not without its contradictions: earlier, the conflict between the wretched world he saw and the beautiful world he wanted and tried to create; later, the interplay between his inherent simplicity and the brilliant, at times violent, imagery of his Surrealist evolution. He resolved these conflicts as a poet and in the process became a greater poet.

His poetry, over a creative period of thirty-five years, reaches its greatest heights in his love poems. The ones he addressed to his first wife, Gala (who left him in 1929 for Salvador Dali), and later, those he wrote to his second wife, Nusch, are among the finest our time has produced:

> We have spent the night I hold your hand I watch
> I buoy you up with all my strength
> I engrave on a rock the star of your strength
> Deep grooves where the goodness of your body will bud
> I repeat to myself your hidden voice your public voice
> I laugh again at the proud one
> Whom you treat like a beggar

At the fools you respect the simple ones in whom you bathe yourself
And in my head which softly makes its peace with yours with the night
I marvel at the unknown you become
An unknown like you like everything I love
Forever new.

In 1946 Nusch died, very suddenly. Using the name Didier Desroches, Eluard wrote her epitaph in *Le Temps déborde:*

> You made our life it is swallowed up
> Dawn of a city on a morning in May
> On which the earth has closed its fist
> Dawn in me seventeen years brighter and brighter
> And death invades me unresisted. . . .

For three years Eluard was tortured by the image of Nusch. Another slender book, *Corps Mémorable* (issued first under a pseudonym, "Brun"), showed the extent to which he was racked by her death. In "A Pound of Flesh" he wrote:

> I am a man in a void
> Deaf blind dumb
> On an immense base of black silence.

But Eluard was also the poet of the Resistance. His poem "Liberté," which first appeared in the pamphlet *Poésie et vérité 1942*, printed under the Occupation, falls on the modern French ear with all the fire of "La Marseillaise" stripped of its rhetoric:

> . . . .
> . . . .
> On the foam of the clouds
> On the sweat of the storm
> On the thick and tasteless rain
> I write your name
> . . . .
> . . . .
> And by the power of a word
> I start my life anew
> I was born to know you
> To name you
>
> Liberty.

From his proto-Surrealist days Eluard had subscribed to revolutionary principles but in spite of a flirtation with the Party in the late 1920s,
he was essentially anti-Stalinist. In 1931–32 came a break with Aragon
and soon after, Eluard was out of the Party. However, under the
influence of his role in the Resistance and the suasion of Communists
beside whom he worked and fought, he became, in 1942, a dedicated
Party man.

* * * * *

On Wednesday morning, the day after Eluard's death, *L'Humanité*,
the "central organ" of the French Communist Party, carried, in the
upper-left-hand columns of its front page, a photograph of Eluard and
the headline, "Our comrade Paul Eluard is dead." Underneath, a
black-bordered farewell message, followed by the signatures of the
French C. P.'s Politburo, said adieu to "the great poet, the great French
humanist . . . the friend and comrade-in-arms of Maurice Thorez."

By Wednesday messages of condolence were pouring in from all
corners. Thursday's issue of *Les Lettres Françaises*, the Communist
weekly newspaper of the arts, directed by Aragon, printed tributes from
Palmiro Togliatti, Pablo Neruda, Frédéric Joliot-Curie, Georges Auric,
Francis Poulenc, Marc Chagall, Berthold Brecht, and dozens of others,
including a group of ten Soviet writers, among them Constantin Si-
monov and Ilya Ehrenburg.

Thursday morning's mail brought me the traditional black-bordered
faire-part—the invitation to Eluard's funeral. "The Comité National
des Ecrivains," it read, "begs you to be present at the convoy and interment of Monsieur Paul Eluard, Medal of the Resistance . . .
Saturday, 22d November, at 1:45 P.M. sharp. The body will be on view
on Friday the 21st at the Maison de la Pensée Française and Saturday
morning at *Les Lettres Françaises* . . . Interment . . . at Père-
Lachaise cemetery."

The Maison de la Pensée Française, a once-elegant mansion, now
rather shabbily maintained, on the Avenue Gabriel between the American Embassy and the presidential Elysée Palace, had been used for
some years as the headquarters of a number of Communist-sponsored
organizations. Some of the more lively openings of the Paris art world
were held there for artists friendly toward the Party's program. Picasso,
Léger, and Lurçat had been shown there recently.

When I reached the Maison that Friday afternoon, the garden entrance was shrouded in the customary black drapes, crowned by a monogrammed "PE." At the door, as I signed my name and address, the funeral director, in black cape, buckle shoes, and two-pointed hat, was urging a few stragglers, *"Avancez, avancez, Messieurs'dames."*

Inside, on a raised platform, Eluard the patriot lay in state under the French flag. Behind the catafalque hung a recent photograph enlarged to about nine feet by six and a Lurçat tapestry into which was woven Eluard's line, "Hope still lives on earth."

Four of Eluard's friends stood guard. The bier was banked with huge wreaths sent by, among others, the Société des Gens de Lettres, the Comité National des Ecrivains, *Ce Soir, Les Lettres Françaises, L'Humanité,* and Albert Skira, the Swiss publisher with whom Eluard had worked in his Surrealist days.

On one side, an anteroom had been improvised with black draperies for walls. The black-covered chairs were empty; men and women stood silently in little clusters. From an amplifier high on the opposite wall issued a recorded version of Bach's *Cantata in F Minor.* I had been standing in the little room for a minute or two when the needle stuck and the chorus went on repeating itself. For a while no one seemed aware of the grotesqueness. Then one of the honor guard raised an eyebrow in the direction of the amplifier and suddenly everyone was conscious of it. No one moved. The sound became intolerable. Finally a man on my right probed for an opening in the drapery and disappeared inside. The record stopped.

As I left the elegance of the Avenue Gabriel behind me and made my way back home through humbler neighborhoods, I saw that the Party had posters up on all available walls announcing the funeral details and urging Eluard's comrades to pay their respects on Friday afternoon or Saturday morning and to join the procession at Père-Lachaise cemetery at 1:45 Saturday afternoon.

In a season of gray skies, intermittent rain, and raw, biting wind, that Saturday was no exception. By 1:30 the rain had settled down to a steady drizzle and the crowds outside Père-Lachaise huddled together in two main groups in front of the gates. Scattered small groups sought shelter in shop and building entrances across the Boulevard de Ménilmontant.

By 1:45 the rain was coming down more insistently. A group of women workers moved through the crowds pinning black-edged passport-size photographs of Eluard onto lapels, at ten francs a head.

A little after two o'clock the cortège arrived. The draped coffin, with Eluard's death mask on top, was placed on a platform in the center of the driveway. The giant photograph of the poet was set up at one side and the hearse and the cars bearing the flowers drove inside the gates. The other cars pulled up before a small covered grandstand at the right of the entrance. First to step out and take their places were the family and close friends: Eluard's third wife, Dominique, whom he had brought back from Mexico three years before on his return from the Mexican "peace conference"; his daughter, Cécile, at that time wife of the artist Gérard Vulliamy; Picasso, Eluard's "sublime friend," hatless, a voluminous blue scarf flowing from his loose-hanging trench coat; Jean Cocteau, whose head barely rose above the upturned flared collar of his fitted camel's hair coat; the writer Claude Roy, Royalist-turned-Communist; Aragon and his wife, novelist Elsa Triolet, who, as vice-president of the Comité National des Ecrivains, was in charge of the funeral arrangements; Tristan Tzara, Rumanian-born founder of the Dada movement and good friend of the Party. The painter Fernand Léger sat down in the rear.

To the right of the inner circle of family and intimates, the Politburo of the French Communist Party took their seats: Jacques Duclos, acting head of the Party; Jeannette Vermeersch, wife of Party chief Maurice Thorez (who had not yet returned from his prolonged convalescence in Russia); Laurent Casanova, and others.

The limousines moved ahead into the cemetery. A black-clad funeral official climbed onto the black-draped rostrum and announced the first speaker: "Monsieur Aragon, in the name of the Comité National des Ecrivains."

Aragon, Eluard's friend for thirty-four years (with time out for ideological differences) and the Party's main bridge with the world of arts and letters, mounted the platform. With oratorical grace he rose to the "tragic honor." As he read Eluard's lines from *Tout Dire* (1950), his voice took on added fervor. Then, abruptly, his manner changed. Monsieur Baylot, the prefect of police, had sought to prevent this gathering, he said. For three days the Comité National des Ecrivains had struggled against the

> chicanery, the coarseness, the despotism of the police, who wished to forbid any cortège, any possibility of a gathering. . . . For three days Dominique Eluard . . . was obliged to wait from hour to hour to learn whether she would have the right to hear [her husband's] verses read. The

prefect of police had decided that order would be maintained if the body of the poet Paul Eluard were carried off at 40 an hour . . . without a cortège, without a pause, from the Rue du Louvre [offices of *Les Lettres Françaises*] to the hole dug in the ground.

In that way the people of Paris would not have been able to associate themselves with the mourning of Dominique Eluard, with our mourning. . . . Paul Eluard would have been thrown at top speed into a hole, without a word.

As he spoke, Aragon's face contorted into a snarl, his jaw shot forward, and his voice rose to the pitch of frenzy. Somewhere behind me, someone whispered, "Hitler."

My attention returned to Aragon and I heard him say, "The immortal lesson he bequeaths to us speaks louder than the dwarfs and the madmen. The lesson of Eluard is the lesson of peace, of the peace served by the People's Congress about to take place in Vienna."

Aragon was escorted back to the stand, and other tributes were read by Jean Bruller, who, under the name of Vercors, had written *Le Silence de la mer*, one of the literary monuments of the French Resistance, and by an official of the Société des Gens de Lettres. Back in his seat, Aragon, from time to time as Jean Bruller spoke, wiped tears from his eyes.

The final speaker—"in the name of the French Communist Party"— was Laurent Casanova, swarthy, thick-set, heavy-lidded minister-without-portfolio in the Communist high command, big boss of all its cultural activities. Speaking slowly, with a heavy Corsican accent, Casanova paid tribute to Eluard, the fighter for the "dignity of France and the brotherhood of man," the humanist, who, in response to the demands of tomorrow, became a Communist, repudiating "that society which mutilates [and] degrades [man's] finest sentiments. . . . His creative power opened up then to the grandest current of modern thought: Marxism."

A "slow, self-critical purge" began to take place in Eluard's thinking, Casanova said.

He speaks still with love for the simple people, for happy lovers, but his language now is epic in its sweep—broad and majestic . . . concrete.

He scourges the executioners, crushes the cowards. He denounces the savage law of capitalism, the despoiler, which snatches men's tools out

Paul Eluard and his third wife,
Dominique, after their wedding,
Saint-Tropez, 1950, with Picasso
and Françoise Gilot.

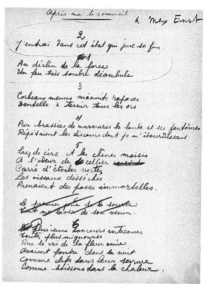

Autograph manuscript of Paul
Eluard's poem "Après moi le sommeil," dedicated to Max Ernst.

Paul Eluard and Gala, his first wife, *c.* 1930. Photograph by Valentine Hugo.

M

Monsieur Paul ELUARD

Médaille de la Résistance

décédé le 18 Novembre 1952 dans sa 57me année, en son domicile 52, Avenue de Gravelle à Charenton (Seine).

Qui se feront le **Samedi 22 courant** à 13 h. 45 très précises 37, Rue du Louvre, Paris-2e.

Le Corps sera exposé le Vendredi 21 de 10 h. à 21 heures
à la "Maison de la Pensée", 26, Avenue Gabriel, Paris-8e

et le Samedi 22 de 10 h. à 13 h. 30
aux "Lettres Françaises" 37, Rue du Louvre, Paris-2e
où un dernier hommage lui sera rendu par ses camarades

REGRETS...

De la part de :

Madame Paul ELUARD, son épouse ;

Madame Cécile VULLIAMY, sa fille ;

Claire VULLIAMY, sa petite-fille ;

Madame Veuve Jeanne GRINDEL, sa mère ;

Marie-Caroline LAURE, sa belle-fille ;

De toute la Famille ;

Et du Comité Central du Parti Communiste Français.

L'Inhumation aura lieu au Cimetière du Père Lachaise

Pompes Funèbres Générales, 66-70, Bd Richard-Lenoir, Paris-XIe
Bureau officiel de Champigny, 100, Rue Jean-Jaurès, Tél. : Pompadour 00-68 - R. MARIE, Chef de Bureau

Eluard's official death notice. The usual formula, "Priez pour lui" (Pray for him), has been replaced by the laconic "Regrets."

of their hands, leaves them in solitude, forced to sell their working strength—that is, their flesh and blood—to greedy merchants. . . .

He has become much more than a sensitive spirit, something other than an announcer of prophecy; he is a man who has resolved the contradiction between dream and action. . . .

Good-bye, Paul. Your comrades salute you. They will justify your hopes. Our ideal will conquer.

Casanova stepped down from the rostrum. Those in the stand returned to the cars and the long procession started off. It wound slowly up the hill, past the crematorium, down the other side, and came to a halt before the open grave. First the giant photograph was removed and placed at the head of the grave. As the attendants carried the coffin from the hearse, the crowds began to move toward the grave. Guards joined hands to push them back, shouting, "Respect for the dead. Stand back. Respect for the dead."

The sky had cleared. It was almost bright. The coffin was lowered into the ground. Eluard's Resistance comrades held their banners over the grave and the poet's intimates filed by, each to drop a red carnation: first, Dominique Eluard, with incredible calm; then Picasso, ashen under his deep tan; Cocteau, distraught, and the others. When the last carnation had been dropped, the cars moved on and the crowds closed in.

As I walked down the hill, I thought of Eluard's Resistance poem, "Avis," about the dying man who began to smile with the realization that "he had not one comrade, but millions and millions to avenge him." The guards' cries echoed in my ears: "Respect for the dead. Respect for the dead."

I left the cemetery by the side gate, which leads into the Rue du Repos. Across the road I could see a group of workers who had stood by my side at Eluard's grave. They had congregated in front of a bistro, laughing and pointing up at the awning over the entrance. One of them went inside and the others soon followed. When I reached the bistro, I read, printed in red letters across the front of the awning: "You're better off here than across the street."

*   *   *   *   *

Over the years following Eluard's death, I was able to acquire a substantial body of Eluard material. I would have preferred to have his entire archive but that was not possible. There were a number of reasons why. For one thing, poetry had never given Eluard a living. For that he fell back on his avocation: the book trade. He collected books—and pictures—and he bought and sold when he needed money. He made fair copies of many of his poems and sometimes got painter friends of his to decorate the manuscripts, thus making them more salable. And he had been living off those collections for years. After his death, his widow, Dominique, needed to draw on that resource from time to time. People in her position often prefer to sell slowly, knowing that the longer they hold onto their treasures, the more valuable they become. Since Eluard had sold many things in his lifetime, a number of dealers who had long ago found their way to his apartment continued to buy from that same basic source. Also, Eluard's daughter, Cécile, had become a dealer in rare books. So there was no chance for any one person or institution to get everything, by any means. But through one channel or another, I managed to get a fair amount: prose manuscripts; manuscript poems—none of them fair copies, but manuscripts that showed the poet at work, some of them unpublished; letters to Eluard from writer, artist, and musician friends, such as André Breton, Le Corbusier, Jean Dubuffet, Pierre Reverdy, Jacques Villon, Francis Poulenc, Valentine Hugo, Man Ray, Cocteau, René Char; books with Eluard's woodcut bookplate designed by Max Ernst and bearing the motto: *"Après moi le sommeil"* (the title of a poem Eluard had dedicated to Max); books and drawings by Dali; books decorated by Chagall and Picasso, and so on.

Of all this material the most affecting was a group of 185 letters I bought from the Paris book dealer Marc Loliée. They had been written by Eluard between 1911 and 1919 to his parents and to his "first friend," the binder A.-J. Gonon, who published Eluard's first book, *Le Devoir et l'inquiétude.* More than seventy of them are unpublished, and they give a very moving picture of the young poet in his early creative years.

At the beginning of the correspondence Eluard is sixteen, in Switzerland on vacation. He has begun to cough up blood and is obliged to remain in a sanatorium near Davos for about a year and a half. There he meets a young Russian girl, Elena Dmitrievna Diakonova, whom he calls Gala and who becomes his fiancée. She goes back to Russia in 1914, but is prevented by the outbreak of war from returning to Paris as they had planned. Eluard is mobilized.

The letters show Eluard as very idealistic and openhearted. He speaks freely and naturally about his affections, both in writing to his parents and to Gonon, who is seventeen years older than he and whose friendship means much to him. At first, Army life is rough going for Eluard, with his sensitive nature and fragile health, but he is given a job at a medical-service evacuation station, writing news of wounded soldiers to their families. As a result of seeing so many maimed and psychically shattered men, he begins to feel ashamed of having such a sheltered job and after insistent requests for transfer, he is finally shifted, in spite of his chest weakness, to an infantry regiment. But the body is not equal to the spirit. There are a few more hospitalizations and Eluard is returned to the auxiliary services.

Gala, meanwhile, has been able to arrange her return to France. She will wait out the war in Paris because they are planning marriage by the end of 1916. During his early months in the Army, while he was hospitalized at Rosny, Eluard had decided to take his first Communion. He wrote to his mother that the bishop would come to officiate and "the ceremony may serve to convince the unbelievers." But by the time Gala gets back to France, Eluard's faith, under the impact of his war experiences, has eroded to the point that he no longer wants a religious marriage service; a quick civil ceremony will do nicely. He feels all the rest is time and money wasted and the money could better be devoted to improving the quality of the room they will have for their brief honeymoon and to buying "an excellent bed, a vast, high, soft, country bed in which we will live and die."

Gala, however, is still deeply religious and so the religious ceremony stands (February 21, 1917)—large guest list, white bridal gown, and all. In fact Gala gives up her Russian Orthodox affiliation and is converted to Roman Catholicism.

After four days with Gala, Eluard returns to the front. Forced marches and three days without food put him back in the hospital. He has a few days' convalescent leave at Easter, but a month later he is once more hospitalized.

In June, Eluard returns from leave thirty-six hours late and is given a six-day prison sentence. On release he is shifted back to the infantry without medical examination. After more illness, in hospitals and evacuation stations, he is finally given a clerical post in Mantes and Gala joins him there. Their daughter, Cécile, is born in May, 1918.

Before entering the Army, Eluard had had two small booklets of poems printed at his own expense, *Premiers Poèmes* and *Dialogues des inutiles*. The poems that grew out of his wartime experience took their first form in a twelve-page mimeographed pamphlet entitled *Le Devoir*, which he printed in the summer of 1916 in an edition of twenty copies, most of which he sent to Gonon for distribution. As the poems increased in number, he arranged with Gonon for a new edition called *Le Devoir et l'inquiétude*, which included eleven new poems and a group of prose poems to which he gave the title *Le Rire d'un autre*. In July, 1917, Gonon had an edition of 206 copies printed, illustrated with a woodcut by André Deslignières.

As the end of the war moves into sight, Eluard's letters become rhapsodic. He is writing *Poèmes pour la paix* and sends Gonon a sample:

> Splendide, la poitrine cambrée légèrement,
> Sainte ma femme, tu es à moi bien mieux qu'au temps
> Où avec lui, et lui, et lui, et lui et lui,
> Je tenais un fusil, un bidon—notre vie.

On the eve of the Armistice Eluard writes to Gonon: "We are going to fight for happiness, after having fought for Life." He has now printed his *Poèmes pour la paix* in the form of a broadside and sends him a copy. But his elation is tempered: "I am writing somber poems . . . as somber as nothingness. . . . I have been greatly shaken by the death of Apollinaire. . . . No one will give what he endlessly promised. . . ."

The final letters show a "stronger and more intelligent" Eluard. Although he was not to be demobilized until mid-1919, he was already embarked on the new life that would take him to the center and one of the peaks of the French literary world during a period in which his was the sweetest voice, the most tender, in French lyric poetry. It was a voice nourished by Paul Verlaine and Guillaume Apollinaire, a voice that, in its turn, nourished us all—until the Party took it over.

In one of the manuscripts I had bought, which Eluard addressed to the future of poetry, he wrote:

> We need only a few words to express the essential;
> we need all the words to make it real.

I have no doubt that he thought, between 1942 and 1952, that he was making it—"the essential"—real, that he was moving from words to deeds, from the dream to reality. But all the words he used to make it real during that decade of dedication to the Soviet ideal are far from being the equal of the "few" he had used before then to express the essential. Funeral oratory to the contrary notwithstanding.

Chapter 3

Rose Adler, one of the most subtly effective bookbinders of our time, was for years a neighbor of mine on the Ile Saint-Louis. One early-summer day in 1953 she came to lunch, bringing with her a copy of a newly published novel, *Jules et Jim* by Henri-Pierre Roché. Rose and Roché had been friends for many years and she wanted me to read this delightful book by her old friend Pierre, then seventy-four. I read it and was as delighted with it as she was. I had heard about Roché forever, it seemed, through mutual friends and had read things he had written about Marie Laurencin, Kandinsky, Wols, and other artists, but somehow we had never met. Soon after reading *Jules et Jim* I was invited to call on him at his apartment in the Boulevard Arago, near the Lion de Belfort. He was then living most of the time at his house in Sèvres, just outside Paris, but he still came in, a few days a week, to that Paris apartment. He had grown up there, continued to live there with his widowed mother until she died (when he was fifty), and he used it as his social and business headquarters until almost the end of his life.

Jules et Jim captured the hearts and imaginations of a great many readers, but even so, it had a limited audience. In 1955 François Truffaut picked up a secondhand copy of the book in a shop across from the Comédie Française. He read the blurb and was intrigued by the idea of a "first novel" published by a man in his seventies. From the first page he was fascinated. The style made him think of Cocteau, he later told me, but a stronger Cocteau, because of Roché's simpler vocabulary and short sentences. He thought it one of the finest modern novels he knew. At that time Truffaut was a film critic with a burning ambition to make films. Eventually, in 1961, he made *Jules et Jim* and almost overnight it became one of everybody's favorites. But Roché had been dead for two years by then.

In 1956 Roché published a second novel—*Deux anglaises et le continent*—which Truffaut thought an even greater achievement. That, too, he made into a film, in 1977. But in 1953, as Roché and I talked about *Jules et Jim*, there was no thought of films or of the wide audience that *Jules et Jim* would eventually capture, not only as a film but also in translations that the film would bring about. He showed me some of the letters friends had written him about the book: Rose Adler, Jean Paulhan, and the painter Marie Laurencin, one of his earliest friends. Marie's letter thanked him for the book and went on to say:

> What memories and how true! We grow old, our feelings remain. Your book thrills me. I read it in one night. With all my heart, your friend Marie.

The novels are not Roché's only claim to fame. Early in the century it was Roché who brought together Picasso and the Steins—Gertrude and her brother Leo—and, in a sense, started the modern movement in art on its way to America. Later, he acted as bird dog and agent for the Irish-American lawyer John Quinn in the formation of what was to become the finest modern-art collection in private hands. Among dozens of other great paintings, that collection included the Douanier Rousseau's *The Sleeping Gypsy* (now in the Museum of Modern Art in New York), Seurat's *Le Cirque* (which Quinn bequeathed to the Louvre), and Cézanne's celebrated portrait of his father (now in the National Gallery, London). Roché was an intimate friend and early collector of Brancusi and Marcel Duchamp. His Brancusis are now numbered among the crown jewels of New York's Guggenheim Museum. An unfinished novel he called "Victor" celebrates Duchamp, whom he called "Totor," and was published posthumously for the Duchamp exhibition that marked the opening of the Pompidou Center in Paris. Among his close friends were musicians with whom he collaborated at times, such as Erik Satie, Albert Roussel, and Georges Auric.

In 1959 Roché died. Over the years that followed, his widow, Denise, spent a good deal of her time putting his estate in order. He had accumulated hundreds of paintings and sculptures and those had to be disposed of. Being of an extremely orderly nature, she went through all his papers, organized them in systematic fashion and then, in the late 1960s, began to turn them over to me in accordance with conversations I had had with Roché, directed toward that end, in the final years of his life. In due course, I made my way into the mass. In talking with me he used to refer to the letters he had received as "documents," sometimes as *"graphologie,"* since he set great store by people's handwriting (on occasion, going so far as to submit a new acquaintance's handwriting to a graphologist for an analysis of character traits). And, I discovered, the letters were indeed "documents," in the best sense of the word. They charted the course of art and literature in the first half of the twentieth century with a precision and a breadth equaled by no other archive I had encountered.

Marie Laurencin, for example, was represented by 268 pieces totaling 600 pages—a more revealing correspondence than any other of hers. It shed new light on Guillaume Apollinaire, Picasso, Francis Picabia, Diego Rivera, Gertrude Stein, Georges Braque, André Breton, and many others. Some of the letters included original sketches in pen-and-ink and watercolor. There were manuscript poems by Marie and original photographs of her by Man Ray and others.

Roché's Marcel Duchamp correspondence came to 228 pieces, over 350 pages, and is unquestionably the finest Duchamp correspondence known, rich in details concerning Breton, Fernand Léger, Yves Tanguy, Man Ray, Hans Richter, René Clair, Katherine Dreier, Max Ernst, Walter and Louise Arensberg, and many more.

There were other major correspondences from Erik Satie and Georges Auric, and long, crotchety letters from John Quinn. There were large groups from Gertrude Stein, Brancusi, Picasso, Braque, Cocteau, Jacques Doucet, Jean Dubuffet, Félix Fénéon, Jean Paulhan, Wols, and scores of other writers, sculptors, painters, musicians, and collectors.

Among the papers in Roché's Gertrude Stein file, I found one of the most extraordinary letters ever written by her, one that might well be included in any anthology of prime documents of the feminist movement. But first, a bit of background.

In *The Autobiography of Alice B. Toklas* by Gertrude Stein, there is an account of a visit Gertrude and Alice made to the studio of an English sculptor named Kathleen Bruce, who was going to do a bust of Gertrude's nephew Allan:

> . . . There, one afternoon, they met H.P. Roché. Roché was one of those characters that are always to be found in Paris. He was a very earnest, very noble, devoted, very faithful and very enthusiastic man who was a general introducer. He knew everybody, he really knew them and could introduce anybody to anybody. He was going to be a writer. He was tall and red-headed and he never said anything but good good excellent and he lived with his mother and his grandmother. He had done a great many things, he had gone to the austrian mountains with the austrians, he had

gone to Germany with the germans and he had gone to Hungary with hungarians and he had gone to England with the english. He had not gone to Russia although he had been in Paris with russians. As Picasso always said of him, Roché is very nice but he is only a translation.

Later he was often at 27 rue de Fleurus with various nationalities and Gertrude Stein rather liked him. She always said of him he is so faithful, perhaps one need never see him again but one knows that somewhere Roché is faithful. He did give her one delightful sensation in the very early days of their acquaintance. Three Lives, Gertrude Stein's first book was just being written and Roché who could read english was very impressed by it. One day Gertrude Stein was saying something about herself and Roché said good good excellent that is very important for your biography. She was terribly touched, it was the first time that she really realised that some time she would have a biography. It is quite true that although she has not seen him for years somewhere Roché is probably perfectly faithful.

But to come back to Roché at Kathleen Bruce's studio. They all talked about one thing and another and Gertrude Stein happened to mention that they had just bought a picture from Sagot by a young spaniard named Picasso. Good good excellent, said Roché, he is a very interesting young fellow, I know him. Oh you do, said Gertrude Stein, well enough to take somebody to see him. Why certainly, said Roché. Very well, said Gertrude Stein, my brother, I know is very anxious to make his acquaintance. And there and then the appointment was made and shortly after Roché and Gertrude Stein's brother went to see Picasso.

This, of course, is typically Gertrude Stein: half-facetious, half-malicious; superficially full of good humor, but very close beneath the surface, unmistakable evidence that she is settling accounts. Why should she be settling accounts with Roché? After all, he had liked her first book, *Three Lives*, and praised it to all his friends as far afield as Germany. There is a clue in a letter that Picasso wrote to Roché on April 7, 1911:

My dear friend,
    I didn't see you at our friend Sam Langford's but today I saw Gertrude Stein. She and I would like you to help us translate her portrait of Mr. Picasso.
    I hope that we shall see you soon at my place. In any case Saturday (to-morrow) we are going to the Cirque Medrano and Gertrude Stein will be with us.

Yours sincerely,
Picasso

Over the next few months Roché read that portrait and others by Gertrude Stein and he began to have second thoughts about her work. Finally, he made so bold as to address the following letter to her (the English is his):

Dear Miss Stein,

The other day you told me about this girl at Vendôme's Tea Room. . . . It was a good story. I had a good laugh. Then, suddenly, you say it again, shorter, but the same. You spoil my laugh. I ask myself: "Why does she say it again?"

I get angry with you to spoil it for me by those d . . . . . repetitions. . . . Many repetitions have great purpose and efficiency, but they have a sea of sisters, which, I think, have perceivable meaning for nobody but you.

I start reading your style only when I feel very strong & want in a way to suffer. After a few minutes I am giddy, then sea-sick, though there are islands to be seen. It is no river, no sea, c'est une inondation l'hiver dans la campagne. Rythm [sic]? Ah yes. But that sort of rythm is intoxicating you—it is something like masturbation.

Of course it is very enjoyable to let one self go & write heaps—but . . . why don't you finish, correct, re-write ten times the same chaotic material till it has its very shape worthy of its fullness? A condensation of 60 to 90% would often do?

Do you know any one (human not literary) who, without knowing you, or the models of your portraits, or both, has understood something in them?

Melanctha is great in my memory. I was quite at home with her, though I had already some toil. I thought your style would concentrate, it has enormously expanded.

The last things stand upon the strength of your personality. Far from your eyes, they fall to pieces.

Your own right faith in yourself shakes other people's doubts about your ways of expression—they probably do not tell them much in front of you?

Are not you after all very lazy?

With frankness, humility and perhaps huge stupidity

Yours very sincerely
H P Roché

That letter was written and mailed on February 6, 1912. In those days and for years after, a letter mailed in Paris before noon to a Paris address was delivered the same day. So Gertrude Stein received it that afternoon. And on that same day she wrote Roché the extraordinary letter I referred to earlier:

My dear Roche [sic],

I made an epigram the other night. I said that women take their impression to be an intuition, men take their impression to be a construction. Now it is perfectly true that more men construct than women and so we might say that construction is a man's business. Being beautiful is a woman's business but there are a great many women who are not beautiful and they act stupidly the ones that are not beautiful if they act as if they were beautiful and xpect [sic] to achieve the results of one being beautiful. Now to take the instance of yourself and myself. You are a man and I am a woman but I have a much more constructive mind than you have. I am a genuinely creative artist and being such my personality determines my art just as Matisse's or Picasso's or Wagner's or any one else. Now you if I were a man would not write me such a letter because you would respect the *inevitable* character of my art. It would be very much (if I were a man) as if [Patrick Henry] Bruce were to advise Matisse. You would not do it however you might wish my art other than it is. But being a man and believing that a man's business is to be constructive you forget the much greater constructive power of my mind and the absolute nature of my art which if I were a man you would respect.

Do you see why I think your letter unimportant and stupid. I have often felt much pleasure and much encouragement as you know from your appreciation but that is as far as any outsider can be of assistance to any one genuinely creative.

Sincerely yours
Gertrude Stein

Poor Roché! He must have felt as though a ton of bricks had fallen on him. He crawled for cover and after several experimental drafts, sent the following letter:

Dear Miss Stein,

Please believe that I have written such letters to men. I have spoken to you as a man-friend, and I have given a true impression, without meaning advice. I thoroughly respect and much like your work and your mind.

I agree with you upon the quality of your art, though not upon the inevitable character of the whole of its form of today.

Yours as before,
HPR

A few days later Gertrude Stein grudgingly and grumblingly replied:

Alright Roche [*sic*] we will just agree that you as you are now and I as
I am cannot agree either to agree or to differ.

Sincerely yours

Gertrude Stein

Her next letter to Roché was dated almost eight years after that one.

So much for Gertrude; what about Leo Stein and Roché? In his book
Appreciation: Painting, Poetry and Prose, Leo tells of visiting the art
gallery of an ex-clown named Clovis Sagot, in the Rue Laffitte, and of
buying from him Picasso's painting *Famille d'acrobates avec singe.*
"Soon after," Leo wrote, "I learned that a friend, Pierre Roché, knew
Picasso. Roché, a tall man with an inquiring eye under an inquisitive
forehead, wanted to know something more about everything. He was a
born liaison officer, who knew everybody and wanted everybody to
know everybody else. He introduced me to the literary band at the
Closeries [*sic*] des Lilas—Jarry, Moréas, Paul Fort and others who had
recently made literary history—and once a month or so he came to see
me, and tell me his news and hear mine. We talked the whole night
through. I was always having ideas, and as the same neurosis that kept
me from painting kept me from writing also, it was nice to have someone
like Roché, who was more ear than anything else. He was delighted to
know that I had seen the work of Picasso, and a few days later led me to
the Rue Ravignan."

In another place, Leo tells it another way:

> I had a friend in Paris—H.P. Roché, a man of little originality but much
> curiosity—who used to come to the house about once a month over a
> term of years before the war to hear my latest news. He generally came
> about ten at night and I talked to him till early morning, and there was al-
> most always something new. He made notes at times for a projected
> book of "Conversations with Leo Stein," but nothing came of it as with
> many other plans of his. . . .

Leo was half-right about Roché, who was, indeed, a man of "much
curiosity." But he was also a man of not "little" but much originality.
And although Roché was a remarkable listener (as all his friends would
agree), he was more than just an "ear," as Leo put it. That "inquiring
eye under [the] inquisitive forehead" that Leo referred to made him a
much finer art connoisseur than either of the Steins. And the combination of the curiosity, the originality, the ear, and the eye was turning
Roché into an extraordinary diarist, as well.

* * * * *

Roché spent his life in three principal ways: (1) making friends, (2) being a kind of private art dealer (guiding people like John Quinn, Hilla Rebay, and other affluent collectors who benefited from his judgment and connections), and (3) keeping a journal. Transcribed single-spaced on 8″ x 11″ sheets, his journal runs to about seven thousand pages. Among other things it establishes two facts: (1) Roché was, without any doubt, one of the greatest lovers in the history of literature, and (2) he documented that aspect of his life in such a thoroughgoing and convincing manner as to make him—in the judgment of the few who have read even some portions of his unpublished journal—one of the greatest diarists in the history of love. Roché kept his journal from the turn of the century until he died, in 1959. Since, as Gertrude Stein put it, "he knew everybody, he really knew them," everybody—or nearly everybody, under a variety of pseudonyms—passes through its pages. Great numbers of French writers have kept journals, often for the purpose of periodic publication, and their content generally ranges from literary gossip to philosophical primping. Roché's journal had a very different function. He had early assigned himself the mission of studying women, and his journal is, above all, the mirror of that uninterrupted preoccupation.

By arrangement with the Roché family, François Truffaut kept a copy of Roché's journal in his office (as I did in mine). He told me that hardly a week passed that he didn't dip into one part or another, just for the pleasure. The two Roché novels he made into films—*Jules et Jim* and *Deux anglaises et le continent* (known here simply as "Two English Girls")—were drawn from Roché's journal. In the case of *Jules et Jim*, Jules's real-life counterpart in the journal was a German-Jewish writer friend of Roché's named Franz Hessel. Jim, of course, was Roché. The young German woman of the triangle—called Kathe in the book and Catherine in the film—was Helen Grund, later Helen Hessel. But she was not the only woman that Roché and Hessel shared. At a slightly earlier period they had shared a French girl, the young artist Marie Laurencin, whose serene work and unquiet nature interested Roché, and that relationship prefigured the three-cornered friendship which forms the basis of *Jules et Jim*. Marie was then at the beginning of her career as a painter, a fellow-student of Georges Braque and Francis Picabia at the Académie Humbert. Drawings she had done caught

Roché's eye and he bought several, along with some of her engravings. In every sense, he was her first collector. Marie appears in Roché's journal under several code names. In the following passages (which I have translated from Roché's original French) he refers to her as "Flap":

> *March 26, 1906.* Flap is twenty [twenty-two] years old. Her black dress molds a body which is a ripple of vibrant flesh. Her arms are bare below the elbow, the skin rather dark, with delicate hands; her hair dark chestnut, slightly curly; a long nose almost too fine; high, mobile brows; flashing, almond-shaped eyes, which go well with the wide mouth turning up at the corners, and then suddenly, right in the middle, the lower lip becomes very full. She is direct, frank, plays the tomboy, talks tough, a mixture of boldness and naïveté, very much the young girl, the virgin. She is a painter, does portraits of herself, very original ones.

Roché and Flap and a friend he calls Gyo go out to dinner and then to the Bal Tabarin to watch the quadrille. Flap is excited by the dancers' legs. She says she will try the dance when she gets home. "My legs are rounder than my arms," she tells them.

The next entry is dated April 1. Roché and Flap are with Gyo at his studio. The two men take turns dancing with Flap, then ask her to show her legs, since she promised she would when they were at the Bal Tabarin. "They are beautiful legs," Roché writes, "long, well-rounded, slender at the ankle, graceful and noble. The legs of an eighteenth-century Diana. She is delighted with our delight and to add to it, she lets down her hair. It falls in heavy, thick tresses below her waist." Roché again observes that her lower lip thickens and puffs out in a way that drives an arrow straight into his belly.

Gyo picks up his violin and begins to play gypsy melodies. Flap stretches out on the divan. Roché turns down the lamp and sits on a cushion at the foot of the divan. He touches lightly one of her feet and she moves it into his hand. He takes off the small dancing-pump she is wearing and caresses her foot rhythmically to the violin accompaniment. He feels her foot quivering. She raises her other leg and places that foot in his other hand. He caresses her calves and finds he is ecstatically happy. The violin music stops and Gyo comes over to join them. Flap sits up and puts her hand in Roché's and leaves it there. "She has frank, naïve, appealing ways," he notes, "like a little girl. She is flirting, independent, capricious."

They go out for dinner and afterward walk across Paris together. Gyo leaves. Flap tells Roché her ideas about love, starting from the time when she was twelve years old and lay awake all one night after a boy told her—in English—"I love you."

The next week there is another dinner and a walk around Montmartre, the streets deserted under a full moon. Flap gives Roché her hand. He caresses it with his and asks her, "Are we friends?" She hesitates, then says, "I don't really think so." He: "You know I'm falling in love with you." She: "Ah—in that case, what's going to come of it?" He: "I don't know." She thinks that over silently, then tells him very simply and without preamble about her first menstrual period and what a surprise it was to her and how the older girls at her school guessed it right away. By now she and Roché have reached her door. Roché wonders whether she will move closer to him as a sign that she might like to have him kiss her on the cheek. She doesn't; so he takes her small hand in his and kisses it.

On April 16, Flap comes to Roché's apartment. She walks around inspecting everything, then asks him, "Who are the women who come here?" He tells her about his two closest women friends. She listens, nods. He moves closer, touches her hands. She asks, "Have you already had a virgin?" He tells her yes. "That disgusts me," she says and pulls away from him. "I'm wrong; it's stupid," she adds, "but that's the way it is." She asks him more about the virgin. As he talks, she becomes more and more interested in his story and soon is in his arms. "I talk on and on," Roché notes. "She understands everything, occasionally summarizing things quickly and neatly and in a most original fashion. It is a pleasure to follow her mind."

He follows not only her mind but also her lips, especially the lower one, which continues to exert its special fascination over him. She says, "Men have an exaggerated notion of young girls' vices. I've heard them talk, and I've read their books. At the *lycée* I never ran into anything like that. One girl told me how she masturbated. I tried it but I didn't like it and so I didn't keep it up." They kiss and her cheeks grow redder, up to her temples. Roché senses that she is feeling pain. He thinks back to a girl he calls Mauve, one of the sisters whom he later wrote about in his novel *Deux anglaises et le continent*—the virgin he had referred to in answering the question put to him a few minutes earlier. He sees the same tragic quality engraved on this face as on the earlier one at a comparable moment. "The female is being born and is trembling inside her," he reflects. He thinks back to his puberty, to "the sensation"

Henri-Pierre Roché by Man Ray, c. 1925.

Marie Laurencin. The artist has added ink sketches of a plumed hat and her dog, Coco. With autograph note to Henri-Pierre Roché, c. 1914.

H.-P. Roché, practicing his swing, c. 1921.

Franz Hessel, the Jules of *Jules et Jim.*

H.-P. Roché. Opening page of the first draft of his manuscript of *Jules et Jim*.

surging up in a dream, the first time, almost like a form of pure pain, leaving him in a stupor afterward. And so he begins to feel sorry for her. Almost as if she were reading his thought she says, "Don't think you're going to take me. That will never happen. Not you, or anyone else, even if I were to love. It's out of the question." They move apart, have tea, laugh happily, as they had been doing before they began to kiss, and then she grows silent, looks up at him and says, "What's it like to make love?"

"Love?" Roché asks himself. "I search for an answer. I talk on and on, just as if I were thinking out loud. I speak of using a light bow against her delicate nerves, of a storm and lightning and rain. I don't know what else I said. I stop talking. I look at her. She is as flushed, as inert, as she had been after the kissing. Her lips are open, her eyes heavy. Finally she says, 'That's all for today. It gives me too much of a headache.'"

In her letters to Roché, which start at this point, Marie has recurrent visions of death and finds her virginity oppressive. Her good friend Georges Braque sits and stares at her through blue-tinted glasses, doesn't understand her moods, accuses her of being a Lesbian. She looks ahead and wonders how things will be with Roché and her in six months. She wants to see him—just wants to relax, up against him, but do nothing that will tire her out. She goes to the country with her mother and misses Roché terribly. She suffers from a number of neurasthenic afflictions—among them, tachycardia. Noises and strong light bother her. She cries a lot. She takes one of his letters out to the back of the garden to read and finds she is as moved as one is by some sudden, well-loved fragrance from the past. She reproaches him for not writing often enough. She tries to keep their correspondence secret. Her mother would never understand. She is sure she is going to die—bad enough by itself but she hates the thought of dying a virgin. She has heard from Braque and thinks of him often because he suffers from the same kind of mood swings as she does. The days seem long and she goes to bed early to make them pass more quickly. She studies her lips, her body, and is afraid of growing old. She twists her ankle, it swells, and her once beautiful legs are now badly matched. She thinks the swelling will move from her ankle to her knee, from her knee to her belly, from her belly to her heart and then she will die.

Back in Paris, a girl named Raymonde enters the correspondence. She tells Marie she admires her body. Marie wouldn't mind making out with her, but Raymonde is rather conventional. And besides, where could they go—"not to her house or mine either." Marie sees another girl on the tram, who exhilarates her, "but I'm very shy." She hasn't written to Braque lately. A lot of stupid stories are going around about his being hooked on opium. That exasperates her. Roché does, too, because he has too many women. At the Louvre she sees a Tanagra figurine with hips and buttocks that round out just like her own. She has voluptuous Lesbian fantasies. She writes poems and sends Roché some. Many of her letters are prose poems, written in a suggestive, elliptical style.

Inevitably, Marie's oppressive feelings about her virginity and Roché's not entirely selfless concern for her troubled, transient state lead them to the edge of the traditional solution, with reservations on both sides. Soon after, Roché introduces Marie to his friend Franz Hessel and she warms to Franz. Roché encourages both of them and before long Marie and Franz are lovers—up to a point.

26 November 1906. Franz's room. He, Flap, and I. . . . Flap . . . begins to rummage through Franz's closet, shows off his neckties, and makes us laugh. Tea. Flap dances, shows her lovely legs, lets down her hair, throws herself across Franz's big bed. On each side of her, at a distance, Franz and I stretch out and each of us takes one of her hands.

She and Franz sing softly to each other. . . . With her eyes fixed on Franz, Flap moves closer to me, and the movements of her hand ask for caresses. I caress. First her arm, then her leg and her thigh. Darkness is falling. They continue to sing. My finger reaches her sex, closed then suddenly half-open, and Flap, still singing, trembles a little. My caress is light.

I get up to leave. Finally she looks at me. Her expression frightens me.

I leave them together for the evening.

13 December. On Franz's bed. Franz, Flap and I. They are a delight to look at. We talk. It's almost unreal. Franz finishes my sentences, I finish his. They play cat and mouse. Franz is the cat, Flap's hand the mouse and my vest the mousehole.

Flap leans back against me. I growl a few indistinct words into her shoulder and my arm slips around her waist and brings her mouth over to mine.

Franz is now on the chaise longue. My mouth brushes up against, then nibbles at, Flap's. Our lips dance back and forth. She bends into me. "I love you," she says. Franz excites her but doesn't take her. I pick up Flap like a little child and set her down on Franz.

She doesn't move; her face is flushed, as though she were sulking.

16 December. Things to do. I slept only a moment. I go to Franz's place, still drowsy.

Flap is there. She tells me, "I love you. I've been thinking of you," and her eyes are beautiful.

17 December. Farewell dinner for Franz. He leaves tomorrow. He is sitting across from Flap and me. Flap says to Franz, "You and I, we love in the same manner and I know what that is." To me she says, "I don't know how you love. You must love some woman but probably not me. . . ."

Franz and I enjoy the same women, but we desire different things from them. I don't think there has ever been any rivalry between us. . . .

We go to a gay bar. Flap grows ecstatic over one of the boys as she watches him dance.

We walk home. At her door I drift away so she can say good-bye to Franz. They kiss. They are sad and yet they laugh.

20 December. My place. Flap. We talk about Franz. We miss him.

Lips, without haste, deeply. Flap trembles. My hands remain chaste. No desire today, neither she nor I.

She says: "When we are together, even with others around, I sense your desire for me, great or not. Do you sense mine? You love several women, but I think you grow tired of them quickly. That makes it easier for me to put up with. . . ."

We talk of our future love, and that brings me her passionate mouth. She fits herself into my arms, my elbows, my legs, slides underneath me. Once again her mouth. Nothing more.

I miss Franz, especially when I'm with Flap.

23 December. Flap. I hold out my hands to you, washed, brushed, scented.

Flap . . . you are good for me. I want you. . . .

You say no. And yet you go to bed—with me up against you.

The flow of your body, those slender lines that move out from your eyes. I want you. I'll take you. . . .

Your face changes. You take your arms away from my head, spread them, your lips soar, your eyes come wide open, and out of your mouth, a slow cry of harmony and joy. You say: "More . . . don't stop. . . ."

I look at you, without thinking of myself.

"Take me—hard," you say.

I take you. Hard.

And then you strike me and hide your face. You're afraid.
I find my pleasure in obeying you.

While Franz is away, Marie writes to tell Roché how much she misses
Franz. On his return, subtle problems of triangularity arise. Marie's
moods change with the days. In one short note she writes to Roché:

> I'm sick for you. All night long, not a wink. I've never thought about you
> so urgently. I want your arms. Answer soonest—I beg of you. Sunday I'll be
> free only after four. I love you. My sweetheart, how are you? Your own.
> Answer.

In another: "I love Hessel. I'm ill because I must leave for four days
and I won't see him until Thursday. If you see him before I do, watch
over him for me. He is my dear, dear lover." And in the next, she sets up
a meeting with Roché at the Trocadéro for a "sentimental stroll, because
here we're swimming in sentiment. Franz is in love with you and all the
other men are in love with one another, which leaves me out in the
cold. . . ."

Trying to come in out of the cold, Marie becomes more sexually
aggressive, and Roché and Franz begin to back off. "Something about
her is dying in us," Roché confides to his journal. Franz tells her he no
longer loves her; she tells *him* she loves him anyway. "She is suffering,
in her fashion," Roché writes. "She needed that; she's been spoiled."
The old camaraderie creeps back in at times but things aren't quite the
same. Marie seems abstracted and authoritarian toward both of them.
One evening in a café, Roché tries to pin down the change. "At last I've
got a lover I can love," Marie blurts out. Since when? Roché asks her. A
week, she tells him—which would situate her first encounter with the
new man somewhere during the first days of July, 1907. She makes
them guess at his identity. The game goes on a long time; finally, with
help from Marie, Roché comes up with the right name: Guillaume
Apollinaire. Marie had met him through Picasso at Clovis Sagot's
gallery. Roché knows him well, finds him a mixture of "somewhat
bestial organic power and ingenious mysticism." Roché and Franz fall
silent: surprise, shock, jealousy? She taunts them with Apollinaire's
maleness: he is "full of temperament." She's taking her revenge for
their neglect, Roché realizes. She doesn't even worry about getting
pregnant any more, as she did with them, she says. "I don't give it a

thought. It won't happen to me." Roché's love has cooled, but his pride is wounded. Even so, the three remain in contact.

On October 15, 1907, Marie writes to Roché:

> Dear Friends. Don't be angry because I haven't answered your sweet cards. I've been sick—for a month I was in bed nearly all the time. Now I'm getting better, but not yet out of the woods. If you see any friends of ours, don't say I've been sick. That would oblige me to go into details that seem very disagreeable to me now.

That cryptic reference to her condition, and others that follow, point to the consequences of Marie's recent indifference to the risk of pregnancy and, along with it—given her disinclination to bear children—the invariable result. But she continues on a more cheerful note:

> If you are in Paris . . . come see me, in a little house with books, port wine . . . in a room with beautiful paintings of me all alone, very pretty . . . and Wilhelm de Kostrovoitzsky [i.e., Kostrowitzky, Apollinaire's real name] whom you will ask for at the concierge's lodge. This letter is also for Franz Hessel. I want him to come, too. . . .

The next letter, written five or six days later, is on the letterhead of Apollinaire's short-lived review *Le Festin d'Esope.* Marie has crossed out the title and written in "9 rue Léonie," Apollinaire's address.

> Dear Roché and dear Franz. Come Thursday around 8 or 8:30—after dinner—for a first confrontation. Wilhelm wanted me to ask you for dinner, but I think that for a first time, this way is preferable.
>
> I'm feeling pretty well—supposed to see a doctor on Monday, because the one who came to see me at my mother's was no help at all. I've been losing blood for a month now, with repeated hemorrhages. Well, see you soon. It's understood that Franz will come too. . . .

There is no record in the correspondence of that "first confrontation," but in letters that follow, Marie seems chastened. There are hints that the honeymoon with Apollinaire is wearing thin. She asks Roché to come see her, giving precise times when she will be free to have him call at her place or asking him to write and tell her what afternoon she can come to his, and there are meetings at the Trocadéro and in the Bois de Boulogne. Weaving their way through this increasingly complex relationship, there are other men and other women with whom Marie flirts, by whom she is tempted. Sometimes she writes, "I am not tempted to give in." On the other hand she is not tempted to remain faithful to Apollinaire. If she is faithful to anyone—in her fashion—it is to Roché and to Franz.

Early in the New Year 1910, Marie tells Roché she wants to "get away from Apollinaire and all the influences of his Bohemian circle"— Cremnitz (the poet Maurice Chevrier), André Salmon, Picasso, and his mistress Fernande Olivier. She finds them "a little noisy . . . effete . . . people one can't count on." She still has dinner with Apollinaire but says there's been nothing more between them for some time. He's all right, she says, but so confused and disorderly, and she finds he is coming to take on the manner of [the classicizing Greek-born poet] Jean Moréas. She no longer quotes Apollinaire as though he were Holy Writ, Roché notes.

Marie has a new lover now—Eugène Montfort, editor of the literary review *Les Marges* and a friend of Apollinaire. They are well matched, Roché thinks. They see each other only on Sundays, for highly gymnastic workouts. Roché sums up Montfort: "very French, solid, discreet, quick, precise, can be counted on, free-spending—very different in that respect from Apollinaire." Toward the end of May, 1910, Marie is in trouble again:

> I have another problem, the only real one I ever seem to have. I'm having it taken care of next Monday. I'll let you know how it works out. I hope I'll be all right. I want to see both you and Franz as soon as this matter is taken care of. What a nuisance to be a woman with such normal inner construction.

Apparently it didn't go well, because on June 4 she writes:

> I could have seen you because so far nothing has happened. My nerves are shot. I can't work. I'll expect you Tuesday at 3. I'd prefer to have you take me to your place for tea. I need to be distracted, and there are so few people I can stand. If you write to me, don't mention this problem. One never knows. . . .

Marie's nerves and her "normal inner construction" get patched up, finally, but by October 27, 1910, she is on the verge of a new crisis with a new lover—another "M," one of several—and things have reached the point where he seems to be trying to get rid of her. He is "vile . . . brutal" but although she has dear, witty friends like Apollinaire, Picasso, and Fernande, she likes him better. She is ashamed to admit that she will never love a man worthy of her love as much as she loves this one. She lies awake all night with wet cloths over her chest to stop her heart from beating so fast, she has lost weight and is very sad. But in the next breath: "My love life is calm and I'm waiting for an elegant adventure. Will it come? I'm having a dress made, split up the side so you can see my whole leg. Your friend for life, Marie." Then there's another big row with Apollinaire. She's tired of the way he blows up at her. Her nerves are in awful shape and she's losing confidence in her own work. She wants so badly to see Roché. On July 20, 1912 she asks him for help in getting rid of one young admirer who's making a nuisance of himself, and she needs his advice about a new star on the horizon who's coming on so strong she's almost sick over it. She's decided not to see Apollinaire any more and wants to talk about that. And so it goes.

Two years later, Marie decided to marry a German painter named Otto von Wätjen, one of the Montparnasse crowd, whom she had met through Roché. She told Apollinaire and he took the news badly. She was married on June 22, 1914, with Roché as one of her witnesses. When war broke out, Marie and her husband—now enemy aliens—fled to Spain and were stranded there for five years. Her letters to Roché from Spain show her career flourishing in spite of her enforced absence from France. Diego Rivera carries her canvases to Paris on the train and she has several successful exhibitions at Paul Rosenberg's gallery. She becomes a careful manager of her finances and arranges to have money sent regularly to friends who are less well off, in Paris and at the front—including Apollinaire, about whom she worries a great deal when he doesn't write. Yet when he does, he often gossips about her friends in a way that she considers a betrayal.

A young poet named André Breton—who is unknown to Marie—writes to her about her painting. He sends her a poem, which she finds a little silly (*"un peu bêta"*). A few months later she refers to him as "the charming, lovesick medical student." Old friends from Paris turn up in Madrid, Málaga, and Barcelona: Gertrude Stein, who interests her greatly; Albert and Juliette Gleizes; Francis Picabia, whom she takes to bed briefly but finds very "bourgeois" and unreliable. She and Picasso make a play for each other, take a "sentimental stroll" to a church (". . . real lowlife, both of us . . ."). She reads an article by Apollinaire in a recent issue of *Le Mercure de France* and spits on it. But no matter how turbulent her relations with others, Marie's friendship with Roché remained untroubled, lasting until her death in 1956.

* * * * *

From a very early age Roché had planned to write about all the varieties of love—unconscious, chaste, poetic, subtle, philosophical, and all shades of carnal ("the taste of an eyelid, the texture of muscles, the geography of the skin . . .").

In a diary entry for Saturday, 13 September 1919, he wrote:

> My desire [is] to write the story of my life one day, basing it on these note-books, like Casanova but in a different spirit.

The women who pass through the pages of Roché's journal—before and after Marie Laurencin—are without number. The "appeal of polyg-amy" which Roché noted in a journal entry during his teens, never dwindled. He kept seeking and finding "different qualities in different women." His first tentative transposition of that body of experience—long before his two novels—came in a collection of short stories on the theme of seduction which, with the encouragement of the critic Félix Fénéon, he published in 1920, under the title *Don Juan*, using a pseudonym ("Jean Roc"), rather than his own name, to appease his mother. Freud read the book and wrote to Roché that he had noticed its "correspondences" with "our psychoanalytic insights." And he added, "This is not surprising since we know that the poet and the analyst draw from the same sources." Had Freud known more about Roché's life style and his unbroken umbilical connection, he might have suggested a consultation.

In 1927, Roché married a woman who, in 1906, had answered an ad he had inserted in the newspaper (150 other women answered that ad and there were many other ads). He called this young woman "Viève," and she was the one he always returned to, across the years, from the myriad of others who wound their way through his nomadic existence. After their marriage, she stayed in her apartment on the rue Froidevaux and Roché went on living with his mother at 99 Boulevard Arago, just a few hundred yards away. Two months earlier, however, Helen Hessel—the Catherine of *Jules et Jim*, with whom he had maintained a passionate and turbulent relationship over the past dozen years or so—had moved in from the suburbs to an apartment equally close to Roché's. Roché continued to shuttle, a little more easily now, between patient, long-suffering Viève and restless, aggressive Helen, with regular stopovers "in Arago," as he put it. But by the time his mother died, two years later, Roché had taken up with Denise, also. Denise lived a bit farther away, in the Rue de Rennes. She wanted a child so badly, she told me years later, that life without one didn't seem worth living and she was almost ready to do away with herself. So Roché came to her rescue and gave her a child. He couldn't marry her but they did have their son and were at peace, momentarily, in spite of Viève's growing bitterness and Helen's outraged shouts of *"Lügner!"*—"Liar!"

Roché never stopped writing his journal—his one concession to fidelity. There were occasional gaps ("Twenty days without writing! And so much to write.") He returned to the earlier volumes time and again over the years, adding comments and summaries ("Rather interesting." "A bit daily and scattered." "Good simple recital.")

When Roché died, women everywhere mourned him—all except violent Helen and poor, gentle Viève, who had died eleven years earlier, in 1948, making way for Denise to become the widow. In spite of his ambitious plans to write the story of his life, basing it on his journal, he had only begun when death intervened. There had been too many travels, too many paintings, too many sculptures, and too many women.

Alas.

Chapter 4

The leading rare-book dealers in Paris after World War II were—in alphabetical order—Pierre Berès, a very shrewd and successful businessman; Georges Blaizot, a courtly and dignified gentleman; Georges Heilbrun, a man of scholarship, if somewhat pompous; Edouard Loewy, a good-hearted, incurable romantic; Marc Loliée, and H. Matarasso. Of all six, the fairest and least greedy was Marc Loliée. From some points of view, the most interesting was Matarasso. Why was that so, I ask myself, and there is no easy answer. Others were more suave, more erudite, more gracious, but nobody had Matarasso's special style. Not everyone would want it, I'm sure, but what he had, he had to a unique degree. He had gall, nerve, unlimited imagination, and a kind of equivocal charm that wound up by taking possession of you against your training, background, judgment, instincts—however one thinks of those protective devices we acquire throughout life which come tingling to warn us when danger lurks nearby. He had come from Belgium—not originally, but before the war—and had a large, blond Belgian wife, a former opera singer who looked like Brünnhilde but was called Carmen. He had been involved with the Paris/Brussels artbook publisher van Oest. Rumor had it that earlier on he had been a wholesale fruit dealer. But to a degree greater than most he had the sacred fire, and he had an incandescent passion for Arthur Rimbaud—the poetry, the life, the legend.

More than any other poet who ever lived, Rimbaud has inspired that kind of passion: a schoolboy from the Ardennes region near the Belgian border who sprang full-blown from the brow of Apollo and between the ages of fifteen and twenty wrote poetry that had no precedent in literature. At twenty he threw it all behind him and wandered over the world—an adventurer in every sense of the word—eventually buying, selling, trading in slaves, and gunrunning in Arabia and Abyssinia.

In 1891 Rimbaud was brought from the Arabian seaport of Aden to Marseilles suffering from a long-neglected tumor of the right knee. In the Hôpital de la Conception his leg was amputated. He stayed barely a month in the family home at Roche, near Charleville, and then, with the aid of his devoted sister Isabelle, he returned to Marseilles, hoping to get back to Aden and Harar. He was in such pain by the time he reached Marseilles that Isabelle took him back to the hospital. His illness was diagnosed, for the first time, as cancer and after much suffering he died, on November 10, 1891, at the age of thirty-seven.

In 1897 Isabelle Rimbaud married a painter-poet named Pierre [Médéric] Dufour, known to literature under the name Paterne Berrichon, who became, in the process and for all practical purposes, Rimbaud's literary executor and official biographer. He edited Rimbaud's works and letters, occasionally twisted the facts to suit what he saw as his duty to Rimbaud's memory, and fought the battles generally left to what the French call *les veuves abusives*. He wasn't the widow but, as the worshipful sister's consort, he came as close as he could to that role and many of his contemporaries felt he abused it.

Isabelle died in 1917 and Dufour married again. When he died, his widow was left in possession of the sad remains of Rimbaud's flight from Paris and poetry, at the age of twenty, into a life of vagabondage and commercial expediency. In his last journeys from Aden to Marseilles to Roche and back to Marseilles, Rimbaud carried a small, sturdy suitcase—a sacred relic known to every devout *rimbaldien* as *"la valise de Rimbaud."* It held all his worldly goods: his passport, his birth certificate, a few books, photographs and drawings, his copy of the Koran, letters from his mother and his sister Isabelle, a piece of woven material that could serve as a scarf or decorative table runner, papers documenting his commercial ventures—dealings in ivory, musk, hides, gum, slaves, arms—with some of the traders he was associated with, such as Labatut, Bardey, and César Tian. Down through the years those papers had made their way to Rimbaud's mother, to Isabelle, to Paterne Berrichon and, finally, to Berrichon's widow. And one day Matarasso made *his* way to her—Madame Veuve Pierre Dufour. Matarasso was about 5′6″ tall, stocky, swarthy, with dark hair, button-bright dark eyes, a ready, nearly constant smile (with just a hint of the barracuda), a warmhearted manner, an accent neither French nor Belgian, a fast-moving oral style, and, to top it all, a genuine passion for Arthur Rimbaud. In the end, Madame Veuve Dufour ceded—the French euphemism for sold—the famous valise to Matarasso. To its original contents had been added, over the years, other memorabilia, such as letters written to Rimbaud's sister Isabelle and to Paterne Berrichon in the course of their efforts to trace Rimbaud's path through life. Rimbaud's manuscripts are few in number, many having been destroyed by him or his way of life, by his family, and by the poet Paul Verlaine's wife, Mathilde, as a gesture of contempt toward the boy with whom her husband had fallen in love and who was thus responsible, in her view, for the breakup of her marriage. On the rare occasions when any fragment of manuscript by Rimbaud appears on the market, it fetches vastly more than a comparable piece by any other modern writer.

For what he got and for what it represented, Matarasso paid a very modest price, which probably seemed a very fair and reasonable—even tempting—one to Madame Veuve Dufour. It would be pointless to quote it because our sense of money values today, combined with the wild inflation that has affected prices of such rare material, would make it totally meaningless. But the miracle was to have got the valise and its contents whatever the price. And that was Matarasso's genius. In his Eastern-bazaar way he was irresistible.

What did he do with these things? Being a shrewd money manager, he sold off a few things he could bear to part with in the interest of getting his money back and turning a profit. The things he could not bear to part with, he kept. And everything else—no mean residue—he eventually gave to the Musée Rimbaud in Charleville to broaden and enrich their homage to their most illustrious son. In due course a grateful government made him a *Chevalier de la Légion d'Honneur*.

In the early 1950s, I was studying philosophy at the Sorbonne with Gaston Bachelard and Vladimir Jankélévitch and following René Huyghe's lectures on the Psychology of Art at the Collège de France. After classes I would often drop by one or another of the bookshops in the quarter. Sometimes it would be La Maison des Amis des Livres, in the Rue de l'Odéon, for a chat with Adrienne Monnier. Occasionally Sylvia Beach, whose Shakespeare and Company—just across the street—had been closed since the war, would be at Adrienne's. More and more frequently, I would wind up at Matarasso's place.

Mata—as all his friends called him—had a small shop in the Rue de Seine, just above the Boulevard Saint-Germain. His secretary, assistant, and general factotum was a bright, witty, good-humored young woman named Madeleine. On the ground floor of the shop there was just one smallish, square room with Madeleine's desk and chair. The three walls not taken up by the display windows on each side of the front door were covered with bookshelves. Behind that room was a small storage area with a winding metal staircase leading up to the *entresol*—a low-ceilinged second story with windows overlooking the Rue de Seine. The back wall behind the stairway was filled with an enormous painting by Francis Picabia in his early Impressionist manner. At the head of the stairs one entered a room that was immediately recognizable as the inner sanctum, its walls covered with portraits of Mata's holy trinity—Baudelaire, Verlaine, Rimbaud—and with likenesses in various media of André Breton, Paul Eluard, Tristan Tzara, René Char, and other members of Mata's—and modern poetry's—pantheon. A glass-front bookcase held some of the choicer stock, and there was a table facing it, in the center of the room, to which Mata would bring, one at a time, whichever of his treasures he was intent on selling you. Once you were accredited, you could browse at will in that glass-front case. Just beyond was another room, Madeleine's bedroom, large enough to hold a double bed and a massive French provincial armoire with two doors. The armoire contained the *grosses pièces*, things Mata saved for the select list or the dramatic moment. Nobody browsed there, as a rule.

Up until the time I met Matarasso, I had been principally a *book* collector. He was the one who opened my eyes to the overshadowing importance of manuscripts and thus changed the focus of my collecting. He did it in an odd and indirect way. He had a great affection for the Surrealist poets and had an excellent stock of their work. If he wanted to sell me a first edition of Eluard, for example, and I didn't seem immediately interested, he would reach into a drawer, pull out a manuscript poem by Eluard and tuck it into the book, to give the transaction added appeal. It was a successful tactic most of the time. He seemed to have an endless supply of such manuscripts. Whenever he sold one, the price would range from five to ten dollars; today that kind of one-page manuscript would cost a thousand or more.

His charm worked on everybody, not simply on little old ladies like Madame Veuve Pierre Dufour. He had had easy entrée with Eluard and Tzara, who "ceded" to him, whenever they needed money, all kinds of rarities from the heroic period of Dada and Surrealism. I remember one huge lot of rare ephemera he spilled out onto the table one day when he was in a housecleaning mood. There were rare tracts and manifestoes such as "Un Cadavre," in which members of the first wave of Surrealists who had been expelled from the movement by André Breton—among them, Jacques Prévert, Georges Bataille, and Raymond Queneau—in turn lambasted their "dictatorial" and "traitorous" leader; others, like "L'Affaire Aragon," "Misère de la poésie," and "Paillasse!," which dealt with Aragon's Communism; one titled "Protestation," in which Breton and Aragon took out after Max Ernst and Miró for working with the Ballets Russes; the famous defense of Charlie Chaplin, called "Hands off Love"; *Légitime Défense*, in which Breton dissociated Surrealism from Marxist control; a sheaf of papers from the wartime underground group "La Main à plume." There were little reviews in profusion: Tzara's *Dada*; Picabia's *Le Cannibale* and *391*; *Le Coeur à barbe* and *Z*, which never got past their first issue; the Dada review *Littérature*, edited by Breton, Aragon, and Soupault; Pierre Albert-Birot's *SIC*; Cocteau's *Le Coq*; wartime clandestine publications by which the poets of the Resistance circulated their works; catalogues of the earliest Paris exhibitions of Max Ernst, Yves Tanguy, Giorgio de Chirico, and Salvador Dali; prospectuses and invitations. In all, nearly two hundred pieces that documented many of the high points of avant-garde activity in Paris between the two world wars.

I looked through them carefully and Mata made me a price, which I accepted. He was alone in the shop, it was lunchtime—the most sacred moment in any Parisian's day—and he asked me to come back later so that he could have the papers packed up for me. I returned at the end of the day, picked up my package, and took it home. When I looked through the papers the second time, I found, in addition to what I had seen earlier, an envelope labeled *Papillons* in ink in Matarasso's hand and containing a number of those small rectangular pieces of colored paper the size of a calling card that the Surrealists used to stick onto walls in highly visible public areas, together with a small stack of cards about twice that size, each bearing a message such as "If you like love, you'll love Surrealism," "Parents, tell your dreams to your children," or "If you're not a priest, a general or an ass, you'll be a Surrealist" and—from a pre-zipper day—"Unbutton your brain as often as your fly." Since the *papillons*—literally, butterflies—were printed to be glued onto walls (there was an adhesive on the back) and were committed to the weather and the fate of all such public messages, they had always been among the scarcest of Surrealist artifacts. A note tucked inside the envelope read:

Dear Mr. Lake,

I have collected these *papillons* over the years from Eluard, Tzara, Arp, Valentine Hugo, and who knows how many others. I went through them all and took out the duplicates and now add one of each, with my compliments, to the lot you bought from me this morning. You weren't here when they were being pasted up all over Paris to shake up the bourgeoisie and I doubt that they ever got as far as Boston. But the ideas are still good and I commend them to your attention. Don't paste them up, however; they're too scarce for that. Just read them from time to time.

With cordial good wishes,
H. Matarasso

With little gestures like that Matarasso managed to get under your skin. And in the heady atmosphere of that private sitting room on the *entresol*, where Baudelaire, Verlaine, Rimbaud, and the Surrealists closed ranks with him as he passed back and forth from bookcase to table and armoire to table, there were times when you hoped that even though he *was* a barracuda, he would prove to have a light appetite. For him these encounters were moving experiences. He felt deeply everything he told you as he showed you his wares. He breathed harder, almost like an asthmatic at times; his hands (with one very short finger) trembled a bit, and you were drawn closer and closer into that communion of spirit which, if uninterrupted, can only result in total capitulation.

Having sprung from a long line of Yankee horse traders, I grew up with the pounding surf of the Maine coast in one ear and the dry nasal tones of Governor Calvin Coolidge in the other. That protected me from being an easy mark. But not all Mata's customers were so fortunate. For example: In France there are several categories of lawyers, each of which performs different functions. One subspecies, the *notaire*, is concerned with transfers of property. As a result, *notaires* are often entrusted with large sums of money over long periods of time in the course of settling estates, liquidating assets and, coincidentally, investing cash for their own and their clients' benefit. A *notaire* from the south of France, without great sophistication in the matter of rare books but well aware that they often showed a more dramatic increase in value than savings accounts or shares of stock, became a client of Matarasso. He was captivated by all he saw and heard and in no time at all, like Saul Bellow's Eugene H. Henderson, he was hearing a ceaseless voice in his heart that said, "I want, I want, I want, oh, I want. . . ." The French, great eaters, put it metaphorically: *L'appétit vient en mangeant.* The *notaire*'s appetite grew and grew; he spent and spent: rare first editions, principally of the Surrealist writers, then fine bindings and illustrated books—the best of everything modern. He spent his own money, and he spent his clients' money, and then one day he needed cash, lots of it, fast. An auction sale was scheduled at the Hôtel Drouot. It was the end of the season and buyers were beginning to think in terms of summer vacation. So the Right Bank firm of Coulet-Faure had to work around the clock to produce a catalogue, and did—just under the wire. There were four sessions and they included the best and most expensive of the *notaire*'s purchases: important autograph manuscripts by Guillaume Apollinaire, Louis Aragon, André Breton, Blaise Cendrars, Paul Eluard, Alfred Jarry, Henri Michaux, Benjamin Péret, Albert Camus, and others; moving letters from Antonin Artaud, written from Rodez, where he was undergoing psychiatric treatment; others from Marcel Proust— some of them as long as sixteen pages. The Dada and Surrealist writers were represented by their finest books—and nearly always in their rarest form, on large paper, limited to a small number of copies, the *notaire*'s copy often being No. 1 and, almost invariably, bearing a significant presentation inscription (from Breton to Eluard, for example). Many of the books had been beautifully bound by Pierre Legrain, Paul Bonet, Rose Adler, and other first-rank art binders.

Most of the principal dealers attended the sale. I saw Georges Blaizot, Edouard Loewy's brother Alexandre, Georges Heilbrun, Pierre Berès, Marc Loliée, Jean Hugues, the manuscript dealer Jacques Lambert, and the artbook publisher Louis Broder. Tristan Tzara showed up and bought a number of good things—manuscripts by Robert Desnos and Eluard, Max Jacob and Jarry, but none of his own books. I did, however, along with drawings and collages by Max Ernst, letters by Picasso, and a variety of other books and bindings. It was a long and hectic sale of 750 lots, vigorously fought for under the early-summer sun that poured in through the vaulted skylights of Room No. 9. It was hard, sweaty work for everyone in that hot, inadequately ventilated saleroom, but it was well worth the effort: There have been few sales in the thirty-five years since that week where so many jewels of the modern movement have rolled out in such profusion. Looking back on those prices today—well, it's better not to; nothing among all those great pieces is worth as little as ten times what it brought in that sale, and very little, twenty times. Many

Two pages from Stéphane Mallarmé's retained corrected draft of his letter to Arthur Rimbaud's mother, 25 March 1897.

Arthur Rimbaud photographed by Carjat soon after Rimbaud's arrival in Paris in 1871.

Tristan Tzara by Valentine Hugo. Ink drawing.

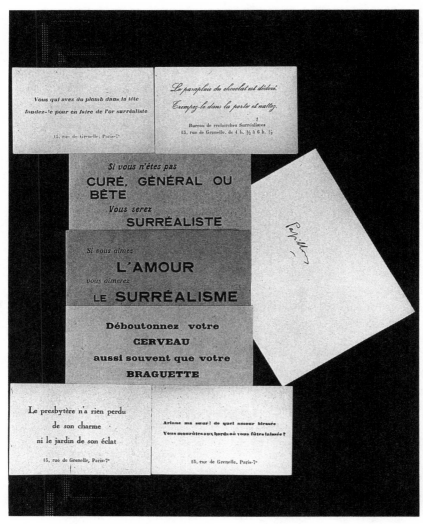

Vous qui avez du plomb dans la tête
fondez-le pour en faire de l'or surréaliste

15, rue de Grenelle, Paris-7e

Le parapluie du chocolat est déloré.
Trempez-le dans la porte et nattez.

Bureau de recherches Surréalistes
15, rue de Grenelle, de 4 h. ½ à 6 h. ½

Si vous n'êtes pas
CURÉ, GÉNÉRAL OU
BÊTE
Vous serez
SURRÉALISTE

Si vous aimez
L'AMOUR
vous aimerez
LE SURRÉALISME

Déboutonnez votre
CERVEAU
aussi souvent que votre
BRAGUETTE

Le presbytère n'a rien perdu
de son charme
ni le jardin de son éclat

15, rue de Grenelle, Paris-7e

Arianne ma sœur! de quel amour blessée
Vous mourûtes aux bords où vous fûtes laissée?

15, rue de Grenelle, Paris-7e

Surrealist cards and *papillons*.

of those things would fetch a hundred times what they did then; some much more. The main problem, though, is that things as good as that have all but disappeared from the open market: Of that quality and in that quantity they are simply not available at any price.

Oddly enough, I didn't see Matarasso at that sale. I wondered if perhaps his conscience was troubled. Having led the *notaire* down the primrose path and thus precipitated his financial debacle, did he feel out of place, like the poisoner at the funeral? No, I decided, he was not the introverted, *Angst*-ridden type who would be disturbed by such extraneous and, in the end, irrelevant considerations. It seemed more likely that he had decided that, having worked unremittingly to help this unfortunate fellow build up a library far more imposing than he could have achieved without his help, the least the man could have done was to sell it back to him and let him make some other collector as happy as *he* had been before his own private crash came about. Instead of which he had taken the auction route—perhaps in the hope of raising even more cash than he had originally laid out! So why should Mata attend the sale and put money into his pocket after that? True or not, I don't know, but, on reflection, it seemed more realistic than the first hypothesis.

After the auction was over, that Thursday afternoon, I dropped in to see André Faure, who had managed the sale and whose shop was then just down the street, a block or two, from the Hôtel Drouot. He had a cherubic smile, his gold tooth glistened, and he was obviously pleased with the results—and for 1954 they were very good indeed. Money had been raised in substantial quantity and fast. There was just one problem: Although most of the best of the *notaire*'s books had, for obvious reasons, been catalogued and dispersed under the auctioneer's hammer, there were a great many lesser but still fine things that just couldn't be squeezed into the sale, as well as a few duplicates of some of the books already sold. André had pushed the possibilities to the limit by scheduling a sale with four separate sessions on four successive days of the week. He hadn't dared go beyond that; the market isn't infinitely extensible. He took me out to a storeroom on the other side of the courtyard. Books were piled up everywhere; we could barely get into the room. It was nearly closing time, so I went back the next morning. We redistributed some of the piles and made room for two chairs. I went through the mass, book by book. Whenever I found one that interested me, I showed it to André. He suggested a price. If I could accept it, I did. If not, we dickered and settled on another price that both of us could accept. We followed that routine, with a few brief interruptions, for most of Friday and Saturday. Toward the end of the afternoon on Saturday—a low-traffic day for that area—I moved my big, lumbering American gas-guzzler to the front of his shop and we loaded it up with the results of our labors. Mine was, at the time, about the largest American car in Paris and it needed to be. I had come away with hundreds of books: such things as Georges Hugnet's *Oeillades ciselées en branche*, with illustrations by Hans Bellmer; Eluard's *Les Jeux de la poupée*, with hand-colored photographs by Bellmer; a fine lot of Jarry books and ephemera; a copy of one of the rare early Kahnweiler publications, Max Jacob's *Les Oeuvres burlesques et mystiques de Frère Matorel mort au couvent*, with original woodcuts by André Derain; a large-paper copy of Tzara's *Midis gagnés*, illustrated by Matisse, signed by author and artist; Japan-paper *exemplaires de tête* of Raymond Roussel's principal books, all with long presentation inscriptions, and on and on. There was no doubt about it: Whatever his other qualities, Mata's taste in literature and art was beyond reproach.

But to buy good things he needed more than just good taste; he needed, also, good sources, and those he had in profusion. I would occasionally see Tzara and Valentine Hugo at Matarasso's shop and I know, because of what I saw there, that he bought a good deal from Eluard. Jean Arp, Mata told me, didn't like to sell. "I sell to him but it's hard to buy from him. He's too much of a collector. Sometimes I can make a swap with him, though, and get things that way."

He had made one such deal with Picasso of which he was particularly proud. He had seen in a boxful of odds and ends in a grubby bookshop near the Rue de Seine frequented mostly by *courtiers*—runners without shops, on the lookout for sleepers in odd places, which they can sell to more established dealers—an autograph manuscript that was unsigned but that he had recognized at once as being in the hand of Alfred Jarry. The *bouquiniste* who ran the shop had no idea what it was and when Mata, in an offhand way, asked him the price, the man said he could have it for 300 francs—pre-1958, pre-de Gaulle francs—i.e., about 85 cents. Not to appear too eager, Mata asked him for the customary 10% professional discount. He agreed and Mata bought the manuscript for about 77 cents. He knew of Picasso's keen interest in Jarry and took the manuscript to him at his studio in the Rue des Grands-Augustins. "He was thrilled," Mata told me. "He looked through his portfolios and pulled out a beautiful gouache of the Minotaur embracing Diana—I think it was Diana—and he gave it to me. Just like that." I asked him if he had the gouache in his shop.

"*Pensez-vous!*" he said sarcastically. "I sold it right away for two million francs" (at that time, a little under six-thousand dollars). I asked him if he had shared the profit with the *bouquiniste.* He gave me his most barracuda-like smile and changed the subject.

Soon after, Mata was joined by Jacques, his son from an earlier marriage, a very pleasant, likable small man who, in appearance and personality, seemed to have little in common with his father. A small desk was set up facing Madeleine's in the downstairs room, and Jacques made three. Not long after that, Mata decided he had had enough of Paris and would move to the Riviera. He had been living in an apartment in a very unfashionable and somewhat remote section of Paris— the 20th *arrondissement.* Even so, his Midas touch didn't fail him. He found someone who owned a comfortable, hillside villa in Nice who wanted to come to Paris and either didn't know or didn't care that the 20th *arrondissement* was not the Garden of Eden. They made an exchange. Meanwhile Mata sold his shop to Marc Loliée. After the deal went through, Marc decided he didn't want to move out of the shop in the Rue des Saints-Pères where he had spent a good part of his life and so he turned over Mata's place to his son, Bernard, who had worked for Georges Blaizot, for Winnie Myers in London, for Madame Vidal-Mégret, one of the more active government-accredited *experts* at the auction end of the Paris book market, and was now ready to branch out on his own.

Mata then bought an attractive bookshop in Nice and—to everyone's surprise and delight—Jacques and Madeleine were married and started a new life together as booksellers there, in partnership with Mata—or so they thought. When the dust finally settled, they discovered they were not partners, they were employees, managing *his* shop, as his agents.

The art market was beginning to move into overdrive and so Mata bought a large apartment in the center of Nice that he arranged to have zoned for professional and commercial use. It had ten rooms. He chopped it in half and sold off the half he didn't want for more than the original price of the whole. The remaining half he converted to an art gallery. In his Paris days he had published several illustrated books, one of which brought together, under the title *Le Soleil des eaux,* René Char's poetry and original etchings by Georges Braque. The publication of prints and albums now was a logical next step. Mata had good connections with Picasso, Chagall, Jacques Villon, Cocteau, and many other very salable brand names and in his new location he was able to mount a number of highly successful exhibitions.

"Picasso can't do enough for me," he told me on one of his trips to Paris. "I called on him in Cannes just a few weeks ago and brought him a copy of *Hélène chez Archimède* to have him inscribe it for me. [*Hélène chez Archimède* is a book by André Suarès, whose illustrations the art dealer Ambroise Vollard had commissioned from Picasso twenty-five years earlier but which had been published only in 1955, long after Vollard's death.] He told me to leave it; he'd do it later. When I went back to pick it up, he'd decorated one of the preliminaries with a beautiful pen-and-ink drawing worth at least half a million francs." Mata smiled seraphically. "It's a real Capernaum, that place. It's like Ali Baba and the Forty Thieves. Cases of everything all over the place. He's got more millions than anybody could count. But he won't make a will. He's superstitious and he's afraid that as soon as he does—that's the end. But that new wife, Jacqueline, she's charming; small, completely devoted to him; simple—like him." He sighed. "I think he's found the woman of his life. In fact, he told me so. But imagine anyone living in a place that looks like that."

I was already familiar with Ali Baba's cave—"La Californie," Picasso's villa up in the hills behind Cannes—and I could empathize with Mata's yearning to get into those cases strewn around the premises. I don't think it was greed—or solely greed, or even principally greed—that made Mata lust after the contents of those provocatively half-open cases; it was his frustration at not knowing what, exactly, they held and imagining all kinds of probabilities—letters from everybody; manuscripts of Apollinaire, Jarry, Reverdy, Max Jacob; multiple copies of all the books Picasso had ever illustrated; first editions and other rare books he had bought or swapped over the years. More than greed, it was Mata's overheated imagination—the torment of not knowing, with everything so near and yet so unapproachable. Like Tantalus, up to his chin in water which receded whenever he tried to drink and standing under branches of fruit that drew away when he reached out to take them, Mata had a hunger and a thirst that could not be assuaged.

Mata suffered other frustrations, too, from time to time. "The most unkindest cut of all," *I* inflicted on him, involuntarily but inescapably. A large collection of important material relating to Rimbaud one day fell into my waiting arms: letters, manuscripts, and drawings by Paterne

Berrichon, including a drawing of the village of Roche done from the window of the attic room where Rimbaud had written *Une Saison en enfer;* another drawing of Isabelle Rimbaud reading at her brother Arthur's bedside; letters and manuscripts by Isabelle, all concerned with her brother, including her account of his deathbed return to the Church under her ministry; notebooks kept by the Gindre sisters, the lice-hunters of Rimbaud's poem "Les Chercheuses de poux"; hundreds of pages of manuscript by Georges Izambard, the single most influential figure in Rimbaud's life and his teacher at the moment of the bursting forth of those early great poems—among them, "Sensation," "Ophélie," and "Soleil et chair." They included a copy in his own hand of the letter Rimbaud wrote to him on 2 November 1870 after running away from home for the second time. And there were many other things of the same kind. The news reached Mata. Obviously he felt those things should have come to him, perhaps not by divine right but at least on the basis of priority, seniority, fidelity, or some other consideration, rational or otherwise. After all, he was the man who had carried off Rimbaud's valise. The thing he wanted most and hounded me for interminably was a letter written by Stéphane Mallarmé to Rimbaud's mother on 25 March 1897 in reply to one she had written earlier asking for his judgment of the suitability of Paterne Berrichon as the husband of her daughter Isabelle. It is a beautiful and moving letter, all six pages of it, but the aspect that made it incommensurably more desirable than anything I have said about it above was the fact that it was Mallarmé's retained draft of the letter he sent to Rimbaud's mother, with all his additions and emendations. Mallarmé, the greatest stylist in the history of French literature, the consummate artist, the perfectionist to whom every mark of punctuation was a matter of infinite concern, is here shown correcting himself in three dozen different ways and places to bring his letter up to the standard every line of his had to meet so that every letter, just as every poem, emerged a seamless garment. The letter Madame Veuve Rimbaud received is a great and valuable letter, but this original version of it is incomparably greater and it hurt Matarasso not to have it wind up in *his* hands. But . . . he recovered. And thrived. And eventually paid me back.

In a surging market Mata sold his gallery, by now a highly profitable going concern. From then on he devoted most of his time to improving his private autograph collection, in the fields of literature, art, history, and especially music. Years earlier, he had explained to me that music manuscripts were the ideal collecting area. Music was not only the universal language; it was the universal currency as well. "They're as sought after in London as they are in Paris; in Geneva as much as New York. They're pure gold all over the globe. If you have to pack up and leave in a hurry, you can stick the equivalent of a million dollars in your briefcase and nobody's the wiser. No worries about crossing the frontier with gold or banknotes. No customs problems at all. Debussy, Ravel, Stravinsky, Mozart, Beethoven—there's a very limited supply, everybody wants them, and prices just keep going up and up."

On his trips to Paris, Mata would generally call me. If I wasn't busy, I would sometimes sit with him for a while at the Deux Magots café, near his hotel, and let him brag a bit. He knew all the latest book-, manuscript-, and art-world gossip and he loved to tell stories. Sometimes if he had heard about something I had bought that he wanted, he would try to soften me up to see if I wouldn't pass it on to him. But I always resisted.

I saw him not long after the publication of the French translation of *Life with Picasso*, the book I had written in collaboration with Françoise Gilot. He was full of compliments about the book and had brought with him a copy for me to inscribe. The French Communist Party had orchestrated a propaganda campaign against the book and circulated a petition among artists, writers, and theater people, some of whom were Party members, to show Picasso that they were on his side. No matter that the book wasn't on any side; it just wasn't the usual incense-sprinkling, hushed-tones kind of treatment that the Party and the camp followers unfailingly turned out. Most of the signers were acolytes, Party stalwarts or the commercially interested; very few respectable, independent figures put their names to the petition. Giacometti, for example, was asked to sign and flatly refused, he told me. The great exception was Miró.

"I was with Miró only a few days ago," Mata said, "and I told him how surprised I was to see his name used in that way. 'But it's a bad book and it's anti-Picasso,' he said. I told him it certainly wasn't a bad book; it was a very good book. And it wasn't anti-Picasso. I asked him how he could do such a thing. Miró shrugged. 'That's what they told me, anyway,' he said. 'But have you read the book?' I asked him. Miró shook his head. 'Not yet,' he said, 'but I intend to. I just bought a copy.' 'Then why did you sign the petition?' I asked. He looked embarrassed. 'They asked me to, and I didn't want to hurt their feelings.'"

That sounded like Miró. I felt better, somehow. And I felt a surge of benevolence toward Mata for telling me the story. In the relaxed conversation that followed, I told him about a beautiful manuscript of Stravinsky that I had just bought—small but complete, a real gem. I had bought it by telephone and was going to pick it up later that afternoon.

When I got there, the dealer who had offered it to me had gone for the day. And the manuscript, oddly enough, wasn't there either. The dealer's clerk didn't seem to know anything about it and suggested I call back in the morning. When I did, I heard a long, complex story about the owner's having taken it back—changed his mind, second thoughts, and so on. Regrets. I later heard, via a very reliable stem of the grapevine, about a beautiful little Stravinsky manuscript that Mata had purchased on that very trip to Paris.

I learned a great deal from Matarasso over the years; not least, the truth of that slogan we used to see on posters during World War II: Loose lips sink ships.

Chapter 5

Across three decades I bought a great many books from Edouard Loewy, who had come from Hungary as a young man to study at the Sorbonne and stayed on to become one of the leading Paris rare-book dealers. He had started out, like many others, *"en appartement"*—in his case, selling from a small furnished room with his stock spread over the furniture, even the bed. He graduated to a Left Bank shop on the Boulevard Raspail but, being Jewish, had to go underground during World War II. When I knew him, after the war, he had re-established himself in a shop on the Right-Bank Boulevard Haussmann, near the end of the Faubourg Saint-Honoré, and did a thriving business both at auction, as an accredited *expert* working in tandem with the *commissaire-priseur* Champetier de Ribes, and through the catalogues he issued to an international and, in the main, affluent clientele. He loved books and wrote about them in an amorous way, sometimes tenderly, sometimes ecstatically, but always at great length and not always without hyperbole. But for a lover, hyperbole is a very small sin. He was proud of his indulgences and would often say, *"Je vends ma littérature"*—I sell my literature—a play on words, since he was, of course, selling literature in the form of books, but referring, rather, to *his* literature: what he wrote about those books in his catalogues. He was about 5'8" tall, with wavy gray hair and a large nose that twitched at frequent intervals the deeper he became involved in any kind of serious conversation. He was almost invariably good-natured, with plenty of time for talk about books and their authors, regardless of the likelihood of its leading to a sale.

For many years Edouard drove a well-maintained vintage Auburn coupé with rumble seat. It set him off, in the eyes of his fellow citizens, as a man of distinction inasmuch as (a) the import tax on American automobiles at the period was 58% and (b) since French tax collectors in each *arrondissement* based their assessments on what they called *signes extérieurs de richesse*—i.e., what street you lived on, the number of rooms in your apartment, servants, cars, summer home, and so on—it was assumed that anyone with the nerve to buy an American car was rich as Croesus and an audit was assured. Beyond that, a French tax collector had the power to decide, on the basis of such "external signs of wealth," how much tax you ought to be paying and could make an arbitrary assessment all on his own. And if you couldn't prove he was wrong, you paid up—or else. But by that time Edouard had moved himself into the position of being taxed *au forfait*—a system whereby you made a deal in advance with the tax man. Once you had arrived at a mutually agreeable figure, you didn't have to produce any documents for the year ahead. You simply paid the amount you had both agreed on. And if you made twice as much money as it was assumed you were going to make in any given year, you still paid only the amount you and the tax man had settled for. Which helps to explain why French dealers sometimes refuse to take checks and, in the case of the more timorous of them, to give written receipts—at least for the full amount involved in a sale.

So Edouard's Auburn—he gave it the French pronunciation, O-'byürn—was not a problem for him; it was an asset, and when he drove along the broad sidewalk of the Champs-Elysées in search of a parking space in front of one of the cafés he frequented, he was—in those early postwar years and up into the Fifties—the target of a good deal of attention. Much of it was female, given the nature and function of a sidewalk café—and the fact that Edouard's browsing was not by any means limited to books. Sometimes his finds could type and sometimes they were merely decorative, but one way or another, a number of them found their niche in the Librairie Edouard Loewy for longer or shorter periods.

The Champs-Elysées had its advantages for Edouard: heavy traffic of the right kind, the sort of glitter that appealed to the playboy in him, and close proximity to his shop—easy in, easy out. But when he felt in a more leisurely or nostalgic mood, he would slide into *l'Auburn* and head for Montparnasse and the Coupole. The Coupole was within spitting distance of Edouard's old shop on the Boulevard Raspail and had its share of fragrant memories. Of all the Montparnasse cafés—the Dôme, the Rotonde, the Select, and the Coupole—that had been the scene of the main action in the Twenties and the Thirties, the Coupole was the only one that—at that time—hadn't changed a bit, and in a city that in the Fifties and Sixties was beginning to strain at the seams with well-nigh insoluble traffic problems, high-rise distortions of the skyline, and every other urban manifestation of prosperity and human greed, the Coupole was a rare oasis for a *grand sentimental* like Edouard.

In addition to his café-cruising, Edouard was also a great walker and swimmer and although he kept himself in good physical trim, he was a bit of a hypochondriac. He worried about shaking hands with just anybody, didn't like to have people cough or sneeze in his bookshop, and was exceedingly—even excessively—sensitive to odors. The breath of someone talking to him would sometimes cause him to step back out of range and when that person left, Edouard would leave the heavy glass front door wide open until the atmosphere had returned to normal. Strangely enough, his own breath was often of the kind featured in Scope television commercials. All body odors were a matter of great concern to him and he had both racial and physiological theories about them. In the matter of food he was categorical: The steak had to be *saignant*—rarer than rare; the salad had its invariable prescriptions, the wine, the cheese, and so on. It became harder and harder for him to get satisfaction at his favorite lunchtime café, Le Colisée. Finally he found a girl who could cook. He installed a mini-kitchen in the basement of his shop and from then on, during that sacrosanct period from noon until two, doors were locked, shades drawn, and Edouard enjoyed the kind of lunch his young lady had been trained to produce. When the long table was cleared, Edouard sipped his camomile tea and re-read something by one of his favorite authors, generally Paul Valéry.

A few yards down the Boulevard Haussmann from Edouard's front door was the bookshop of Georges Privat, a very traditional, even old-fashioned kind of shop that seemed anchored in the prewar period. Monsieur Privat, a lively old gentleman with a merry twinkle, was assisted by two sons and by his second wife, who walked with a cane because of a hip problem. Madame Privat was in charge of the auto-graph department and worked all by herself belowdecks. If you wanted to buy a letter or a manuscript, you couldn't go down to her; she had to come up to you. She was a large, rugged-looking woman, and since the basement, where she worked, and the ground floor of the shop were joined by one of those narrow, creaky, spiral iron staircases, her progress upward, in view of the hip condition and the cane, was slow, no doubt difficult, and was inevitably followed by a rest period during which, over an interval varying from ten minutes to a half-hour, Madame Privat brought you up to date on her numerous aches and pains.

I didn't go to Privat's often because I always felt rather unhappy about putting Madame Privat through that ordeal. And there weren't a great many occasions when I had to go, because her catalogue offerings were not very exciting, for the most part. Early on, I had bought a good Benjamin Franklin letter from her, an interesting and sassy manuscript by G. B. Shaw, and—best of all—two important manuscripts by Colette. But these were separated by long dry spells and eventually—since one couldn't go in and just browse among her papers—I gave up going there almost entirely. Edouard Loewy, on the other hand, was one of the Privats' most faithful clients. He referred to their shop as his "annex," because, he explained, since they were years behind the rest of the pack, whenever they had anything good he was sure of being able to buy it at a price he could mark up for quick and profitable resale. So he went there often, under the umbrella of the good-neighbor policy, chatted, browsed, and almost always returned with at least three or four, perhaps a half-dozen, sleepers.

I was in Edouard's shop one afternoon in the early 1960s when he returned from one of those excursions, bringing with him, among other things, an illustrated letter by Henri de Toulouse-Lautrec. I admired it. He told me it was already sold. But, he suggested, why not go back and see Madame Privat? There might be more where that came from. I did. After the customary discussion of Madame Privat's health—bad and rapidly getting worse—I learned that she and her husband were in the habit of driving down to the south of France twice a year: at Eastertime and during the summer vacation. A friend in the southwest had put them in touch with an elderly lady who was a relative of Toulouse-Lautrec and the last person alive who had actually known him. She had been a little girl when Lautrec had died at Malromé, one of the family's châteaux. In recent years she had arranged a small museum in Henri's memory at the Château du Bosc, another of the family properties in that area. She had installed memorabilia of various kinds—letters, drawings, toys, clothing—and she showed interested visitors through the rooms on request. But the château's roof had numerous leaks and there were other urgent repairs crying out to be made. So she had sold the Privats a small group of illustrated letters, some early drawings, and a mass of family correspondence that had considerable importance inasmuch as all of the letters related to Henri. Madame Privat had sold a few of the illustrated letters, was keeping the remaining few for herself, but would be willing to let me see the other things when she had finished going through them, she said.

When that day came, I looked at the results and was impressed. There were nearly four hundred letters and Madame Privat had not only read every one of them—and some of them were very long indeed—but also had priced each one separately, factoring in the length, the quality, and the usefulness for research purposes of what that particular letter contained. A dozen of them were written by Henri himself; about 275 by his mother to her mother, her husband's mother, and her sister-in-law; about sixty by Henri's grandmother, and more than forty by other members of the immediate family and household. They totalled 1,520 sides with approximately 210,000 words. Along with them, she had brought back an album of eleven drawings, on separate sheets, most of them covered with sketches on both sides; also, a notebook of about thirty-five pages with drawings and sketches from several periods (as was the case with the album). They included the earliest known drawings by Lautrec. It is generally recorded that he began to draw at the age of ten. Some of these had been done, demonstrably, when he was eight; some, when he was six, and a few probably even earlier. Others, principally from among those of larger format in the album, were from his teens. The most interesting aspect of the drawings was the fact that even the very earliest of them showed the same sharp wit and intelligence that characterize Lautrec's mature work. There were animals— goats, monkeys, horses, dogs dressed as boys and wearing spurs, others bearing arms; a costumed rider (probably Henri's father, Alphonse) on horseback or astride a large dog; representations of the devil, duellers, men in medieval and seventeenth-century costumes, the family's Château du Bosc, and a sketch of the family priest with the head of a dog smoking a pipe. They all had a precocious self-assurance, along with the full flavor and incisive observation of his later work, however "childish" some of them might be considered from a technical standpoint.

Like the letters, each drawing—even each page in the notebook—had its own price. And to get all those prices melted down into one figure was a long job for the venerable Privat adding machine, because in the end I bought everything. It was the kind of acquisition one would make at almost any price, a once-in-a-lifetime opportunity. Over the days that followed, as I read the letters in detail, taking notes as I went along, my excitement grew with each discovery. Because, in essence, it was a voyage of discovery. The story they told had never been told before. The insights they gave into the family life, the character of the mother and father, their relationship with each other and with their son, enable—in fact, force—one to make a complete re-appraisal of the standard analyses of the effect of Lautrec's upbringing—in particular, his relationship with his mother—on his later behavior.

The family spent much of its time traveling back and forth to visit other units and generations in one or another of their numerous châteaux and country houses. Between visits they wrote, and the letters I had bought related in profuse detail the interim lives they led in Paris, at watering-spots and spas, and with other relatives. Every one of the letters, just as Madame Privat had told me, was concerned, to a greater or lesser extent, with Henri. They began a few weeks after his birth, in November 1864, and carried through until after his death, in September 1901.

The most significant group—those written by Henri's mother, Adèle—gave to her correspondents detailed reports of every phase of Henri's life: his health as a baby and a young child, his early inclinations toward drawing, his interest in animals, his lessons, his accidents and medical therapy, his studies at home and with his art teachers—René Princeteau, Léon Bonnat, and Fernand Cormon. Eventually, when he was nineteen, he stopped living with and traveling with his mother and set out on his own. After that, there were frequent reports of his life in Montmartre and his visits home.

The earlier books about Lautrec took their cue, with respect to vital matters of family relationships, from the recollections of surviving family members and servants—views that were often embellished, after Henri's death, by the pious reminiscences of his mother: in short, the family's own presentation of itself. And in the case of books by friends— for example, the two-volume work published in the mid-Twenties by Maurice Joyant, Lautrec's lifelong friend and testamentary executor— there was an understandable discretion in the references to family background. Writers since then have reproduced intact from their predecessors the conventional clichés about "the gay, comfortable confusion" of Lautrec's family life and they speak of Adèle in such terms as "this sainted woman." One writer rubbed out whatever reservations one might have about Henri's father, Alphonse, by simply summing him up as "the incomparable sportsman." Those labels were, of course, in some degree true, or half-true, but the real truth, it now became clear to me, lay much deeper than such superficial embalming techniques would suggest.

In a family where inbreeding was commonplace, Adèle and Alphonse were first cousins. Adèle was a romantic, sexually frigid woman, saccharine, namby-pamby, with a cloying religiosity that would have driven almost any husband up the wall. That excessive piety formed and clothed her every thought and provided her every satisfaction—other than the supreme satisfaction of breathing for and living through her only son. She was neurasthenic, hypochondriac, an anxious, medically hysterical type. In practical affairs she was penny-pinching and, although the family possessed very great resources, she was constantly preoccupied with the cost of everything and niggardly in her dispensations. When her clothes were worn-out, she sold them. When she made a bad bargain, she reneged on it. The one exception to this was her marriage to Alphonse. Her romantic dream had vanished but her penance continued *in perpetuum.* She was a martyr to her marriage, a martyr to her son's ill health, broken legs, long convalescences, and the modifications they imposed on her way of life. But they did, at least, make it easier to avoid Alphonse, and the exquisite masochism of her Florence Nightingale role was only occasionally marred by a peevish revolt against the necessity of choosing one's vacation spots and limiting one's stays in accordance with the recommendations of Henri's doctors.

Adèle's only other child died when Henri was four. After that the marriage was a dead letter and all her attentions were focused on Henri. Adèle's brother had married Alphonse's sister, and with them one child followed another. Even if one disregards the stillbirths and early deaths, their offspring reached a total of fourteen. How much this may have troubled Adèle was not easy to see, any more than one could quickly decide how much of her exasperating religiosity was due to inherited superstition, how much to a well-disciplined hypocrisy, and how much to sheer desperation. And it would take more digging to learn to what extent Alphonse's "eccentricities"—kite-flying, falconry, a penchant for outlandish costumes, and his compulsive, year-around killing (this "incomparable sportsman")—were intensified by the behavior of this possessive, overprotective mother—Adèle—who was in no sense a wife.

Adèle poured out her heart to her "Mama" and could stay away from

Prime Minister Georges Pompidou, Edouard Loewy, Robert Couturier, and Alexandre Loewy at the Foire de Paris.

Henri de Toulouse-Lautrec. Pencil sketches, *c.* 1871, drawn when Lautrec was seven years old.

Henri de Toulouse-Lautrec with his mother at Malromé, *c.* 1899–1900.

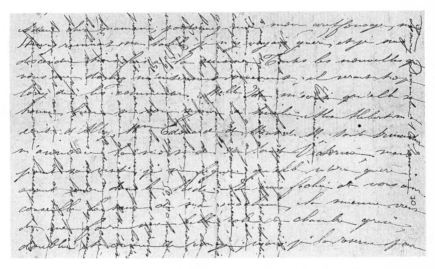

Letter from Toulouse-Lautrec's mother, Adèle, to her mother, 16 January [1870]. To avoid "wasting" stationery, when Adèle had filled the four pages of a folded letter sheet, she would turn it ninety degrees and continue her letter by writing across the already fully covered pages. *"Ça fait de petites économies."*

her only so long. In her letters she yearned to revert to the happier days of her childhood when Mama solved all her problems. Totally dependent herself, she battened on Henri in the classic reaction which unknowingly, pathetically, and ultimately tragically, could only have made him as helpless as herself.

Henri's health had always been delicate and his growth, slow. A first fall, at age thirteen, broke his left thighbone; a second, a year later, fractured the right. At that point, the long bones stopped growing. Many writers have seen "the tragic fall at Barèges"—Lautrec's second accident—as the decisive factor in his evolution. But that was, after all, only an accident. The real determinant was his genetic weakness—and Adèle. Fortunately, Lautrec's genius fought hard for expression and he was able to break loose from "this sainted woman" and her deforming touch. But in his reaction against her life-denying, smothering embrace, he went as far as one could in the other direction. In his twenties she was still referring to him as "my little man." But by now Henri was trying to prove to himself and to the world that he was *not* Mama's little man by launching himself on the road to alcoholism and by cohabiting with women who were polar opposites to Adèle and all she represented. And yet the real reasons for his dedication to such a devitalizing and eventually fatal way of life had never been realistically explored. On the basis of this archive, I could see that, sooner or later, the Toulouse-Lautrec story would have to be rewritten.

Even though the letters are filled with cameos of life in France under the Second Empire and Third Republic—political crises, fashion notes, involuntary social insights—it is the character of Adèle and the pathetic nature of her emotional responses and conditioning that give them their special value. In all her letters there are two parallel sound tracks: her detailed recitals of the facts and the insistent overtones provided by her nature and her reactions. Listen to her now, in these few extracts taken at random from her letters, and see how, as she passes along the news about Henri, she sketches in her own self-portrait.

After the death of her second and last baby, Adèle writes: "It is the hand of God . . . in His infinite wisdom. . . . May He compensate me by concentrating my happiness in Henry, who grows daily in intelligence and wisdom. . . . May God's will be blessed. . . ." [In writing about her son, Adèle nearly always used the English spelling of his first name.]

"The great advantage that this overactive life has for me is that it does not leave me too much time for thinking. . . . Can one complain at being judged worthy of bearing a heavy cross? . . ."

Adèle leaves Henri, aged eleven, to go visit her mother: "My heart is heavy already at the thought of leaving my Henry. He is very understanding, though, and realizes full well that I, too, have need to see my Mama once again. . . ."

Henri is now twelve and pains in his legs make it difficult for him to walk. "Pray God that this testing-time be not long. It is harder perhaps on me than on Henry, who is happy to spend his time reading or drawing and greatly enjoying the visits of [his cousin] Louis and is in no pain at all as long as he remains seated. . . ."

Henri continues to suffer—calves, thighs, and one side of his head. He can't walk a step, but whenever the pain subsides somewhat, Adèle takes him in a carriage to the church of La Madeleine to enjoy the Easter masses, "even though the cab fares are ruining me. . . ." She keeps returning, however, and writes of her pain to see him suffer so, moving around inside the church, limping first on one foot, then on the other. Afterward, at the hotel, her "arm is sore all over from helping to support him. . . ."

Adèle and Henri (now fourteen) are back at the Château du Bosc. She hopes Alphonse won't be in too much of a hurry to take Henri to Arcachon for a vacation, after his ordeal, although she had agreed to let him do so. "No place is as nice as Le Bosc at the moment. . . ." She orders from a jeweler a ring to be made from Henri's first four baby teeth. Later we learn that she doesn't like Arcachon (a favorite of Alphonse and Henri) but prefers Nice. She writes: "Henry hasn't the shadow of a pain, eats like an ogre, and seems to continue his little progress. I thank God and find therein an encouragement for a trip to Nice. . . ."

Everywhere they go, Henri is visually stimulated and draws constantly. At Le Bosc, it is the animals—horses, monkeys, dogs—and the servants. At Villefranche he is excited by an American warship. At Monte Carlo he is disappointed not to be allowed inside the gambling halls because of his age. Adèle doesn't find the sight of gambling immoral, she says—". . . it is too sad for that. . . ." Predictably they do go to Nice, and it is carnival time. Adèle is taken with a new church dedicated to the Holy Virgin and much frequented by the "foreign aristocracy." The priest is "very nice" and has promised her dispensa-

tions for Lent, "understanding my problems here. . . ." Henri is "wild
with joy" at the flower battles, can walk now as far as the Russian chapel
but "is still quite a burden for me to drag around, in spite of the many
benches. . . ."

They go to Barèges for the waters. Henri's swimming skill is much
improved and he comes out of the water "all red, warm, and hungry. . . ." The doctor is very pleased with his progress, but "I have told
Henry flatly that if the improvement is not immense, I am saying good-
bye forever to Barèges. Mlle. Duplessis and I are the only ladies in the
salon after dinner. You can imagine the fun! . . . Henry isn't bored,
however, thanks to a few acquaintances (including two dogs) and his
paints. . . ."

After Henri's second (and more serious) accident at Barèges she
writes: "I understand only too well the shock that my misfortune has
given your hearts; I suffered for it in advance . . . but it is also
consoling to feel oneself loved and supported when one has a sad life
like mine. My morale, I confess, is flattened out. . . . I never expected
to start out on a second ordeal. However, the good Lord, who well knows
that the pain of the last year would have been beyond my strength, has
softened this recurrence. Henry is coming along marvelously well, not
suffering, eating and sleeping well. . . . But how many have already
gone and will continue to go to take the waters [at Cauterets], while I am
glued here at Barèges—for nothing. What can one do other than submit
blindly to the will of God, yet when I reflect on the uselessness of my
afflictions, I am very discouraged. . . ."

Back in Nice: "Father Félix has done much good by his fine sermons,
so logical and consoling. He makes us forget our sorrow in this life, since
God alone and eternity are our goal, so beautiful and so near. Henry
appreciates the sermons, too, although he finds that they are very long
and the seats not very comfortable. He dreams more than ever of
painting and is making remarkable progress with portrait sketches; that
amuses the guests at the hotel and I must say his good disposition makes
people love him. . . ."

The family moves on to Paris in April, 1881, Henri now sixteen:
"Alphonse is very busy with Henry, and Princeteau [Henri's first
teacher, a deaf-mute animal painter] is literally transported by the sight
of Henry's masterpieces. It didn't take that much to transport my little
man to the third heaven and his Mama is happy to see him
happy. . . . Alphonse is still talking of going to see his horses at

Orléans, but I can't go now; we are really too busy. . . . Alphonse has been on the point of leaving six times but we still have him with us. It is impossible to make the slightest plan with Alphonse, who drags his heels more and more and dreams up projects it would take three lifetimes to execute. Meanwhile he does nothing. . . ."

The following year she writes from Paris: "What commotion! Henry spends much time with Princeteau, who is putting the final touches to his big painting for the Exposition. As soon as he delivers it, he is going to see about getting Henry into Bonnat's atelier. Bonnat is Mme. de Gironde's favorite master [Mme. de Gironde, a socially well-placed Parisian hostess Adèle looks up to] and it seems to us that Henry will have with him more advantages and fewer disadvantages than at the Beaux-Arts. Anyway, he can always change over if it doesn't work out. Pray for us, dear Mama, at this important moment, which may be decisive in the life of your grandson. . . ."

The following week: "Henry is launched, full sail, on his vocation of artist as of Monday. He seems most eager to work seriously and doesn't allow the difficulties of the beginning to discourage him. As luck would have it, a young American who has traveled a great deal with Mr. and Mrs. Moore [also Americans; Mr. Moore, a deaf-mute and an artist] started in with Bonnat the same day as Henry, so that the customary pranks weren't directed at Henry alone. . . . They simply hoisted the two new students up onto stools and sang some rather indelicate songs to accompany a few drinks that [Henri and Watson, the other new student] were obliged to pay for. Henry and Mr. Watson leave at quarter to eight each morning, full of enthusiasm. Since there are two life classes each day, Henry chose the morning class this week. But the studio is so far from here that he has to lunch in a restaurant before returning to the hotel. Today he will spend the whole day there. . . ."

A fortnight later Alphonse arrives in Paris "as surprised as can be at not having reached here earlier. Naturally Henry had a great deal to say about his new life, which he is taking more and more seriously. To listen to him, you would think he plans to spend the entire year in Paris. . . . I'm afraid our vacation will be very short. Bonnat plans to get rid of the majority of his pupils, and in order to be allowed to stay on, one must really dig in. . . ."

And at Ascension: "Our vacation will be very short this year in order not to miss the opening of Bonnat's atelier in October. Since he will choose a very small number from among his pupils, Henry is doing everything possible to be singled out. . . ."

But when Henri and Adèle returned to Paris after the vacation, Bonnat had closed his studio, having been named professor at the Ecole Nationale des Beaux-Arts. Henri and a few friends begin to study with another painter, Cormon. "Henry is preparing to submit to Cormon a sketch for a subject from The Song of Songs. This composition . . . has involved me in a good deal of correspondence with [the château of] Le Bosc, in order to have my Bible sent to me. I didn't want to be obliged to have recourse to a Protestant Bible, [the only kind] easily come by in Paris. . . ."

One day, the following spring, Adèle and Henri are out walking. A sudden squall comes up and both are knocked down by the wind. Neither one sustained any broken bones but Adèle is laid up for weeks with vague and mysterious ailments. She is convinced she has barely escaped peritonitis. "Henry heroically hid his own discomfort from me to minister to my needs and showed me what a little man he is. . . ." She returns to the château of Malromé to convalesce but is plagued by fevers. A doctor looks her over and administers a purge. She improves but goes back to Paris under medical escort. The second floor of the hotel is full and she is obliged to stay on the third floor. "I hate it from every point of view. . . ." The stairwell is drafty and she catches cold and is confined to her room. "Henry doesn't mind as he is hardly ever here. He spends all his time looking for a private atelier for his afternoon work. Models come to Cormon's only in the morning and Cormon wants Henry to work evenings on his own. The expenses of all this have grown very heavy but Henry's future comes before everything else. Pray God, dear Mama, that all this trouble is not without result. . . ."

20 October 1883: "Henry is at Montmartre from eight in the morning until dinnertime. Alphonse is so busy I never see him. You see how much is left for me. . . . Henry is thrilled with his atelier, where he works all afternoon with two friends. He has carried there all his drawings and paintings, which were so much in the way here at the hotel. . . ." She thanks her mother for a gift of money and says she will wait until Christmas to hand over Henri's share to "my dear little baby." (He is now nineteen.)

New Year's Eve: "Henry has been talking with concierges and landlords and since his lease is up on January 15, he has finally taken a big atelier nine meters long in the Rue Lepic in Montmartre. Now we must buy all the furniture—divans, curtains, chairs, etc., not to mention a stove and getting a cleaning woman to sweep up and light the fire. That is no small affair and I'm not sorry to have my artist learn that bread doesn't grow already baked. . . . There is a bedroom adjoining the studio, which he has been able to sublet. That cuts the cost to 1100 francs a year—even then, it's too much. Henry couldn't resist buying a beautiful Chinese hanging with your New Year's present. . . . He's been running around to all the old Jews in Paris to buy Oriental rugs for his divan, the central motif in his decoration. . . ."

The next June (1884): "Henry has decided not to enter the competition for the Beaux-Arts. He feels he has too little time. However, he has received from his teacher, Cormon, a very flattering assignment . . . chapter and page headings for an edition of the poems of Victor Hugo and he will be working with the best-known contemporary artists. To give you an idea of the unusual importance of this edition, each copy will cost 6,000 francs! You can imagine Henry's joy and excitement. There is one disadvantage: If Henry's work is accepted by the publisher, we are tied to this big job for an indefinite period. If Rachou [another young painter from Albi, a former pupil of Bonnat, who, the year before, had done a portrait of Henri] were to accept a part of the illustration, I would do everything possible to arrange to have the two artists work at Malromé during the hot spell we shall surely have. . . ."

Difficulties increase in connection with the ambitious edition of Victor Hugo, but the work does go on at Malromé, so that Adèle has her summer there, as planned. After a while the project falls through. "Henry is philosophical about it. Cormon's approval is all he was interested in. . . ." Adèle had feared a cholera epidemic in Paris, but Alphonse, although he has been packing for two months, is still there. "Henry paints mornings, framed by our lovely hortensias." There are trips to another family place at Respide, archery and rowing, the races at Brède, trips with Henri's cousins in their carriage.

In Paris that fall, Henri is racing back and forth between their new hotel in the Rue Cambon and Montmartre. "He is still the busiest student in the world, and in excellent health despite his active life. . . ." Henri spends less and less time at the hotel. Adèle grows more nervous and fatigued; goes on a strict diet. "The new hotel is excellent for that. The food here is very expensive but first-class. Imagine—the chef had the honor of directing the stoves of Queen Victoria! . . ."

Henri is often absent nights now. "He spent last night as Cormon's deputy checking the votes of the painting jury at the Palais de l'Industrie. An important affair. . . ." Another vacation approaches, but this time Henri, thoroughly weaned, stays put. Summer in Paris would be a fate worse than death for Adèle, so she reluctantly returns to the Midi to make her usual aimless rounds, sadder, more and more resigned. Life, from here on, grows steadily bleaker for her. For Henri, it centers increasingly on bars, music halls, and brothels. In the end, though, the umbilical cord proved to be the strongest bond. When alcoholism and its accompaniments finally overpowered his fragile physique and he suffered a stroke, he returned to Malromé to die in his mother's arms, sobbing, with his last breath, "Mama, you, only you."

* * * * *

At the beginning of his Montmartre life Henri wrote to his father's brother, Uncle Charles, who had encouraged his art studies from the first, "I feel myself held back by a great load of sentimental considerations that I must absolutely forget if I wish to achieve anything." Just how great a load it must have been, this archive lets us see.

What it let *me* see—beyond the immediate and specific clarification of "the Toulouse-Lautrec story"—was the fact that one should never believe anything simply because a biographer or several biographers have said that *that* is the way it is. Too often they are drawing on or repeating the same mistaken or biased secondary sources. There is no substitute for primary sources—and a healthy dose of skepticism.

Chapter 6

I have referred to Marc Loliée as the fairest and least greedy of all the booksellers I frequented over the years in Paris. I think of that as a pretty high distinction all by itself, given the aggressively contagious nature of human greed. But there was a great deal more to Marc than just that. He knew books not only in their bibliographical aspects or as commercial commodities; he read them, and when he liked them he sometimes held onto them. Occasionally, if he liked you and you liked the writers he did, he would let you have one of his own—not just something stashed away for that purpose in the back room, but something he'd bring from his library at home. He liked to buy and he liked to sell, but trade, for him, was an exchange of goodwill and shared enthusiasm, more than just a financial transaction, and sometimes the margin between cost and selling price was rather slender. I know because in the course of dealing with him over several decades, I had cracked his code and I always knew from his markings just what any book or manuscript had cost him.

In his narrow little shop in the Rue des Saints-Pères, just off the Boulevard Saint-Germain, with books everywhere but on the ceiling, Marc sat at a broad mahogany desk in the back, generally writing descriptive catalogue entries. He was a tall, ruggedly built man, balding, with an easy grin, and he wore tortoise-shell-framed glasses which he pushed up onto his forehead whenever he wanted to examine something closely. To his left, a step led up into a tiny back room where he kept *les grosses pièces*—the more expensive books. In addition to shelving, it had a series of locked cabinets in which he stored his folders of autograph letters and manuscripts. There was room for just one chair; a window-seat served as a table. Only one client at a time was allowed in—indeed, could fit in. But the number of *grosses pièces* that changed hands in that cubicle over the years had no relation to its square footage.

One of Marc's favorite writers was Alfred Jarry, whose *Ubu Roi* (1896) did more to change the course of theater in our time than any other play. Like Jarry, Marc rode a bicycle. In the end it was the bicycle that did him in. He had always been very athletic, and well into his seventies he was taking long walking tours in Switzerland, playing tennis even in the hottest weather, and riding his bicycle in city and country alike. In the fall of 1979 he was cycling along a country road outside Paris when an approaching car caused him to draw too close to the edge of the roadway. He struck a stone mileage marker, went over the handlebars, landed on his head, and died.

In May, 1968, right at the time the barricades were going up and the new revolutionaries were massing at the Odéon and the Sorbonne, I was dropping into Marc's shop several times a week. In looking through his autograph folders, I began to find an occasional postcard written by Jarry to Alfred Vallette, director of the literary review and publishing house *Le Mercure de France*, or to his wife, the novelist Rachilde. The cards were always photographic reproductions of scenic or architectural highlights of the town of Laval, Jarry's hometown, in Brittany. Whenever I saw one, I bought it. In a few days, there would be another. When dealers have a sizable correspondence by one writer, they sometimes dole it out, bit by bit, just like that. For one thing, the total of the individual prices is generally higher than the single price they could set on the whole group. Then, too, the number of people in the market for an entire correspondence is very limited. But if you *are* interested in having it all, as I was, it's frustrating to have to buy it piecemeal over a long period of time. So I chided Marc about putting himself in a class with Jacques Lambert, an autograph dealer in the Rue Bonaparte who was famous for those tactics.

"But that's all I have," he protested. "I got just a few from Georges Hugnet. He often owes me money for things he buys; if I push him hard enough, he gives me something on account. Sometimes, instead of cash, he gives me a book or a manuscript. That works out even better for me."

I asked him if he thought there were more of the Jarry cards off in the wings. He shrugged. "I'll see what I can do," he said. "You never know with him. He's not always very easy to deal with."

I waited, more or less patiently, over the late-spring weeks that followed but saw no more Laval postcards from Jarry to the Vallettes. One day I raised the question again. Marc shook his head.

"No sign of life from Hugnet in a long time," he said. "But if you're so interested, why don't you call him up and ask him?"

I told him that although I knew about Hugnet, I had never met him and wasn't sure he'd welcome the intrusion. Besides I'd heard for years about his temper. Perhaps I should write to him.

"He probably wouldn't answer you," he said. "Give him a call. He can't do any worse than bite your head off."

So I called—and Hugnet bit. I called at what I thought would be a reasonably propitious moment: between two and two-thirty the next afternoon. Hugnet roared into the telephone, asked me who I was, what I wanted, and who or what gave me the right to interrupt his siesta. He was a sick man, all alone in the house with nobody to answer the telephone and besides, where did I get the idea that he was a dealer, interested in selling anything to anybody?

He didn't slow down for several minutes and then, sounding out of breath, he grew quiet and let me try to explain myself. When I had finished, he started all over again but this time more calmly, almost plaintively. I made all the apologies that seemed called for and he gave me an appointment to come see him in mid-morning two days later.

Georges Hugnet had been in full view on the Paris literary scene for a very long time. As a teen-age poet he had been taken up by the people who at that time would be likely to take up precocious young poets— Marcel Jouhandeau and Max Jacob, among others—and when he was about twenty he met Virgil Thomson. Through him he became a member of Gertrude Stein's entourage. He was in full revolt against his father, a furniture manufacturer in the Faubourg Saint-Antoine, near the Bastille, and he began working a small publishing operation called Les Editions de la Montagne. He published books of his own and those of a few writers who were his friends. In 1929 he brought out his translation of a portion of Gertrude Stein's magnum opus—*The Making of Americans.* The following year, in collaboration with Virgil Thomson, he translated a group of ten portraits by Stein, including those of Picasso, Apollinaire, Erik Satie and, of course, the two translators.

Gertrude, meanwhile, had grown rather fond of Hugnet and had agreed to translate a book of his into English. It was a poem cycle about childhood to which he had given the title *Enfances*. Gertrude Stein's French was not exactly idiomatic or even precise and Hugnet's English was even more approximate. But with the help of a French-English dictionary she made a stab at translating what was intended to be one-half of a bilingual edition of *Enfances*. Then she decided to call her versions not translations but "adaptations," and finally, "reflections." A prospectus for the book was drawn up and Georges showed Gertrude a copy. His name and the book's title were in large type; the French equivalent of "followed by Gertrude Stein's translation," in smaller type. She demanded equal billing. Hugnet refused; he didn't see the work as a collaboration to that extent. Then the first proofs appeared. Hugnet's name was set in 12-point type; below that was the line *"Translated by* Gertrude Stein"—in 9-point. Gertrude was outraged. Virgil Thomson tried to arbitrate the differences but failed. Gertrude—pushed by the determined Alice B. Toklas—walked out. When Christian Zervos's firm, Editions "Cahiers d'Art," published Hugnet's *Enfances* in 1933, with three original etchings by Miró, it had no translations, adaptations or reflections by Gertrude Stein. Gertrude's answer to *Enfances* had already come out two years earlier under the title *Before the Flowers of Friendship Faded Friendship Faded*, published by Plain Edition, an imprint established by Alice Toklas for the exclusive purpose of publishing Gertrude Stein.

That episode marked the end of a close friendship. Hugnet later told me he felt the whole maneuver had been engineered by Alice, who had come to resent his influence on Gertrude. Gertrude herself had acknowledged that Hugnet's work had had considerable influence on her poetry. And history records a number of incidents in which Alice Toklas's ascendancy over Gertrude Stein resulted in other friendships' being broken off when Alice felt they were too invasive. "Gertrude was in love with me; it's as simple as that," Georges said quietly, the day he told me the story.

Others besides Gertrude Stein had been taken with the young Georges Hugnet. After reading articles Hugnet had written in Zervos's review, *Cahiers d'Art*, about the Dada spirit in painting, André Breton invited him to become a member of the Surrealist group. He remained one until 1939, when Breton, with his characteristic papal arrogance, excommunicated him for "intellectual dishonesty." That term, in such contexts, generally meant disagreeing with Breton. In this case it was applied because Hugnet had refused to end his friendship with Paul Eluard, who, in 1938, had broken with Breton and the Surrealist movement.

Hugnet was continually involved in all varieties of exploits that lay open to an ambitious and energetic young poet: he wrote and acted in a film (*La Perle*); he published a large-format little magazine (*L'Usage de la parole*), and he brawled with dissident factions created by political and other ideological schisms inside and outside the Surrealist group—with Roger Vitrac, Marcel Jean, Noël Arnaud; and after the death of Breton's close ally, Benjamin Péret, with Péret's ghost. On several occasions he suffered physical aggression as a result of what had begun as merely journalistic squabbling.

Poetry aside, Hugnet had always been on the fringes of the rare-book world: as a passionate collector and trader, a designer of Surrealist bookbindings, a publisher of limited editions. During World War II and after, he had in fact been installed as a bookseller in a small, gray frame dwelling near the beginning of the Boulevard du Montparnasse, which housed also the Jeanne Bucher art gallery. He lived there with his wife Germaine and, later, with his young second wife, Myrtille, and their infant son Nicolas. In that period I sometimes used to go to exhibitions at the Jeanne Bucher gallery—it showed Hans Reichel, Vieira da Silva, and Arpad Szenes, among others—but I never tried to enter the Hugnet compound. I find that hard to explain, even to myself.

By now Hugnet and Myrtille were living in the Rue de la Gaîté, in a small two-story *pavillon* at the back of a courtyard, and that is where I went to keep my appointment with him that Thursday morning. It was a sunny day, verging on summer, and there was a leafy, willowlike tree just outside the door. The *pavillon*'s ground-floor windows were wide open. I rang the doorbell. A dog barked, a man's voice shouted *"Tais-toi,"* followed by a few less repeatable injunctions. There was noise and scuffling and finally Georges Hugnet opened the door. He was short, heavy, unshaven, wearing a bathrobe and slippers, a somewhat Ubu-esque figure, which I found very appropriate in view of the fact that it was Ubu's creator—or, at least, exploiter—who had brought us together via those Jarry postcards from Laval that Marc Loliée had sold to me.

With a few inarticulate grunts—mostly about the dog, now peering out from around a corner—he invited me inside. We passed through a tiny vestibule and then, through a room to the left, into what seemed to be an all-purpose family room/kitchen with a stove, a sink, a large round table and chairs in the center and, just beyond, a pantry and a *lavabo*. The place was a bit dark because of the larger building on the other side

Marc Loliée in his bookshop in the Rue des Saints-Pères, Paris.

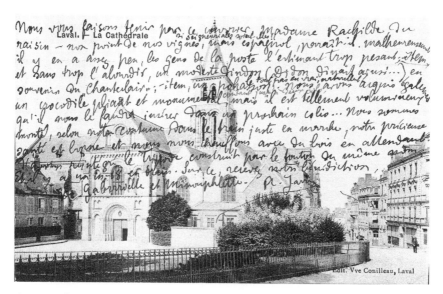

Autograph postcard, signed, from Alfred Jarry to the novelist Rachilde (Mme. Alfred Vallette), written on a view of the cathedral in Laval, Jarry's hometown in Brittany.

Paul Eluard, Georges Hugnet, Robert Valençay, in the late Thirties.

Gertrude Stein and Alice B. Toklas in the printshop after Alice had established the imprint "Plain Edition" for the publication of Gertrude's work, c. 1930.

of the courtyard but rather cheerful in its way. The fact that the large double-frame window in each of the two rooms was thrown open to the leaves of the tree and the fresh air in the courtyard created a pleasing illusion of space.

We sat down, facing each other across the table. Hugnet poured himself a glass of red wine, lighted a *Gauloise*, and asked me once again, in a relaxed manner this time, some of the questions he had asked me in our telephone conversation. I had told him then about the Jarry postcards and my interest in buying any others he might have, and now I talked more at length about Jarry. As he smoked, he manipulated his cigarette with pins he had stuck into it, refilled his glass, and occasionally offered a comment, not unfriendly, merely restrained. We talked about America and Americans. He had never been there but he had known many of them. He talked about Gertrude and Alice and "Virgile"—giving their names the French pronunciation—and someone I finally identified as Donald Gallup, a friend of Gertrude's and then still a curator at Yale.

He smoked more cigarettes—always with the help of the pins—and drank more wine and finally, after half an hour, picked up a small packet wrapped in very old brown tissue paper. He unwrapped it carefully and laid down before me a small pile of illustrated cards— perhaps twenty-five or so—which I recognized at once as the brothers and sisters of the Jarry cards Marc Loliée had sold me. They were all addressed to "Madame Rachilde" or to her husband, Alfred Vallette ("Monsieuye"). Only one was signed in full, "Alfred Jarry"; many were signed "A. Jarry," but the majority were signed with initials: "A.J." or "P.U." (Père Ubu). Nearly all of them, with the notable exception of an action photograph in color of the Manneken-Pis in Brussels co-signed by Jarry and his friend Eugène Demolder, were views of Laval: the château, the cathedral, the viaduct, the prison, the barracks, the main street, the town hall, the funeral parlor. One was an eerie quayside view of the town under a full moon and scudding clouds—a photograph that might almost have been reproducing something painted by Laval's other famous native son, the Douanier Rousseau. In a few cases Jarry had used only the side intended for the message; most of the cards, however, were covered on both sides, some with writing in all directions and some with more than a few of his characteristic inkblots.

I asked Hugnet if those were all. He nodded. And what were they worth? "You tell me," he said. I made a quick calculation, added a margin for safety's sake, and pronounced a figure. He thought, pinned another cigarette, and refilled his wine glass.

"You think that's what they're worth?" he asked. I told him I did. Another pause. He reached over to a side table, picked up a fresh whole Camembert that was to be his lunch, and sniffed it appreciatively.

"Let me think about it," he said finally. "Come back tomorrow at the same time."

I returned the next morning. Hugnet was more outgoing than he had been the day before. He handed me the packet of Jarry cards, with a kind of nod that indicated they were mine. I looked at them again, admired the Rousseauesque *Clair de lune*, then paid him the money.

Over the next half-dozen years I spent many mornings facing Georges across the kitchen table. Beyond the kitchen was a large room into which I was never invited in his lifetime. It was his library and, as I was to see only after his death, it was tightly packed with his very choice copies of all the modern writers whose work interested him, along with manuscripts, sometimes bound sumptuously by his favorite binders. Whenever I called on him, there was a small pile, on the kitchen table, of things he had preselected for me. Sometimes what he had chosen said nothing to me: for example, a group of fair copies of manuscript poems by his old friend Paul Eluard in a brilliant mosaic binding by his newer friend Mercher was a splendid piece for a private collector to show off. But its research value was nil. And since I am not so much interested in buying objects for display as in acquiring documents—in the broadest sense of the term—that are useful to scholarship, when I buy a manuscript I prefer one that gives clues to the creative process at work. When Georges came to understand—or to accept—that, he was more likely to bring out a different kind of manuscript by some other old friend, such as Georges Bataille, whose pages, covered with revisions, told the story of a work in progress.

One of the things Georges had that I was eager to relieve him of was his correspondence with Gertrude Stein and one day he showed it to me. It was housed in a broken saffron-yellow cardboard carton, precariously held together with rubber bands. I took the box apart as gently as possible. Inside were 114 autograph letters totaling 263 sides, each letter in its own envelope, originally closed with sealing wax and stamped with Gertrude Stein's crest. The correspondence covered the full period of their "honeymoon," which had been a long one, dating from March, 1928, to December, 1930. The growth of their friendship could be measured in the progression of Gertrude's salutations: "Dear Hugnet," "My dear George [*sic*]," "My very dear George," "My very dear little George," "My very dearest George," "My poor dear darling George."

Years earlier, Donald Gallup had been after him to give the letters to Yale, Georges told me, then to sell them, and he had resisted. But they should be somewhere in America, he supposed. So we worked out a price—a process which generally consists in a buyer's paying somewhat more than he wants (or thinks he ought) to pay, and a seller's accepting, with a martyred look, somewhat less than he'd like to get. And we did it all that same day.

A few days later I had a phone call from Myrtille Hugnet. They needed the letters right away. The Public Broadcasting System was making a film about Gertrude Stein, and Georges figured in it, along with Janet Flanner, Virgil Thomson, the literary agent Jenny Bradley, and other friends, including the sculptor Jacques Lipchitz, who had done a bust of Gertrude. For his segment, Georges wanted to be filmed with his letters from Gertrude. So I spent the better part of a morning sitting in Georges's kitchen with some of the crew while Perry Miller Adato and the rest of her team worked in the library with Georges. When they had finished shooting, I left—with all of the letters carefully accounted for.

Sometimes Georges wasn't in a selling mood, or he would want to sell me some of his own manuscripts. Since I knew he had an inexhaustible supply of those, I would agree to take some only if they were accompanied by other things. So he would bring out some early Dada manuscripts by Philippe Soupault or a manuscript by the influential Belgian Dadaist Clément Pansaers or manuscripts by Paul Eluard and André Breton of unpublished definitions they had prepared for the *Dictionnaire abrégé du surréalisme*—things designed to give added luster to his own fresh-from-the-mint-looking, beautifully calligraphed manuscripts—and we would make a deal. And if he was very happy, as he almost always was whenever I bought any of his own manuscripts, he would search out a copy of one of his books, inscribe it gracefully with a tribute to my intelligence, humor, or whatever he thought would please me most, and add that as lagniappe.

One morning, as we were sitting at the kitchen table, we began talking about Erik Satie. Georges knew, by then, that what interested me most was unpublished correspondence. He got up and opened the door to his library, went inside, closed the door behind him and emerged a few minutes later with a small-quarto volume. With loving care, he removed a slipcase covered with Japanese paper and edged in crimson morocco, then a wraparound sleeve made from the same materials. The binding itself, finally revealed, was in the same crimson morocco, with an inlaid saffron-hued facsimile of Erik Satie's monogram on the front cover. Inside, tipped to sheets of heavy handmade paper were sixty-two autograph letters from Satie to Valentine Hugo.

Valentine Hugo was the wife of Jean Hugo, a great-grandson of Victor Hugo. They were married in 1919, with Cocteau and Satie as witnesses. Both Valentine and Jean were highly respected as painters, designers, and illustrators, and it was Valentine who had brought together Satie and Cocteau to set in motion the chain of events that linked them to Picasso and Misia Sert and led to Diaghilev's 1917 ballet *Parade*, one of the watershed adventures of the modern movement.

Earlier, as a budding young artist (and handsome young woman), Valentine had presided over a salon frequented by Léon-Paul Fargue, Jacques Copeau, Paul Valéry, Gaston Gallimard, Jean Giraudoux, and other stars in the contemporary literary firmament. Later she became very friendly with Cocteau (whose mother dreamed, as only a doting mother could, that her son would one day marry Valentine). Later still, she was very close to the Surrealists—André Breton's mistress for a time and a good friend of Paul Eluard and René Char. But at the period of the letters Georges was showing me in their elegant Mercher binding (which Georges himself had designed), Valentine was caught up in the hectic preparations for *Parade:* Cocteau not always dependable, Diaghilev wily beyond belief, Picasso independent as always, Misia playing her role of *grande dame* right up to the hilt, and Satie, the most delicate and sensitive of them all, suffering the acute anguish known only to one with a temperament like his.

Satie's letters are never long; each is a jewel of the kind of understatement and sly/wry humor that give his music its unique zest. The earliest letters—notes, really—were written on cards with a heading of his own composition and draftsmanship: *Erik Satie / Compositeur de Musique.* After that, they filled skimpily the small *carte-lettre* and *pneumatique* forms that, folded in half and sealed around three sides, were opened by tearing off the perforated margin on those sides. The handwriting was like no one else's; the capitals and some of the letters with tails were

ornately shaded and convoluted. Nearly all were signed with the monogram which had been reproduced on the front cover of the binding.
Each letter told its story suggestively, by implication. Other news, on the
fringes of the Ballets Russes, crept in from time to time: Debussy, Ravel,
Léon-Paul Fargue, Matisse (Very nice fellow, Matisse. He *admires me*
and has told me so. How polite!). But when someone displeased Satie,
he could be rough: at one point, he was calling Misia Sert the abortion-
ist. By now, Valentine—my big girl, my good big girl—was the only one
of whom Satie could speak favorably: Can one come see you—for a
second? We'll speak softly, so as not to tire you. . . . I love you always
and admire you more and more.

Cocteau, in the first letter admirable, had now become a brute, a
bastard, a mug, disgusting, a fathead, a lout. But weaving a path around
and among the maneuvering and manipulation, Satie hints at his
progress and then, just after New Year's, 1917, writes: *"I've finished
'Parade.'"* Soon Diaghilev and his crew are off to Rome and Satie is
wrapped up in his "Vie de Socrate." But since nothing is ever really
finished, the wrangling went on. Eventually Cocteau—my son Jean—is
restored to a state of grace in Satie's hierarchy and *Parade* is published
by Durand. Satie is at peace—so much so that he doesn't write again for
three months. Then no work, no money and a note to Valentine: Can
you do something for an old gaffer? He broods about the war and the
death of his friends and two months later: Can you, for me, a little? A
fortnight later: I'm really flat: resources, none. I have *nothing*. What to
do? Yes? Couldn't one help me? Try, dear friend. In a week he is asking
her to speak to anyone about a job for him. He'll do anything—night
watchman in a factory. Very urgent. *Very urgent.* Finally a friend of
Valentine's comes through, by mail, with an anonymous donation. The
crisis is eased and his spirits are lifted. And on it goes, up and down,
never long in either place.

Originally there had been eighty-nine letters. From time to time when
the need arose, Valentine had sold one, so that now, here and there
throughout the correspondence, in place of Satie's original letter was a
transcript in her hand, copied from a photograph made at the time of the
sale. Nearly a third of the original correspondence had slipped away like
that. But the blue, green, and white tissues bearing her transcripts and
comments, bound in at the appropriate places, helped make up for the
loss of the originals.

"Valentine had promised me for years that if she ever sold her Satie correspondence, she would sell it to me," Georges said morosely. "In 1955 she wrote these pages that complete the correspondence, with the idea that one day I would have them bound in with the letters, just the way they are now. But when the time came, she sold the letters to Matarasso. I didn't even know they had been sold until I saw them at Marc Loliée's. Loliée had bought them from Matarasso and I got them from him." He sighed, then shrugged. "I can't really blame her. She was up against it and whenever she needed money, Matarasso was always right there with what she needed. She told me that more than once." He looked over at me grimly. "I waited years for those letters. And I've just waited nine months more for Mercher to finish this binding. If you think I'm going to turn them over to you now, you're crazy."

Crazy is not the word; patient is. The conversation continued, longer than for Jarry, longer than for Gertrude Stein. Meanwhile, Georges was having to face up to his accumulated unpaid binding bills, his debts to various booksellers, and the installation costs of an expensive electronic security system designed to protect his library. And so before he left for his summer place on the Ile-de-Ré that June, he sold me the Satie letters.

Four years later, on a morning in the summer of 1974, Georges was writing in his garden on the Ile-de-Ré. He looked up, started to speak, and then stopped breathing. No one who collected modern books knew more about them, cared more about them, than he. What a pity he couldn't have taken as good care of himself as he took of them.

Chapter 7

In the making of books, Jean-Gabriel Daragnès had done it all. The Compleat Printer, he had designed type, been compositor and pressman; designed the book and illustrated the text; engraved the illustrations, using every technique ever developed. In the process he produced some of the finest books of their kind to come out of the France of his time. Occasionally he took the ultimate step and designed a book's binding, to be executed by Georges Cretté or some other contemporary master. The strength of Daragnès and of his more successful books stemmed from his being that rare combination of artist and craftsman—a hands-on architect, in the special sense in which that term applies to the book.

Daragnès produced more than a hundred books. Sometimes they were texts written by such friends of his as Colette, Léon-Paul Fargue, Paul Valéry, Jean Giraudoux, or Francis Carco. Others were by writers he admired as a reader of books: Baudelaire, Verlaine, Goethe, Rilke, Nerval. By the mid-Twenties Daragnès had already reached the peak of his success—a peak which became a plateau and sustained him in his position as a major designer, illustrator, and printer of *éditions de luxe* until after World War II.

In November, 1924, Daragnès selected from his own library fifty-nine books for an auction sale. With one exception (a first edition of Baudelaire's *Les Fleurs du mal*) they were his own copies of all the books he had thus far designed and illustrated. Each copy was in the fullest sense unique, since Daragnès had added to each of them his original drawings, his maquette, and the unpublished trial states of his engravings—whether drypoint, burin, aquatint, woodcut or whatever other process was involved. In some cases he included the author's manuscript and related letters. Some of the books had been bound by Pierre Legrain and other binders such as Marius Michel, René Kieffer, and A.-J. Gonon.

Even the catalogue was more in the nature of an *édition de luxe* than of an auction catalogue. It had been printed by one of the best French printers, Coulouma. Its illustrations were perfect facsimiles of Daragnès's original drawings and were made by the master of that craft, Daniel Jacomet. And the frontispiece was an original etching by Dunoyer de Segonzac which showed Daragnès working over a copperplate.

The sale was so successful that, with its proceeds, Daragnès built a handsome, broad, neo-Palladian villa on the Avenue Junot near the top of Montmartre, on the site of a crumbling old landmark known as the "Philosopher's Manor House." It was almost across the street from the Moulin de la Galette, the late-nineteenth-century dance hall made famous by the paintings and lithographs of Toulouse-Lautrec and other artists of the period. He installed his press on the ground floor, his studio and living quarters on the three floors above, and settled into a productive and rewarding second phase of his career.

Until then, most French illustrated books had been the province of professional illustrators, not great artists most of them, and not primarily painters or sculptors. Some were good enough in their way, some merely crowd-pleasers, caught up in the anecdote, the belly laugh, the erotic detail. Most of them had built up a following among publishers and collectors of various kinds and, different as they were, they all fitted into the mainstream of contemporary book-illustration.

But another tradition was forming, that of the painter (and, more rarely, sculptor) who, though not by profession an illustrator, occasionally became involved with a text that challenged his interpretative sense. Even as early as 1828 Eugène Delacroix had produced a series of lithographs for *Faust*. And in the 1870s Edouard Manet had done illustrations for *Le Fleuve* by Charles Cros, for Mallarmé's translations of *The Raven* and of other poems by Poe, as well as for Mallarmé's own *L'Après-midi d'un faune.* Nearer the end of the century, Maurice Denis had done a modest but appealing interpretation in color lithography of André Gide's *Le Voyage d'Urien.*

With the book-publishing activities of the art dealer Ambroise Vollard, beginning early in the new century, the *livre de peintre*, or *livre d'artiste*, as it came to be called, was on firmer ground. Vollard commissioned many of the leading painters—Bonnard, Braque, Chagall, Dufy, Picasso, Rouault among them—to work on editions that, when they were published—generally long years after completion—sometimes came to be ranked with the greatest achievements in the history of the illustrated book.

Most of Daragnès's painter friends who also illustrated books were beginning to lose favor as a result of the changing taste in art that was making itself felt even before World War II and more so in its aftermath. Jean-Louis Boussingault, for example, had been a very good painter and illustrator; likewise, Luc-Albert Moreau. But times had changed. *Their* Ecole de Paris had had its day. The only one of the more traditional painter friends of Daragnès to survive the shift in public favor away from their kind of painting to what one early (1926) Cassandra had labeled "pathological art" was Dunoyer de Segonzac. He was so well entrenched with his loyal French constituency that the books he illustrated (several of which, including Charles-Louis Philippe's *Bubu de Montparnasse*, had been printed by Daragnès) could be purchased by only the favored faithful: there simply weren't enough copies to satisfy the demand, although they were priced higher than most of the others.

Daragnès was at the crossroads. He was a gifted craftsman and had a great sense of design and doubtless would have gone on to make outstanding contributions to the book as it evolved in accordance with the times. But in the early summer of 1950, although a vigorous, youthful-looking sixty-four, he was having difficulties in the genitourinary department. His doctor booked him into a private clinic for observation. They operated but he didn't improve in the way they had expected. He became restless and depressed. His wife tried to talk to his doctor and the surgeon about his condition. She got nothing but double-talk in return, she later told me. One day she spoke to a nurse about it. The nurse gave it to her straight. "He's going to die. You know that, don't you?" Madame Daragnès was stunned. She didn't know that and could hardly believe it. She decided to take him home and there, in a bedroom adjoining his library and his studio, surrounded by his books, he died.

I had seen books by Daragnès and had owned a few before I went to live in France. An article I had read about him after the war in *Le Portique*, a French bibliophile quarterly, had been illustrated with a number of photographs, not only of pages from his books but also of the man himself, painting and engraving in his studio and at work on his handpress. He looked like the actor Leslie Howard, a gentle kind of man one took to on sight. I planned to look him up after I got to Paris.

Early in my stay there, wandering around Montmartre like any other tourist, I came upon his house quite unintentionally. I recognized it at once from my memory of a photograph of it which had been reproduced in the article in *Le Portique*. I decided I would write to him in a day or two. The next morning I read his obituary in the *Paris Herald-Tribune*.

It was many years later before I returned to that house at 14, Avenue Junot. I knew then that Madame Daragnès had continued, to some extent, her husband's printing and publishing activities over the years since his death. I had bought some of the books she had done, each with the familiar Daragnès emblem of a heart capped with the fleur-de-lis. One morning, on an impulse, I called her up. I first got a maid, who then called Madame Daragnès to the phone. She had a low, throaty voice. I told her about my interest in books and manuscripts and she gave me an appointment for the next afternoon. When I arrived and rang the bell from the sidewalk, at the foot of a long flight of stairs blocked by an iron grill, which was locked, little dogs started yipping up above me at the first-floor level. Someone pushed a buzzer, the grill opened, and I climbed the stairs. When I got to the top, Madame Daragnès, barely five feet tall, with close-cropped white hair, was trying to restrain two dachshunds from overdoing their guard-duty antics. We shook hands and she invited me out onto the large terrace, luxuriantly and shelteringly planted, that was built over the street-level garage and print-shop. She was wearing a black bikini and, for a woman in her mid-seventies, was in remarkable shape, all of it deeply tanned. I soon realized she was stone-deaf. She wore no hearing device, but whenever she turned her head away and I started speaking, it was obvious that she was not hearing a word I was saying. She apologized for her costume. She hadn't made a note of the time I was due to arrive and had remembered it as an hour later. She cut short her tanning session and left me the terrace while she went inside to change. In about ten minutes she returned, fully dressed. She invited me to follow her.

Off the terrace was a large reception area with a dining room adjoining. It was furnished with a mixture of Renaissance and somewhat later French provincial pieces, dominated by paintings in profusion. The most notable of them was a nearly life-size oil portrait of Daragnès by Pascin.

Toward the rear was a magnificent marble staircase with a graceful wrought-iron balustrade leading to the floors above. Accompanied by the dachshunds we marched, four abreast, up to the second floor.

Simple rather than ornate, the staircase was wide and altogether one of the most beautiful I had ever seen in a modern house. The black-and-gilt wrought-iron balustrade had been fashioned by Raymond Subes, Madame Daragnès told me. At the landing we passed through double doors into a large, sun-drenched drawing room about forty feet wide with two sets of huge double-doored windows crowned by large demi-lunes overlooking the terrace. On the left, as we entered, I noticed a framed, annotated proof of Rouault's large "Head of Christ" from the *Miserere* series. Beside it hung the masterpiece of Picasso's Vollard suite, the 1934 aquatint "Blind Minotaur Guided by a Little Girl in the Night." At the right end of the room was a loggia and all around were bookcases, print portfolios, and unobtrusively attractive furniture scattered about with a very knowing combination of casual abandon and thoughtful design. At the right rear, just before the loggia, was a small sitting room with more bookcases and folders of prints. At the other end of the drawing room was a double door leading into the library. There, a good part of the front wall was given over to another large set of windows overlooking the Avenue Junot. The rest of the wall space, except for the door connecting with the drawing room and one leading to a corridor, was covered with glass-fronted bookcases. There were tables and chairs and a divan, antique globes and ship models, but mostly there were books. I was to spend a lot of time there over the following weeks and years and for as long as I did, I continued to find things—small, medium, and large—whose presence had eluded me on previous visits.

I had explained to Madame Daragnès in our telephone conversation that I was interested most of all in manuscripts and correspondence. "We have all that," she had told me, in a matter-of-fact way, as though I had just read off a grocery list. And "all that"—or an impressive part of it, at least—was laid out now on a long, narrow walnut table that stretched about a third of the way across the drawing room's width, its long dimension. I took off my jacket and went to work.

There was an extended correspondence from Dunoyer de Segonzac to "Gab" (as Madame Daragnès referred to her husband). The letters began in the early 1920s, during their work on Segonzac's illustration of the classic World War I trilogy by the novelist Roland Dorgelès: *Les Croix de bois, La Boule de gui,* and *Le Cabaret de la belle femme.* Others related to their collaboration on one of Segonzac's major illustrations, the *Bubu de Montparnasse* which the Lyons bibliophile society "Les XXX" brought out in an edition of 130 copies in 1929. The correspondence continued, after Gab's death, with Madame Daragnès ("Ma chère Janine").

There were letters and manuscripts by Colette, Fargue, Carco, Giraudoux, Paul Morand; from Pascin and his mistress, the painter-engraver Hermine David; from Valery Larbaud, Marie Laurencin, and a host of others, including Gen Paul, one of Céline's closest friends, a Montmartre painter who had illustrated an edition of his *Voyage au bout de la nuit.* Gen Paul could have been a character created by Céline. He had lost a leg in World War I, drank heavily, and had become something of a recluse. He lived just a few doors further up the Avenue Junot. Later on, after I had become a regular visitor, Janine took me up the street to meet him on two occasions. The first time, he came to the window, waved, and went away; the second time, he didn't bother. Being a stubborn little creature, Janine slipped a note under his door. He wrote on it the French equivalent of "Go to hell," and slipped it back out. "Oh, well," she said, "he never did have the sweetest disposition in the world."

One of the more amusing groups of letters I found had been written by Jean Cocteau to Walter Berry. Berry was an international lawyer who was president of the American Chamber of Commerce in Paris, a cousin of Harry Crosby's father, and an intimate friend of Edith Wharton, who idolized him. Other close friends of Berry's were Henry James and Marcel Proust. One letter in particular caught my eye. Cocteau had arranged to give a reading of a new work in progress, *Le Cap de Bonne-Espérance*, at the apartment of Valentine Hugo one Thursday evening late in 1918. Valentine had invited several of her *Nouvelle Revue Française* friends, Fargue and Gaston Gallimard among them. Cocteau had invited Marcel Proust, Proust's godmother, Madame Marie Scheikévitch, a prominent literary hostess of the period, and Walter Berry, with whom he was eager to ingratiate himself. Proust habitually arrived anywhere very late. When his party finally showed up, Cocteau, deep into his reading for the other guests, took it all very badly and created a scene, interrupting his reading until Proust and his party had left. Back home, he began to be even more troubled and so at two o'clock in the morning he wrote a letter of apology and justification to Walter Berry:

Dear Mr. Berry,

You *know* you are one of the 7 or 8 people that I respect and love by instinct and by taste (even though I hardly know you in fact). . . . This evening, for me, was a veritable nightmare (like dreaming that one arrives at a ball with nothing but one's shirt on, for example).

But as I think it over, I consider myself *lucky* not to have made a mess of a work [*Le Cap*] that means a great deal to me in the presence of a man I think so highly of [W.B.].

There is only one offender in all this—Proust. He *knew* that his coming after 9:30—it was actually ten minutes to ten—would upset me. He forgot that I too am a *sick man* and a poet. Do you blame me? For my part, *je vous embrasse.*

Jean Cocteau

As for books, there was no end to them. They were dispersed all over that great house in a way that to a librarian might have been confusing but for a digger was exhilarating. There were discoveries to be made every day I was there. No room was without its bookcases. In a third-floor bedroom, I found first editions of Lautréamont's *Les Chants de Maldoror,* of Flaubert's *Madame Bovary* and *Bouvard et Pécuchet,* and the journals of the Goncourt brothers, in fine period bindings. In the sitting room adjacent to that bedroom there were scarce first editions by Aragon, Claudel, Gide, Cocteau, Max Jacob, Julien Gracq; firsts of Gérard de Nerval, all handsomely bound by Semet et Plumelle in faithful reproductions of contemporary Romantic bindings with wrappers preserved; and books illustrated by Pascin, Dufy, Henri Laurens, Jacques Villon, Marie Laurencin, and more. Every room was a cornucopia.

There were extensive collections of Colette, Giraudoux, Fargue, Céline, Paul Morand, and Valéry, among others. These were, for the most part, first editions, often large-paper copies of which only a small number had been printed, all of them bearing warm presentation inscriptions, like the copy of Colette's *Sido,* the book she wrote about her mother. It was one of ten numbered large-paper copies on handmade Dutch paper inscribed, "For Daragnès. I offer him the best that is in me, the portrait of 'Sido,' and the pride I have in resembling her—even if only a bit. His old friend, Colette." Or his copy of her novel *La Seconde,* one of a small number printed on handmade paper in Colette's own special shade of blue in which she had written: "To Daragnès, this 'touch of blue'—because of his eyes, naturally. His old friend, Colette."

The Fargue collection was rich in rarities, from a first issue of Fargue's first book, *Tancrède,* printed at the expense of Valery Larbaud, to scarce offprints of Fargue's articles in *La Nouvelle Revue Française* issued in editions of ten or twelve copies; proof copies of *Pour la musique* and *Poèmes*, the first with poems omitted from the published edition, the second a unique copy on Japan paper, and all with presentation inscriptions. Most of the Fargue books had been bound in apple-green boards by A. J. Gonon, Paul Eluard's binder and "first friend," and most were inscribed to Daragnès; but here the collector in him had reached out to other sources to fill in gaps in his collection. A number of Fargue's books were inscribed not to Daragnès but to Raymonde Linossier, an Orientalist and close friend of Fargue, Sylvia Beach, Francis Poulenc, Darius Milhaud, and Erik Satie. Raymonde was also the stout-hearted young woman who took over the typing of the climactic Circe episode in *Ulysses* to break the bottleneck which had halted the printing of Sylvia Beach's first edition of the book. After that, Joyce "put Raymonde into *Ulysses*," as he told Sylvia.

But Daragnès had not limited himself to collecting books by his friends. There were large groups by a wide range of other writers who interested him, from Remy de Gourmont to Guillaume Apollinaire; Rilke, too, whose books held manuscript poems and letters; and also the late-nineteenth-century poets Baudelaire, Verlaine, Mallarmé, and Jules Laforgue.

The most fascinating aspect of Daragnès's library was its variety. Some collectors buy the high spots of a period or a subject; others collect one writer—even a few—in depth. But Daragnès's tastes and interests ranged more widely. For example, in addition to the extensive literary collections, there were great quantities of the best art-history reference works, from the Renaissance up until the day before yesterday: *oeuvre* catalogues and monographs on Rembrandt, Delacroix, Millet, Manet, Monet, van Gogh, Renoir, Degas, Redon, Rodin, and beyond. There were albums of facsimiles of master drawings by Poussin and Claude, Jacques Callot and Jacopo Bellini; and enormous tomes, all long out of print and very scarce, on the primitive painters of France, Italy, and Germany, Indian art, illuminated manuscripts, bibliography, book-binding, and more.

One day Janine and I had gone down to the ground level to look for something in the printshop. It was dark and silent now, but there were books and more books—typography, lithography, history of printing from its earliest days, facsimiles of incunabula.

In rummaging through a file drawer, Janine came across a group of

Jean-Gabriel Daragnès
in his studio.

The Daragnès house, at 14 Avenue Junot, near
the top of Montmartre.

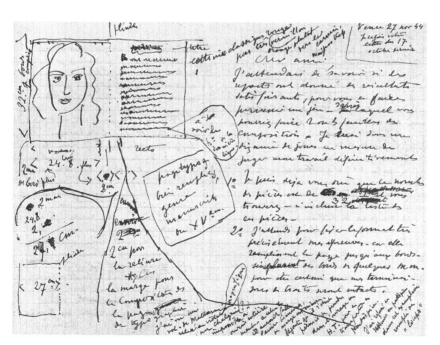

Henri Matisse. Autograph letter dated 27 November 1944, to Jean-Gabriel
Daragnès concerning their work on an illustrated edition of Baudelaire's
Les Fleurs du mal.

Matisse, drawing,
by Brassaï.

One corner of the
library in the
Daragnès house.

three original copperplates engraved by Pascin (one of them un-published) together with a proof of his first etching, done in Daragnès's atelier and under his supervision. It was inscribed in pencil at the lower right, "for Daragnès, his pupil Pascin." She found other copperplates, by Marquet and van Dongen. When she had taken them all out, there remained a box, wrapped and tied, labeled "Matisse."

"Oh, ça alors!" Janine muttered to herself. She pulled the box out of the file cabinet, cut the string, and opened it up. Inside were three linoleum blocks engraved by Matisse. The two smallest showed the head of a young woman in profile and full view. The third, which measured about 11 by 8 inches, was the seated figure of a woman with long hair against a leafy background. The two smaller ones had a black surface, but where the artist's gouge had cut into the block, the lines it uncovered—hair, eyes, eyebrows, nose, lips, facial contours, neckline—stood out in a warm rust tone, the inner color of the block in both cases. There was no trace of ink: no proofs had been pulled.

The large block had clearly been used for printing: black ink was smudged around the edges of the woodblock onto which the linoleum had been nailed. The composition was more elaborate, the woman's features more detailed. All three were magnificent examples of Matisse's seemingly effortless but uniquely precise arabesque.

Janine looked into another drawer of the cabinet, shuffled through a few file folders, and brought up one on which was inscribed, in a hand I recognized as hers, the words *"Documents pour linos Matisse."*

"This is part of it," she said. "We might as well take it all upstairs where we can have a good look."

Up in the drawing room, she turned over to me the papers in the file folder. I sorted them out and began to read. They told a story I had never heard before although I was very familiar with Matisse's work as an illustrator of books. His first great book, one of the monuments of twentieth-century book production, was the edition Albert Skira had brought out in 1932 of the poems of Mallarmé, with twenty-nine original etchings by Matisse. And then came a much less spectacular work, which George Macy's Limited Editions Club had published in 1935, an edition of Joyce's *Ulysses* with six etchings and twenty drawings by Matisse. It was soon after that, as these papers made clear, that Daragnès and Matisse had begun discussing with the bibliophile society "Les XXX" the idea of doing an *édition de grand luxe* of Baudelaire's *Les Fleurs du mal.*

Matisse was beginning to interest himself in engraving on linoleum and early in the correspondence he proposed to use that medium for his illustration of *Les Fleurs du mal.* (Later he wrote that linoleum should not be considered an economical substitute for wood; it actually gave the engraving a special character, very different from that of a wood engraving.)

In all matters Matisse was precise and painstaking in the extreme. He said he would commit himself to the number of plates for the book but not to the subjects. Those he would choose as the work progressed, and in accordance with his inspiration—probably from the section of *Les Fleurs du mal* entitled "Spleen et Idéal." Every detail would be decided by him; his page dimensions, for example, were to be 23 x 28 centimeters. He said that it would be hard to make the page any smaller, working in that medium. He would select the paper, the type, and the wrappers, and would allow no additional suites of the engravings to be pulled.

Occasionally, unable to satisfy himself on some point, he would launch a trial balloon with Daragnès. In composing his pages, he was playing with the idea of running half a line of poetry above the image. In the case of an image with two women, he was thinking of using *"Descendez, descendez, lamentables victimes,"* or possibly, *"Descendez le chemin de l'enfer éternel."* Or then again, he would take the view that it might be better to put nothing at all. In any case, before their next meeting he needed to know how many copies those people wanted and what he would get out of it all. But no suites. Once those issues were agreed upon, they could talk about other questions more intelligently.

Matisse was spending much of his time in Nice at that period. And Daragnès, who had a summer place and a boat at Toulon, less than two hours away, called on him frequently to show him proofs and discuss technical problems. Sometimes Matisse's health forced him to cancel their meetings. His eyes were giving him trouble; his belly, too. And then there would be surges of activity and he would ask for further proofs, revising this plate or that, or wanting his approved proof sheet returned and the plate destroyed.

There was much discussion about a plate Matisse referred to as "La Tahitienne." It seemed likely to me that it was the largest of the three blocks that Janine had found in the printshop, since that one bore evidence of much use and it had a strong resemblance to the pen-and-ink sketch Matisse drew in one of his letters to identify the plate he was referring to under that name.

By mid-1939, Matisse's conscience was beginning to trouble him about "the gentlemen of 'Les XXX.'" His work was going badly. He hadn't been able to satisfy himself on a number of points. And then there was the matter of his health. He hoped they would understand he was still interested in what they were asking him to do but it couldn't be done with a wave of the wand. He needed tranquillity of spirit. He was uncertain how he could adequately apologize to the *lyonnais*—he was thinking of their deadline and their money-raising obligations, no doubt—but the truth was the best excuse, he decided, since there are some things in life that one can't do anything about. And then he dropped it all into Daragnès's lap, with the hope that *he* could find the right words to make this disappointment acceptable, at least.

A year and a half later Matisse confessed he hadn't thought about Baudelaire in a long time. He had expected he would be getting back to it but it just hadn't worked out. If it weren't for the fact that he had to enlist Daragnès's help to get a message to Galanis (a French engraver of Greek ancestry who was a Montmartre neighbor of Daragnès), he probably wouldn't be showing his face now. He was very ashamed of himself, he had to admit.

Paris was now trying to cope with the German Occupation and Matisse hoped that Daragnès was able to work and to accept Paris as it was. By keeping hard at work, he assured him, one finally could accept anything. As for Baudelaire, he just couldn't say when he would get back to it. For that, he would need a kind of calm that he didn't have now.

In 1941 Matisse had major abdominal surgery. And Baudelaire, already on the back burner for over two years, dropped out of sight. But toward the end of 1944, from Vence, where he was then living, Matisse sent Daragnès a long illustrated letter which almost bristled with energy. He had made his selection of the poems and he sent a list of the thirty-two he was going to illustrate. It included some of Baudelaire's finest: "La Chevelure," "Sed non satiata," "Le Chat," "Invitation au voyage," among them.

It was now apparent that at least some of the illustrations were being done in lithography. Matisse was drawing on transfer paper with a lithographic crayon and his drawings were being transferred to the lithographic stones which would be used in printing them in the Paris atelier of the lithographer Mourlot. Since his operation Matisse spent a good deal of his time working in bed and the use of the transfer paper made his work much less taxing than drawing directly on the stone.

Matisse was waiting for proofs of his lithographs so that he could determine the page format with precision. He wanted the image to fill the page right up to the edge, with just a few millimeters to spare, in order to make certain that the endings of his lines would be intact. He wanted the printed pages to be very full, in the manner of a fifteenth-century manuscript.

Since many French bibliophiles have books of this kind bound artistically by master craftsmen, Matisse was very concerned about the effect a binding might have on the proportions of his pages. He told Daragnès a horror story about a copy he had recently seen of his illustrated edition of Mallarmé's *Poésies*. A collector had shown him a copy which had been beautifully bound, but couldn't be fully opened. As a result, the inner margins—called the gutter—were out of proportion to the others. The man had even gone so far as to displace one of the full-page plates, which had been a loose sheet before the book was bound, moving it up front because he liked it better as a frontispiece! Like the art collector who had touched up the sky in one of Corot's paintings because he didn't like the shade of blue Corot had used. The world is full of crazy people—even the world of bibliophiles—and Matisse wasn't taking any chances; so he wanted to have two centimeters added to compensate for the binding, over and above the margin normally required for the composition of the printed page.

The typefaces that interested him most were 20-point Elzevir, 24-point Garamond Roman, and 20-point Didot Roman. He asked Daragnès for a sample composition of each to help him make up his mind. He needed to be able to judge the luminosity that each of the three would give to the lithograph facing it. The text was on the recto—the upper side—of the sheet; the illustration, on the verso—the underside—of the preceding sheet. The margin should be calculated so exactly that text and image would meet but not overlap. And he wanted classic ornamental capitals, red but not too red—vermilion, or perhaps orange, but tending toward carmine. I could see that one of the great modern illustrated books was now building.

Six months later the entire structure had collapsed. Because of the intense heat, Matisse's transfer sheets had dried out. One of the lithographers at Mourlot's dampened them slightly to make it easier to transfer Matisse's drawings from the paper to the stone. In the process each sheet had stretched about a quarter of an inch. When Matisse saw the proofs, they looked, to his critical eye, so distorted that he wouldn't approve them. At first he tried to substitute other, similar drawings. But they didn't seem right to him—not for Baudelaire, certainly. Daragnès urged him to make a fresh start. He simply couldn't. He had given his all—intermittently, to be sure—for seven years and the idea of beginning over again was just more of a burden than he could take on.

Meanwhile, Louis Aragon had had an idea for a volume of *his* poetry which he wanted Matisse to illustrate and the publication committee of "Les XXX" had approved it. Matisse made a wry pun about having been burned with Baudelaire—he *and* his lithographs. He hoped he'd make out better with Aragon. Quite clearly, Daragnès didn't have his heart in that project and he found himself unavailable for meetings that Aragon kept pushing Matisse and him to arrange. Soon Matisse grew tired of the idea and it fell by the wayside rather quickly.

Finally, as a consolation to Aragon, Matisse let him do an inexpensive edition of *Les Fleurs du mal* using reproductions based on photographs of Matisse's original lithographs taken before their distortion. The book came out in an ugly green-and-red slipcase at a price almost within reach of the masses Aragon's political alliances were purported to be concerned with. The chapter was closed. But what could—and undoubtedly would—have been one of the great triumphs of the illustrated book in this century was lost. No record of the project remains, other than the blocks and the letters Janine had disinterred for me from their semifinal resting-place.

In Matisse's last letter to Daragnès I found a phrase which describes the situation aptly. He called it *"un concours de malchance"*—a run of bad luck. Much as I deplore that bad luck, I must confess I'm glad I had the *good* luck to be able to pick up the pieces.

Chapter 8

One afternoon when I was harvesting my weekly quota from the library of Jean-Gabriel Daragnès, I took down his Céline books—prewar, wartime, and postwar—most of them inscribed either to Daragnès or to his wife, Janine. Céline had been a friend and neighbor of theirs, and Daragnès had arranged for the publication of some of Céline's minor works, including a ballet and a satire on Sartre. Many of their copies were *exemplaires de tête*, printed on better paper than ordinary copies and limited, in one case, to thirty; in another, fifteen, and in a third, five. After Janine and I had agreed that I could and would buy them all (and for how much), she left the library, crossed the long drawing room, and went into a small sitting room at its far end. When she returned to the library, she brought with her a thick file folder. It held long folio sheets of letters written in a rapid scrawl that was recognizably Céline's. There were other documents, as well, and I settled in for a good read.

Céline had loyal friends and violent enemies, and knowing what lay in store for him at the Liberation because of the outspoken and sometimes unspeakable treatment in his writings of almost every ethnic group—not only Jews, by any means, but also English, Americans, Russians, Germans, along with Vichyite and every other brand of French—he had left for Germany as the war was winding down. There he was given an exit visa so that he could go to Denmark, where he had some money to live on. But by this time the Allied victory was assured.

For a long time Céline had been receiving letters—an average of three a day, he said later—which threatened his life. "I wanted to be able to speak for myself when the time came. If I had remained, they would have prevented me from doing so by shooting me. Dead men have neither voice nor pen." Céline was certainly right on that score. It was not long after the Liberation that *some* Frenchmen—including *some* writers—were being executed for *"crimes d'idées"*—criminal ideas—in a bloodbath of what soon came to be known as "Liberation justice."

After stays in Baden-Baden, Berlin, Kränzlin, and Sigmaringen, Céline reached Copenhagen, where he was traced and denounced. The French Embassy there requested that he be arrested and extradited on the grounds that in April, 1945, a warrant for his arrest had been issued in Paris based on an accusation of treason. He was picked up and jailed as a "suspicious foreigner." The French kept trying to have him extradited, charging that he had "struck a blow against the nation's morale in time of war." (A forced return to France could have meant five to ten years at hard labor; if he returned voluntarily, it was suggested, the sentence might be shortened.) In the end the Danes refused to recognize the French charges as grounds for extradition and, after fourteen months' imprisonment, Céline was released. Aware that both ends of the political spectrum were howling for his blood (at one end, the Gaullists; at the other, the Communist daily, *L'Humanité*, and several other vengeful left-wing Paris papers), he did not see fit to return to France. A few months later, with his wife, Lucette, he went to live in a small, unheated shack, without water or electricity, near Körsor, about sixty miles from Copenhagen, which his Danish lawyer had made available to him. He was suffering from pellagra, rheumatism, a tumor on his arm, and unremitting head pains. In addition, he had recently come down with a recurrence of malaria, which he had first contracted in 1916. His doctor allowed him out of bed one hour a day, but he was barely able to walk to the yard, even with the help of two canes.

The French government decided to try him *in absentia*. In the meantime, the press was trying him daily. Céline answered his accusers through letters to friends and his wife's parents, who, in turn, passed the word along. The bloodthirsty howled louder. Calmer heads accused the Ministry of Justice of having an "empty dossier": i. e., no real basis for a legitimate trial. Céline had not been accused of collaboration, except loosely by political enemies and certain journalists. But it was claimed that he had written articles for collaborationist papers. The "articles," Céline said in the course of a ten-page memorandum quoted by the writer Albert Paraz in his book *Le Gala des vaches*, were letters, published at random and on the responsibility of the recipients—edited and not authentic. He was accused of having "literary connections" with Germany. But other than a few pages of *Bagatelles pour un massacre*, he said, his works were banned in Germany. And the Germans considered him an "anarchic spirit, a dangerous moral saboteur." He had criticized the Resistance. If so, that was because, at the time, there were things about it to be criticized, just as there were in the other camp, he said. He was alleged to have left Paris under the protection of the Germans. Céline refuted that point by saying he had applied long before 1944 for permission to go to Denmark. (He had actually made his first attempts as early as 1941.) Permission had been granted only in June, 1944, and he had left in July. He said he had been interned in Baden-Baden and in Berlin and then brought to Sigmaringen to serve as a medical doctor (his original profession).

Finally, he was accused of having supported anti-Semitic persecution by bringing back into print during the Occupation *Bagatelles pour un massacre* and *L'Ecole des cadavres*, two of his most strident works, and of having published a third, and similarly unbridled, venting of his spleen—*Les Beaux draps*. But as the novelist Marcel Aymé pointed out later, Céline's publication schedule was controlled by his publisher, Robert Denoël, who was bringing out Céline with one hand and Elsa Triolet, a good Communist and a very commercial writer, with the other. And making money on both.

Le Libertaire, a respectable trade-union-oriented paper published by the Fédération Anarchiste, solicited opinions from a number of prominent figures. André Breton and his chief lieutenant, Benjamin Péret, who were not only far removed from Céline politically but also had no use for him as a writer, gave Céline no sympathy whatever.

Albert Camus wrote that political justice was as repugnant to him as the anti-Semitism that troubled many of Céline's readers. He urged that Céline be left alone.

Morvan Lebesque, editor-in-chief of *Carrefour*, said that he considered Céline and William Faulkner the greatest living novelists, and Céline the only French writer of this century to have closed the gap between literature and the people at large. Let him come back to France, he wrote, with all the consideration that is due him.

Louis Pauwels, another respected writer and journalist with no taint of collaboration, said Céline should simply be acquitted. Politicians, writers, journalists, profiteering businessmen had been whitewashed by the Government. Why pick on Céline?

The painter Jean Dubuffet called on the Government to bring liberty and free speech out of the dictionary and into everyday life, "to absolve [Céline] completely, to open wide our arms, to honor and celebrate him as one of our greatest artists and one of the proudest and most incorruptible of us. We don't have many more like that."

Jean Paulhan, editor-in-chief of *La Nouvelle Revue Française*, pointed out that Céline had shown himself as distant from the Germans and the Vichy government as he had, before the war, from the French (so-called) democratic government. He had turned down, between 1940 and 1944, dinners at the German Embassy, trips to Weimar, important assignments from the hireling press in the same way he had turned down honors and decorations in 1937. If anarchy is a crime, he said, let them shoot him. "If not, leave him alone, once and for all."

Paulhan had a valid point there, but you can't please everybody. Five members of the Sacco-Vanzetti Anarchist Group wrote in outrage to *Le Libertaire*. They had been surprised to see their paper devoting so much space to Céline on the pretext of condemning a witch-hunt. They were sure that the majority of the paper's readers didn't give a damn about Céline. And they didn't need any lessons in the miscarriage of justice; that was an old story to them. What they wanted to read about were the persecuted masses in Spain, Bulgaria, Bolivia, Greece, eastern Europe, India, Vietnam, North Africa—and France: miners, deserters, revolutionary scapegoats, the unknown, unsung rank and file. Let Céline look after himself.

Throughout the debate Daragnès had been one of the most active workers in Céline's behalf. In his view, Céline was perhaps the greatest French writer since Proust. But there was no place in our society for those who didn't wish to play the game, Daragnès reflected. And since Céline never had and never would play anybody's game but his own, he was up against a rigid system of "justice" that would fall back on the famous "empty dossier" rather than tolerate that much independence.

Daragnès had been in correspondence with Céline in Denmark and had done everything he could to sway public and official opinion against the idea of trial. Failing that, one of the most influential voices to be raised for the defense, he felt, would be that of the novelist François Mauriac, friend of General de Gaulle and spokesman for the conservative, middle-of-the-road newspaper *Le Figaro*.

Toward the end of January, 1950, he wrote to Mauriac as follows:

Dear Mr. Mauriac,

I should like, on the eve of a trial in which the health, the life, and the work of Céline are at stake, to meet with you if you could set aside a few minutes for me.

The latest maneuvers of a Court of Justice in dealing with an empty file of essentially meaningless accusations can surely not be a matter of no concern to a man like you.

If you feel it would be useful to receive me, I will be available at whatever time and place suits your convenience.

With best wishes,
Daragnès

From his office at *Le Figaro,* Mauriac replied, on January 26th:

Dear Sir:

I shall be glad to see you, but I must tell you straight off that I don't feel much inclined to defend Céline since he is at liberty in a foreign country and under no risk.

Céline's case is not that of a man who is being reproached for a political attitude: I feel that his anti-Semitism at the period when he did not deny it, that is to say at the time of the crematory ovens, *is a complicity in crime*—and what a crime!

The letter from him which [the newspaper] *Combat* published this morning is disgusting.

You know what my attitude has always been in such matters of criminal prosecution and that from the start I have been on the side of indulgence and forgetting.

If Céline were in prison, this would not be the letter I would be writing you.

With best wishes,
François Mauriac

On the 29th of January, Daragnès sent his reply:

Dear Sir,

I was expecting the kind of letter you have written me. I could not forgive myself if I did not point out a few errors due to a faulty perspective: You speak of a letter just published in *Combat* but written by Céline in 1941—at the time of the crematory ovens, you say. But at that period the "ovens" did not exist (it was only several years later that their existence became known to us). [If we are to censure Céline] we should also censure the writers who, at the time of the ovens, sent their books, with gracious presentation inscriptions, to the German, [Lieutenant Gerhard] Heller, who was then in charge of the distribution of paper for book-publishing.

You tell me, also, that Céline is at liberty in a foreign country and has nothing to fear. It is only fair to point out that he has spent [fourteen] months in prison in Copenhagen and that he is unable to leave Denmark except to return to France, where a warrant for his arrest would bring him right back into a prison cell.

With best wishes,
Daragnès

When Daragnès sent Céline copies of his exchange with Mauriac, Céline sent him a copy of a full-page illustration from a publication relating to World War I. It showed Sergeant Destouches (Céline) on horseback racing under heavy rifle and artillery fire to deliver a message from an infantry regiment to brigade headquarters. Céline delivered the message, but in returning was wounded. He was decorated and cited for his valor by Marshal Joffre.

On the verso of the image, Céline had written in ink:

> To François Mauriac, Christian.
> Pharisaical bastard. Shirker in both wars.
> Shining star in the dictionary of weathercocks.
> Great friend of Lieutenant Heller
> and the mess-of-trash Claudel-the-Francoist!
> A thousand turds and contempt from
> Louis Ferdinand Céline, volunteer in both wars,
> wounded, dying, 75% disability.
> Médaille Militaire, November 1914.

The trial, of course, was a somber farce. The accused was represented by an empty chair. Céline was called by name. Silence responded. A clerk read the charges, a very mixed bag. The presiding judge discussed the background and then, in lieu of the customary interrogation, had the clerk read passages from letters Céline had addressed to the Court. Since Céline's writing is not only—at times—outrageous, but also—at times—very funny, people laughed.

One of the points Céline made was related to the acquittal, on 30 April 1948, of his publisher; that is, the publishing house of the late Robert Denoël, then in the hands of a woman known by her *nom de plume* as Jean Voilier. Not only had the firm been cleared of all charges; it had even been reimbursed for all its costs. After Daragnès had written him about that, Céline had replied to another supporter:

White as snow. . . . Intelligent firm. . . . Intelligent directress. . . . And on the same charges, they want to hang me! And it won't be long!

They didn't hang him; but in spite of favorable testimony from Dr. Henri Mondor (the eminent neurosurgeon and Mallarmé scholar), from Marcel Aymé, Pierre MacOrlan, Henry Miller, Thierry Maulnier (a colleague of François Mauriac at *Le Figaro*), from Jean Paulhan, Daragnès, and a Jewish organization called L'Association d'Israélites pour la Réconciliation des Français, they sentenced Céline to a year in prison, national disgrace, a fine of 50,000 francs, and confiscation of one half of all his property, present and future.

In reporting the verdict, most French papers took the position that, all things considered, Céline had got off lightly and they seemed to be breathing a sigh of relief. The Thunderer of the French Communist Party, the morning paper *L'Humanité*, predictably, was exceedingly unhappy. Under the headline "A hearing in a court of justice? NO! A rehabilitation session for the Gestapo agent Céline," they called him "anti-Semite, collaborator, agent of the Nazi secret service," and more. The trial, they charged, had been rigged in his favor; in short, a characteristic *Huma* story and a model of journalistic bad faith.

A year later, amnestied, Céline returned to France. He eventually settled into a dilapidated nineteenth-century house on the Route des Gardes in Meudon, just outside Paris, up on a hill overlooking the Renault automobile factories at Billancourt. He was a badly scarred survivor of his journey through Hell, surrounded by his cats and dogs and birds and his dedicated wife, Lucette. He began to practice medicine once more. At first, his writing seemed to fall flat. Then, with *D'un château l'autre*, in which he satirized wartime collaborators, he was back on the rails, once again a critical success and an irresistible flame to the journalistic moths. He kept writing, and talking, as outrageously as ever, until the first day of July, 1961, when he suddenly died.

* * * * *

One afternoon in the late 1960s, not long after Madame Daragnès had sold me her Céline documents, I bought a batch of Céline manuscript at the Hôtel Drouot. I say "batch" because it was a group of several chapters of one of the manuscripts of *D'un château l'autre*, the novel based on Céline's flight to Germany at the end of World War II. Céline was a compulsive rewriter of all of his works and *D'un château l'autre* is no exception to that characteristic practice. I have encountered several

Louis-Ferdinand Céline, before World War II.

Céline in Denmark, just after World War II.

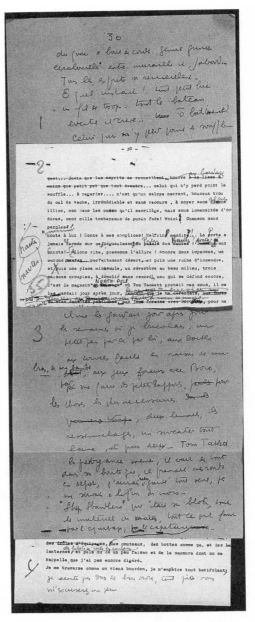

Autograph manuscript of Céline's appraisal of François Mauriac, sent with "a thousand turds and contempt. . . ."

Louis-Ferdinand Céline. *Guignol's Band*. A characteristic assemblage of blue and white pages from Chapter 6 of Céline's corrected manuscript, pieced together with pins.

autograph manuscripts of that book and have seen, in addition, sizable chunks of carbon copies of one or another of them: i.e., copies Céline had made by inserting a sheet of carbon paper between two blank sheets of typing paper, which allowed him to handwrite two copies of a draft simultaneously. The carbon copies were often heavily revised in ink afterwards, providing thereby one more revision for eventual study and analysis by Céline scholars.

It had been clear from the start that someone had been selling off chapters or small groups of chapters of a manuscript of *D'un château l'autre*. For a time such batches were to be found everywhere, almost as copious and as ubiquitous as the research notes written by Jean-Jacques Rousseau and Madame Dupin for her monumentally ambitious but finally elusive History of Women.

Why buy things that are incomplete and so readily available? Among other reasons, because the glut never lasts very long. It stems usually from an ill-conceived dumping on the market of a cache of material that, in wiser hands, would be parceled out more discreetly. When it is not, but simply shows up one day at the Hôtel Drouot in the settlement of some estate, like the Rousseau material or, a bit later on, the love letters of Juliette Drouet to Victor Hugo—all 16,000 of them, written over a period of fifty years—then supply overwhelms demand and prices are low enough to tempt speculative dealers who stockpile such things until the market, under more deft manipulation, adjusts. And then those first-level prices soon double, triple, quintuple, decuple, and so on.

In the case of the *D'un château l'autre* pages, I had another, more basic reason for buying. The more versions one has of any given manuscript, the better one understands the writer's working methods. And with Céline as with Proust—indeed, as with Samuel Beckett—those methods are complex and sometimes all but impenetrable. So we need every scrap of evidence we can lay our hands on in order to formulate or to confirm our understanding of the world they have created.

As I was getting ready to leave the saleroom with my purchases that afternoon, I saw, among the crowd standing behind the benches, the sleek, dapper, portly figure of Jacques Lambert, an autograph dealer with a shop in the Rue Bonaparte, near Saint-Germain-des-Prés. He came over to me. "I see you're interested in Céline," he said. I had to say yes; at that period of glut, anyone with little interest in Céline would hardly have taken the trouble to buy pieces of *D'un château l'autre*.

"I have a manuscript of his that you ought to see," he said. I asked him what it was.

He looked puzzled. "I'm not sure. I haven't had a chance to study it. It could be *Féerie pour une autre fois.*" Whatever it was, it was a very important manuscript, he assured me. I told him I'd be glad to take a look at it, and we made arrangements to meet at his place the following week.

Lambert was an interesting case. Years earlier he had taken over the shop and inventory of the publisher Conard in the Place de la Madeleine, facing the entrance to the church. He knew little about literature and even less about the autograph market but he began to attend autograph sales at the Hôtel Drouot and watched carefully to see what his more experienced colleagues were buying. Whenever he saw the competition heating up and the price skyrocketing in the fight for some strongly contested lot, at a certain point he would step in and buy it. He refused to make deals, participate in the local ring (called *"la révision"*), give discounts or otherwise play along with his colleagues. They all resented his presence and his tactics but had a grudging respect for his buying power. It was rumored that he was related to the family of the Banque Lambert in Brussels and that he owned a thriving wool business to which he devoted a certain part of his time. When he began to be a market-influencing factor in the manuscript field, he bought a shabby, disused bookshop in the Rue Bonaparte just above the Rue Jacob, had it completely refurbished, and became the most active buyer at the Hôtel Drouot of manuscript material in all the more popular collecting areas, such as literature, art, music, history, medicine, and science. Lambert himself was rarely at his shop, which was staffed by a somewhat ponderous man-of-all-work and a very pleasant, buxom woman, Madame Mariani, who knew the stock well and served both her employer and his customers with exemplary efficiency. Lambert attended almost all of the auctions not only in France but in the other European countries as well and occasionally flew over to New York. Once he had started bidding on something, he rarely backed off, and as is usual when the word gets around that someone has money to spend and is willing to spend it, he was offered privately a good deal of first-class material that for one reason or another the owners did not wish to sell at auction. I assumed that the Céline manuscript he had told me about ever so sketchily was in that category.

When I went to keep my appointment with him the next week, we talked for a while and then he showed me a few things—none of them by Céline—that he thought might interest me. Some of them did, I bought them, and then I brought up the question of the Céline manuscript. He pointed to a cupboard in a corner of the room. "It's all in there," he said, "but I have to put it in order before I can show it to you. It's pretty big and I haven't had a chance to get to it." So we made another appointment. When I showed up that time, the scenario followed pretty closely the script of my first visit, except that this time, after other business had been taken care of, he opened the cupboard and pointed to a large cardboard carton resting on the bottom. "That's it," he said. "In that case," I suggested, "perhaps we could take a look at it." He shook his head. "Not yet. Not till I check it out. But don't worry—it won't budge." And he closed the cupboard door. He told me he'd call me when he had done his homework.

A few weeks passed, I didn't hear from him, but at another sale at the Hôtel Drouot I ran into him again. He said he was working on the manuscript and would be in touch with me. Toward the end of June our paths crossed once more. He was still working on it, he said. A very interesting manuscript and very important, assured me. In fact it wasn't one novel; it was two, he said. He didn't think he'd have a chance to finish studying it before leaving on vacation and he'd be gone for most of July and all of August. He wasn't even sure he'd be back in Paris before I left for the States in September. But I was not to worry because—he repeated—"it won't budge." And then he added, as though he were telling me something I didn't already know, "Besides, I'm not in a hurry to sell it."

I returned to Paris the next April. We met often, Lambert and I, at the Hôtel Drouot, on the street, at the post office, in bookshops, and the little ballet went on—one step forward, two steps backward—all through that spring and summer. By the third year I was becoming a little annoyed, not only with the delay but more particularly with his way of making provocative statements such as, "This is probably the most important Céline manuscript in the world." I told him that since it wasn't the manuscript of *Journey to the End of the Night* or *Death on the Installment Plan*, Céline's two major works, I found it hard to see how it could be the most important Céline manuscript in the world. He only looked wise and said, "You'll understand when you see it."

A few more months passed. One morning the mail brought me an envelope from my bank, in the Place Vendôme, enclosing a note from

Lambert, written on Morgan stationery. The note said that he had lost my address and telephone number, had gone to my bank (where he had been before to cash checks I had given him), and had asked the bank to put him in touch with me. They told him they couldn't do that but if he wished to write me a note, they would see that I got it. He wanted me to come see him as soon as I could. When I got there, he explained that he had promised a young woman a trip to America, she was growing terribly impatient, and he could defer action no longer. Did he use the word "niece"? I'm not sure, but even if he did, that wouldn't tell me anything since in French that word has, beyond its primary meaning, a metaphorical usage. In any case, he needed a substantial sum of money, particularly dollars. Was I still interested in Céline? Feeling a rather warm glow toward the young woman—niece or otherwise—I told him I was.

He opened the cupboard, brought out the carton, and removed from it large bundles of manuscript, all very obviously in Céline's hand. He spread them around, in two groups, on a library table and explained to me that one group was the manuscript of *Guignol's Band;* the other, that of its sequel, *Le Pont de Londres.* How did that justify his judgment that this was the most important Céline manuscript in captivity, I asked him.

He pointed to the masses of manuscript. "It's not just bulk," he said. "I've gone through it carefully enough to see that there are at least two complete versions of each of those novels. And there's plenty more, too. Exactly what, I'm not sure. I never did get a chance to finish the job." He hesitated. "If I had a little more time, I could check it *all* out . . . very carefully."

Given his track record over the previous three years, I decided it was time to change the subject. Until that moment, money had not been mentioned. I asked him how much he wanted for the manuscript. He said a number we'll call X. X was a very respectable and hefty sum, but I was obviously in the presence of a very respectable and hefty major manuscript. The question was: Was it *as* respectable and *as* hefty as X? This, as every bookman knows, was the moment of truth.

So I sat down and began to look through the piles of paper. How long that process went on, I don't know. One thing I do know is that by the time you have spent thirty-five or forty years digging out rare books and manuscripts in half the civilized countries of the world, when you pick up a book or a manuscript and you turn the pages and you palpate them and you fondle them, at some point there are vibrations that begin to pass out of the book or the manuscript into your fingers and your hands and up your arms and into your brain, and then, suddenly and very clearly, you get the message: right or not right, good or not good, and if good—how good.

I got the message and I said OK. We made some rather Byzantine financial arrangements involving several countries and several currencies. I gave him several checks and some banknotes and he piled the manuscript back into the carton, tied it up, and I left, somewhat lopsidedly, carrying Céline. As luck would have it, Paris was undergoing a public-transport strike at that period: no subway, no buses. As a result, many subway and bus riders were taking taxis; hence there were no empty cabs in sight, either. I made my way laboriously over to the Boulevard Saint-Germain and finally, mercifully, was able to get a cab as it was disgorging passengers at a corner.

When I got home, I took the manuscript into the bathroom and set it down on the scales. It weighed in at exactly thirty-eight pounds. I laid it out on a long table, sorted it, and began to go through it carefully with the printed texts of the two novels in hand. When I had finished my work, I discovered that *Le Pont de Londres* was represented by not one, not two, but three complete manuscripts, each very different from the others. *Guignol's Band* was present in not three, not four, but five widely varying versions. And they all added up to 4,022 folio pages, many of them joined together with rusty pins into yard-long, fluttering blue streamers which, with Céline's bold, blunt hand, took on the look of a working-class version of a manuscript by Marcel Proust.

I knew that *Guignol's Band* and its sequel, *Le Pont de Londres,* had been written as one novel, but one so long that Robert Denoël had published only the first half in his edition of 1944. Soon after the Liberation, while Céline was still imprisoned in Denmark, his Paris apartment was ransacked and his papers—including a number of manuscripts—disappeared. Among the manuscripts was the second part of *Guignol's Band.* In 1962, a year after Céline's death, his former secretary, Marie Canavaggia, in cleaning out a closet, came across a bundle of typescript. It was the second part of *Guignol's Band* and from that, *Le Pont de Londres* was published in 1964.

But this manuscript I had just bought was the *complete* novel, and with its triple and quintuple versions of both parts, it would allow scholars to trace the thread of the creative process in Céline's work to a degree provided by no other manuscript of his that I was aware of. On that basis

Lambert was not speaking absolute nonsense when he called it "the most important Céline manuscript in the world."

On the other hand, the compulsive rewriter in Céline obliges us to withhold definitive judgment. In 1976, when one of the Paris dealers learned about this blockbuster manuscript, he wrote, offering me another slice of *Guignol's Band*—1,191 pages in all. Three years later, 1,420 pages of the two parts turned up in a sale at the Hôtel Drouot. And I have heard rumors of another batch, so far unconfirmed. With Céline, nothing was ever simple.

Chapter 9

Just as there are certain sacred cows that nobody can knock without risking permanent ostracism by the arbiters of taste, there are some cult figures that it is fashionable to run down: Dali is one, Cocteau another. In Dali's case, the main reason was his unabashed moneygrubbing. André Breton's anagrammatic nickname for him, Avida Dollars—unscrambled, it says Salvador Dali—didn't embarrass Dali a bit. On the contrary, he often bragged about it, orally and in print.

The case against Cocteau is more complex. He was a social butterfly (and therefore not "serious"), exceedingly ambitious, a flamboyant homosexual long before Gay Liberation. It was not that the homosexual writer was a rare or rebarbative species. It was a question of manner. Proust was discreet; Gide, generally dignified. Cocteau was neither. But worst of all, he did too many things, most of them rather well: poetry, criticism, the novel—I see *Les Enfants terribles* and *Le Grand écart* as two of the finest short novels of our time—the theater in its broadest range, film, the graphic arts, and more.

And so in 1955, when he announced his candidacy for the French Academy—that august body of forty "immortals" who have only occasionally elected any of France's great writers to share in their deliberations on the dictionary—it first seemed surprising, even a bit shocking. But since surprise and shock had always been Cocteau's hallmark, in a paradoxical kind of way it could be construed as very normal. On the other hand, normal or otherwise for Cocteau, for the Academy itself it was a nearly unique situation. On one side of the balance sheet stood jauntily Cocteau, a high-wire performer in every medium, a man who for more than a generation had enjoyed—or suffered from—the reputation of being the *enfant terrible* of contemporary French literature. On the other side sat stolidly the French Academy, founded in 1635 by

Cardinal Richelieu as a hedge against seditious literary cliques. It had never, since then, wavered far from its original position. To be sure, it numbered, in addition to its dukes, military heroes, doctors, and assorted other trades, a group of bona fide literary figures, but they had almost always been writers who fitted neatly into traditional categories. And for a writer like Cocteau—anything *but* traditional—that fact raised serious recognition problems, because to run for election to the Academy, one first applies in writing and then campaigns. In view of the average age of the academicians (at that time, the upper seventies) and their widely divergent and often nonliterary specializations, he must have felt at times like the seeker after public office who is obliged to canvass the most remote whistle-stops in his attempts to get out the vote. When it came time, for example, to present Cocteau officially to Georges Lecomte, *secrétaire perpétuel* of the Academy, it was discovered that M. Lecomte had never read anything by Cocteau, although Cocteau had been writing for more than forty years and his bibliography, stripped down to a minimum of detail, covered eight printed pages. Unbelievable? All the more so if you had been told that the Secretary was Cocteau's uncle.

But Cocteau had always made it a habit to be charming and, whatever the opposition, to get what he wanted. The academicians voted him in and he thus had immortality conferred on him by official government decree. His reception was scheduled for Thursday afternoon, October 20. An event with such revolutionary overtones was not to be missed and I was determined not to miss it. "Determined" is a rather large word in the circumstances: there are 700 seats under the cupola of the Institut de France, the Academy's home, and 12,000 requests for tickets had been received. Prices for black-market seats were out of sight. I went ticketless. But having been a practicing art critic in Paris for several years by that time, writing regularly in *The Christian Science Monitor* and other periodicals, I had a government-issued press card. I decided to try that.

A little before three o'clock that Thursday afternoon, I walked down the Rue de Seine and turned in at the arcade that leads to the Quai de Conti. Across the quay, on the Left Bank side of the Pont des Arts, hundreds of spectators were clustered as near to the Institut as the scores of police would allow them. A policeman stationed at the other end of the arcade asked me for my ticket. I showed him my press card. He waved me on. Two more stopped me along the sidewalk leading to the Institut. The same routine sufficed. I walked up the steps and, after showing my card again, passed through the outer door, then the inner one. As I followed the corridor leading to the rear entrance, through which the academic procession was due to pass, I came up against what looked like an impenetrable obstacle: a platoon of the Garde Républicaine, shoulder to shoulder, forming a protective cordon on both sides of the path between the rear entrance and the doors leading into the official chamber. Two women in front of me, heavily laden with mink, tried to find their way around the unmoving guards. An usher attempted to change their minds. They showed him their invitations, to each of which was pinned the *carte de visite* of an important public figure. The usher spoke to one of the guards. He stepped aside. The women walked through and I followed behind them. The second line of guards gave way and we passed through, as far as the door leading to the side entrance to the main hall. At that moment a drummer began a deafening roll, the guards drew their sabres, and through the rear entrance filed the not-quite-forty immortals. Most of them were wearing dark business suits, but when Cocteau passed by, I saw that he was resplendent in his full Academy regalia: the embroidered green uniform (not actually green but midnight blue, with green facing), cape, cocked hat (all by Lanvin), and sword. Cocteau's sword was not the usual academician's sword. Executed by Cartier, its hilt bore various symbols relating to Cocteau's life and work. I was unable to make out all of them as he passed, but I could see the hand guard, at least—a profile of Oedipus— and, at the top, the ivory lyre, symbol of the poet. Flash bulbs popped. Finally the last straggler entered the auditorium and the drum was quiet. I saw the two mink-clad women arguing with the usher guarding the last obstacle—the doors leading to the side entrance to the auditorium. Neither their invitations nor the attached cards affected him. "*Mesdames*, there is just no room," he insisted. The argument continued. Then one of the women lowered her voice. I heard only her last sentence. "Just turn your back; it's very simple," she told the usher. Discreetly, I turned mine, so I cannot guarantee the nature of the transaction that admitted them, but they passed through the door. I thought I'd try my luck with him. I handed him my press card. "What's that for?" he asked. "I'm a member of the press," I told him, with the dignity the occasion seemed to warrant. He threw up his hands. "What do you want me to do?" he said. "You think you're the only one? Everybody is of the press. Look." Holding me off with one arm, he waved the other at the two dozen or so photographers behind him.

"They're from the press, too." Just then, a short, incredibly thick human bulldozer led a wedge of cohorts into the crowd. *"Attention, attention,"* he bawled. "Make way for Marshal Juin." Marshal Juin had been one of the great heroes of the North African and Italian campaigns in World War II. After the war, he reached the peak of the French military pyramid, wrote a book, and was elected to the French Academy. I saw him at the wedge's center, a bald, brown little fellow, looking singularly unmartial in mufti. It was time to help a good cause along. I joined the wedge, we pierced the doors, and when the struggle was over, I was inside. The Marshal turned left and entered the hemicycle. I walked to the end of the dark corridor, opened a door at my left, and found myself staring up into the faces of the small group of elite that filled the low-hanging first balcony, left wing. I climbed the few steps that separated us, closing the door behind me.

Behind an elevated bench at the rear of the jammed auditorium, not more than ten yards from my position, sat three academicians. Like Cocteau, they had dressed for the occasion. André Maurois, erudite biographer of the French and English Romantics, who was presiding over the session, sat in the center. At his left sat Georges Lecomte, *secrétaire perpétuel*, looking very permanent in his long, square white beard. At Maurois's right was Marcel Pagnol. Pagnol looked a trifle uncomfortable in his uniform. One had the impression he would have preferred to be back in Marseilles with Marius and Fanny.

Halfway between the bench and the balcony, in the middle of one of the curved tiers of seats, I saw Cocteau sitting between his two sponsors, the novelists Jacques de Lacretelle and Pierre Benoit, they, too, in full uniform. Maurois rose and opened the session and immediately turned it over to Cocteau for the reading of his speech of thanks. Cocteau read fast, yet it took him a full hour. It is fair to assume that the academicians had never before received a speech of thanks quite like that one. It was the essence of the man: brilliant, subtle, occasionally obscure, some-what scattered, and—at times—a little preposterous. Cocteau was suc-ceeding to the seat of Jérôme Tharaud, who, with his brother Jean, had written exotic novels, many of them laid in North Africa and the Near East. It is traditional for the successor to praise his predecessor but it was evident that Cocteau had had little interest in or familiarity with the Tharauds' works. However, by setting himself the task, he had finally discovered a link to bind him to Jérôme: they were both affable men, he announced.

One could hardly call Cocteau's speech a recantation of his own career, yet one point in his eulogy of the Tharauds sounded suspiciously significant: his prophecy that ". . . youth, discovering that unbridled perversity no longer pays, will wake up to the realization that certain values they once scorned were by no means unworthy and will hail the Tharauds, perhaps, as charming precursors."

All the way along one sensed, beneath the sparkling imagery of his paradoxes, a double apology: one to his old companions for having sought out, in the autumn of his years, the pomp and official recognition of the Academy; the other, to his new colleagues welcoming him to their circle, for the apparent disorder and disrespect of a life and work that had constantly whittled away at the base of everything the Academy stands for and on.

As he spoke, the expressive, fluttering hands with their long, bony fingers, so familiar to us from photographs and films, gestured nervously. Now and then he grasped the hilt of his sword. Finally, after several near-climaxes, he stopped speaking. The applause, as was to be expected from *le Tout-Paris* that filled the hall, was thunderous. After sitting down, Cocteau stood again to acknowledge it with an ecclesiastical gesture of the right hand which he dispensed for well over a minute to each segment of the assembly. His eyes darted from group to group as the spotlights were turned on his gaunt features and taut, parchment-colored skin.

When Cocteau had settled into his seat once again, André Maurois rose and, in his thin, high voice and semi-lisp, and with the grace and charm which marked him on all such occasions, made the traditional response to Cocteau's speech. He thanked Cocteau for having stayed "on this side of what would have shocked us." He gave a longer and more affectionate, more reasoned and more knowledgeable appreciation of the Tharauds, and when he had finished with them, he returned to Cocteau and traced his life from childhood on. From time to time, as Maurois spoke, Cocteau wiped his brow and sipped water. His hands shook. Maurois's speech wasn't endless, but it, too, consumed a full hour. It wasn't dull, either—Maurois wouldn't have known how to be dull—but the afternoon was wearing on, the hall was crowded, and the air was close. I thought it quite a tribute to the durability of the French Academy that I saw only one academician nod and another yawn.

At last the speech and the seance came to an end. I walked down into the corridor and out onto the steps of the Institut. Across the quay the crowds were still waiting. *Que diable allait-il faire dans cette galère*, I thought fleetingly, but realized at once that the answer, after all, was pretty obvious. It was not the first time a tired revolutionary, with shadows falling and the taste of ashes in his mouth, had yearned for home and mother. I couldn't help hoping that in Maurois's final words, *"Soyez le bienvenu"*—"Welcome"—Cocteau would find the comfort he sought. But . . . could he, really?

* * * * *

In my collecting I had never gone out of my way before then to look for Cocteau material. Thinking of Cocteau now, in the context of the Académie Française, forced me to think of him in his earlier incarnations as well, and I began to see him in a new light. He was no longer the "frivolous prince," the perennial playboy of the arts, the tireless experimenter with forms both old and new; he had become a kind of historical monument. But the role he had played between the two extremes had been an important and original one, and however much he may have been denigrated by some of those whose artistic and creative credentials were more acceptable to the power brokers of the intellectual circuits— the Surrealists, for example—Cocteau's contribution could not be overlooked. And so I began to seek out significant and characteristic examples of his work from its very beginning.

One day in the early 1970s, in the back room at the Librairie Gallimard on the Left-Bank Boulevard Raspail, where for years Roland Saucier had guided and encouraged the collecting activities of numberless French bibliophiles, his successor, Raymond Poulin, brought out for me a pile of dossiers of Cocteau manuscript material. They were filled with early poems and fragmentary but fascinating notes made by Cocteau, starting about the time of his association with *"Les Six"*—the six composers he promoted after World War I in every way open to him—Georges Auric, Francis Poulenc, Darius Milhaud, Arthur Honegger, and the two others one hears less about today, Louis Durey and Germaine Tailleferre. The poems, although undated, were very early ones, demonstrably so because of their full, round handwriting and purple ink, both of which were borrowed from one of Cocteau's early influences, the poet and novelist Anna de Noailles. Among the notes in Cocteau's hand was the retained draft of an agreement he had made with another Noailles, Charles, who had backed his film "The Blood of a Poet." There were drawings, tax bills, telephone bills; letters addressed to Cocteau by a number of friends, celebrated and obscure; notes on the film makers Eisenstein and Buñuel; a manuscript about his play *La Voix humaine*, written on the back of menus from the bar-restaurant "Le Boeuf sur le Toit"; notes about the source of his novel *Les Enfants terribles;* fashion notes written on the backs of cigarette cartons—a very mixed bag, but nothing that was not interesting. I bought it all, wondering, in view of the fragmentary and ephemeral nature of some of the pieces and the personal character of others, just where it all came from.

In a week or two, Poulin showed me a similar batch of odds and ends: notes on Cocteau's protégé, the poet and novelist Raymond Radiguet, who had died, barely twenty, at the end of 1923; notes on Stravinsky; a typescript of Cocteau's short novel *Le Livre blanc,* which had been published anonymously in 1928 in an edition limited to twenty-one copies plus ten for its unnamed author. Where *did* all these things come from, I asked myself and, getting no answer, asked Poulin.

He gave me a dusty answer which let me know there was something very unusual about their background. I suggested that if someone was holding a large cache of Cocteau material, it would be to everyone's advantage to bring it all out now, rather than by bits and pieces every week or so. After we had explored that idea for a while, Poulin agreed to talk to his source and see what he could learn.

The next time I saw Poulin, I got the whole story. He was dealing not with the owner but the owner's agent, a man named Henri Pollès. I had often seen Pollès in some of the Left Bank bookshops I had frequented during my earliest days in Paris. He wore what used to be known, in my boyhood, as "plus fours" and rode a bicycle in pursuit of his daily bread. He was a *courtier,* who traveled from one shop to another, covering a whole network of clients for whom he performed a variety of small but essential services. For example, most Paris booksellers kept a list of unfilled orders they had received for books that were in some cases rare, in some simply out-of-print. Pollès—along with others like him—made it his business to know where such books could be found. When he spotted something in A's shop that was on B's list of desiderata, he would offer it to B at a price based on A's marked price less 10% (his professional discount) plus whatever he felt the traffic would bear, depending on his sense of the urgency of B's need for the book. I used to see Pollès most often in a vast, rambling old bookshop in the Rue de

Seine, the Librairie Fischbacher, in whose dark and dusty corners I had made more than one gratifying find in those early days in Paris. He would often be arguing the case for one of his proposals with one or another of the Fischbacher functionaries, sometimes becoming quite excited in the process. The Fischbacher clan—now composed of nephews and nieces with different names—were all Protestants. In strongly Catholic France the adjective "Protestant" is often used to imply tight-lipped, tightfisted, hard-nosed, at best puritanical, often in combination with the term "constipated." So I knew on the basis of the local folklore what Pollès thought of *them*. They, on the other hand, thought of him as being very disputatious and rather whiny, but they put up with him, the manager had told me early on, because he was a writer—"with a lot of talent." And he certainly did prove to have talent in abundance. He continued to make his way around Paris on his bicycle, wearing the same old threadbare plus fours, picking up a book here, dropping it off there, and on the difference between cost and selling price supporting a family and continuing to write. He had won his first recognition even before World War II with the award of the *Prix du roman populiste* for his novel *Sophie de Tréguier*. A few years after the moment of which I speak, he was to receive one of the most prestigious (and richest—$45,000) of French literary prizes, the *Prix Paul Morand*, awarded by the French Academy with funds left for that purpose by the French writer-diplomat whose name it perpetuates.

But right now, according to Poulin, Pollès was representing a man named Henri Lefebvre, a longtime Paris bookseller and publisher. I remembered Lefebvre well. When I had first arrived in Paris and used to wander up one street and down another looking for bookshops to browse in, I had come upon his near the beginning of the Faubourg Saint-Honoré, its large display window filled with all kinds of tempting books. The one that drew me inside was a two-volume set devoted to the drawings of Georges Seurat—two albums of 120 drawings reproduced in facsimile, published by the art dealer Bernheim Jeune in 1928. The price was the equivalent of $28.50, a bit stiff for the period but less than five cents on the dollar in terms of today's value. Lefebvre himself waited on me. Of a little less than medium height, thick through the middle, with a scraggly black beard, he had one feature that riveted my gaze: a weird and wandering eye that seemed lost in its socket and looked everywhere but at me. It had an ominous aura and in its dark,

Levantine setting, made me wonder if this man was really evil or just the hapless victim of some genetic malfunction.

I told him I was interested in the Seurat. He repeated the price, which I already knew from the sign in the window, but he didn't offer to take the book out and show it to me. Everything about him reinforced the initial involuntary prejudice and I left without buying the book. In the twenty or so years between that day and the day of Poulin's disclosure, I had never returned to Lefebvre's shop. But now, quite clearly, I would need to go see him again. From Poulin's story I learned that Lefebvre owned an enormous collection of Cocteau manuscript material dating from the very start of Cocteau's career to the mid-1930s—certainly the most important period for Cocteau. In fact, this mass of material had once been Cocteau's own archives, he said, and through some strange, ill-defined combination of irresponsibility and skulduggery had come into Lefebvre's hands about thirty-five years before. Lefebvre was now in trouble with *le fisc*, the French equivalent of the IRS, and needed money. My proposal, relayed to Lefebvre through Pollès, of making the collection available all at once, had appealed to him—in principle. He passed along to me his financial demands—a very fat price, all in cash, no paperwork. Obviously it would be necessary to compensate the two intermediaries, but Lefebvre made it clear that he would not pay for any of that; his price was *net net*. He was no longer in the Faubourg Saint-Honoré; his shop there had been turned over to a son. He was now a Versailles bookseller, having opened an elegant—Pollès *dixit*—new shop not far from the palace.

We settled on a time and I took a train to Versailles and a cab to the Lefebvre home address I had been given by Poulin. It was a somber nineteenth-century townhouse in need of refurbishing. A maid showed me into a sitting room on the ground floor. The room looked out over a sunny garden in the rear, but the shutters had been pulled and the room itself was shadowy. Lefebvre sat, his back to me, writing at a small table. He turned around and once again I was transfixed by that eye. Older, heavier, but otherwise little changed, he extended his hand. I took it. It was limp and damp. After an exchange of *politesses* he raised himself up out of his chair and walked over to a larger table in the center of the room. It held uneven piles of file folders, which he tapped lovingly.

"That's part of it," he said. Then he pointed to a carved wooden Renaissance chest. "The rest is in there. Except for some of the things I keep upstairs." He opened the chest and I looked inside. In the semi-darkness, I could make out packages of various sizes, wrapped in paper and tied with string. In one corner I could see some loose sheets of manuscript. He closed the chest and ran his hand over the top. "That piece used to belong to Proust," he said. "I took it from his bedroom myself."

I asked Lefebvre if he had an inventory of his Cocteau collection. He rummaged around in the depths of Proust's *bahut* and brought out a sheaf of papers, looked at them briefly, then handed them to me. There were about a dozen quarto sheets, written, recto-verso, in a small, neat, commercial hand, in black ink. Key words and phrases were underlined in red ink. The first page was headed *Collection Jean Cocteau. Manuscrits.* Looking through the pages quickly, I saw that they included descriptions of manuscripts, typescripts, and corrected proofs of nearly all of Cocteau's early and major works from his second book of poems, *Le Prince frivole* (1910), to *Le Coq et l'arlequin* (1918), *Le Potomak* and *Le Cap de Bonne-Espérance* (1919), *La Noce massacrée* (1922), on through the Twenties and into the Thirties. There seemed to be a good deal of unpublished material and there was a section devoted to artwork, with many drawings by Cocteau and others by artist friends of his. It was clearly not only an immense collection; it was an extremely valuable one from any point of view. I asked Lefebvre if he could tell me something of its history. He looked off somewhere beyond me with his good eye and I tried to avoid looking at the other one.

"These were Cocteau's own archives," he said finally. "In the spring of 1935, Cocteau was getting ready to leave for a vacation on the Riviera. He began to put some order to the things he had lived with for years in his room at his mother's apartment in the Rue d'Anjou. But he was soon fed up with the job and turned it over to his friend Maurice Sachs. He told Sachs he could sell a few of his drawings and manuscripts and some of the books that he didn't care about keeping. Sachs and a young friend of his named Robert delle Donne brought some things to me, explaining that they were acting as Cocteau's agents. I bought what they showed me, paid for them, and pretty soon they brought me more. As their work went on, they brought still more. I bought everything. It wasn't long before I had a registered letter from Cocteau, who was staying at the Hôtel Welcome in Villefranche-sur-mer. He was distraught because he had learned that Sachs and delle Donne had sold me a great deal more than he had ever intended to part with. Jean Desbordes, who had been

Jean Cocteau. Self-portrait (caricature). Wash drawing.

A page from the autograph manuscript of Cocteau's book *Le Coq et l'arlequin:* some harsh words for Diaghilev and the Ballets Russes.

Jean Cocteau by Diego
Rivera. Pencil drawing,
1918.

Pablo Picasso. Jean
Cocteau and Marie
Shabelska. Pencil
drawing, done in Rome
in 1917, at the time of
the rehearsals for the
ballet *Parade* prior to
its première in Paris in
May, 1918.

his secretary and protégé, was trying to help him straighten things out with Sachs and the other fellow so that they would buy back everything Cocteau wanted to keep. Then, apparently, Cocteau decided it wasn't safe to let Sachs and delle Donne be involved any further in the transaction. His big mistake in the first place, he told me, was believing that Sachs would not take advantage of a situation of that kind and that delle Donne was thoroughly honest. He planned to have Desbordes sort out the things he wanted back and he asked me to put them aside until he, himself, returned to Paris. Then he said that his current secretary, Marcel Khill, who was at Villefranche with him, would come up to Paris in a few days and try to work things out with me. But he wanted me to understand that he hadn't received a penny from that 'false sale,' as he called it. He said he hoped Robert delle Donne would understand the gravity of the situation and arrange with me to have all of his 'poor treasure' put under lock and key. He pointed out that I had become an accomplice. I got the point.

"I wrote him that I'd be glad to annul the sale—at least for the things they had sold without his permission. All they had to do was return my money.

"Cocteau kept getting more upset and even before he received my letter of agreement, he sent me a telegram begging me to give back to delle Donne what he referred to as 'all intimate documents' and to demand the return of my money from him and Sachs.

"The next day delle Donne came around, money in hand, and took back the 'intimate documents' Cocteau had been so worried about; mostly, they were letters—some from Proust and some from François Mauriac—a few photographs, some of the books, and a statue of Saint Sebastian.

"Of course, the news spread all over Paris, even before the affair was settled. Marcel Khill turned up, looked things over, and when he got back to Villefranche, reported to Cocteau that he hadn't seen everything that was on the list of missing things that Desbordes had sent to Cocteau. But in the end Cocteau decided he was satisfied with the arrangement. I've kept the collection off the market all these years, not wanting to take advantage of Cocteau's bad luck and easygoing ways. But now I need the money and that's why you're here."

I asked Lefebvre if we could check out some of the packages in Proust's chest against the inventory. He pulled out a few bundles and untied one. It held proofs of Cocteau's book *Le Potomak*, written in 1914 but not published until 1919. We looked through the material together. It seemed incomplete, to judge from the description in the inventory. We tried another package. It contained manuscript material that neither one of us could find listed. A third package relating to *Le Cap de Bonne-Espérance*, a book dedicated to the aviator Roland Garros which Cocteau published after World War I, presented similar difficulties. He brought out other packages but nothing seemed to match up satisfactorily. It would be a long, complex job, I could see.

I suggested to Lefebvre that, in order to save time for both of us, we adopt a different method of working, that we forget about the inventory for the moment, but work with the objects themselves, one group at a time. I would come back in the morning and go through as many packages as there was time to examine. Together we would put a price on what we had seen. At the end of the day I would pay him for everything we had covered, take it away, and come back the next morning and start fresh with a new group. We would follow that routine until everything had been seen, priced, paid for, and removed from the premises.

He thought long and hard. I had the feeling he knew what his answer was but didn't know how to put it. Finally he roused himself. He pulled himself up out of his chair. "Let's go up to the library," he said. "There are more things there."

I followed him up to the next floor: books everywhere; paintings, prints, photographs in profusion. I saw a large original photograph of Alfred Jarry fencing. There was a wonderfully characteristic inscription to Jarry's patroness, Rachilde, on its mount. I told Lefebvre that if we followed the procedure I had suggested, we could move out from Cocteau into other realms at the same time.

He smiled without pleasure or humor. "It's very intel-ligent, your suggestion," he said. "I quite see your point. *Very* intel-ligent." He pronounced the word "intel-ligent" caressingly, splitting the l's with precision between the two surrounding syllables. It made me think of Huxley's Mrs. Bidlake, "the only person in England . . . who regularly pronounced the apostrophe in T'ang." I followed him into a room—obviously the *grand salon*—which, just as obviously, was never used. Here he had re-created France's Golden Age. He invoked some of the golden names: Largillière and Lancret, Houdon and Hubert Robert. He showed me miniatures and snuffboxes in locked gilded display cases. He had taken on an added dimension. This was *his* kingdom. He not only lived in the shadow of the Palace of Versailles; he had created a microcosm of it. His fingers rippled gracefully over the arms and backs of the chairs among which we moved. We didn't sit down. He concluded the tour, we left the room, and he closed the door reverently. We went back downstairs. Lefebvre accompanied me to the front door.

"I think I'd better check everything out myself first," he said. "It will take me a week or two, but then we'll know exactly what is here and what isn't. I'm sure it's all here. It's just a question of finding it. Why don't you ring me up in a couple of weeks?" He walked over to a telephone beside the stairway. "I'll call you a cab."

I gave him three weeks, then called. He was making progress, but now his secretary was on vacation. As soon as she came back, he'd put her to work typing the revision, then call me, and we'd get together again. Why bother to type it? I asked. The other one had been handwritten. The typing seemed important to him. He said he would call me at the first opportunity.

I heard no more from Lefebvre but toward the end of July, when I dropped into Gallimard's one morning, Poulin told me that he had heard from Pollès that Lefebvre hadn't liked my suggestion of buying the collection piecemeal, a day at a time.

"He's convinced you want to skim off the best of it and leave him with the odds and ends—the stuff that all by itself is not very salable."

I laughed. I explained to Poulin that for purposes of research, there was no such thing as *"la drouille"*—his term for the odds and ends. Everything has its relative importance. No one can predict what may prove useful to a scholarly investigation.

He shrugged. "I told him I thought he was on the wrong track, but he's a pretty stubborn fellow," he said.

I called Lefebvre and made my point to him in some detail. He understood—or seemed to—but said he thought we'd do better to wait for the new inventory, still untyped. I sensed that the *fisc* had relaxed its pressure on him. There was nothing more to be done. To insist would have been counterproductive. I left France without seeing him again.

The next time I returned to Paris, I went in to see Poulin. The shop was busy, as usual, and he was apologetic about keeping me waiting. Then he told me Lefebvre had died. He didn't know what had happened to his Cocteau collection but he would check with Pollès. When he did, I learned that the Cocteau collection, along with the Versailles bookshop and the townhouse, had been left to one of Lefebvre's sons—not the one who had taken over his shop in the Faubourg Saint-Honoré, but a younger son, Michel, a painter, who, with his wife, had lived on the top floor of Lefebvre's house after the death of Madame Lefebvre.

I called the son and sketched in the background of my Cocteau dealings with his father. He seemed aware of the story. He invited me to come out to Versailles and talk with him. Since he was co-executor of the estate and the direct recipient of his father's Cocteau collection, he saw no reason why we couldn't come to an agreement promptly, he said. He proved to be a very amiable fellow, with no perceptible trace of his father's temperament or physique. He was using the ground-floor sitting room to assemble his recent watercolors for an exhibition he was preparing. It was pleasant, representational work in the tradition of Dunoyer de Segonzac, redolent of the Ile-de-France countryside. He took me upstairs to the library, where he had assembled the Cocteau collection. It filled a long library table and overflowed onto a divan and chairs. Framed pictures were lined up along a wall.

I spent a couple of days going through everything. It was an extraordinary collection. There was the manuscript—unpublished—of Cocteau's "Art Poétique," written in 1916. Its text was laid out in a manner inspired by Mallarmé's *Un Coup de dés jamais n'abolira le hasard*, which had been published in 1914 by Gallimard, sixteen years after Mallarmé's death. There was the beginning of a four-volume maquette for "David," an unpublished, unproduced biblical ballet. Cocteau had tried to interest Stravinsky in collaborating with him on it in 1914. Nothing had come of their talks, but "David" had been the first step toward *Parade*, the "realistic ballet" Cocteau produced, three years later in collaboration with Picasso, Erik Satie, and Léonide Massine, with which he had made waves and history for Diaghilev and the Ballets Russes. There were two manuscripts of *Le Coq et l'arlequin*, the witty, aphoristic little book on music which Cocteau published in 1918 to run down Debussy and run up Satie and *"Les Six."* One of the manuscripts included quantities of unpublished material, which Cocteau had suppressed in the final version:

—Satie often says: The terrible thing is not that they are booing us, but that one day we'll be boring the young just as we're bored with yesterday's hand-me-downs.
—Albéniz: the bullfight trimmed with lace.
—Stravinsky wears the jewels of a black king—his music, also. What saves him are his cannibal jaws and his taste for good wine.

—Don't open your doors to Richard Strauss; he'll rape your daughter and piss all over everything.

Cocteau's book *Le Potomak* had been published in 1919 by the Société Littéraire de France. Along with sets of corrected proofs of the first edition, I found corrected page proofs and a unique unstitched proof copy of an edition unknown to the biographers and bibliographers—the original edition planned and set in type by the Mercure de France in 1914 but never published.

Le Cap de Bonne-Espérance was present in many forms: several first-draft phases, the heavily corrected final manuscript, trial settings with different type faces and different colors of paper, several sets of corrected page and galley proofs—virtually everything that preceded its eventual published state.

There were a number of versions of *La Noce massacrée*, including one which had nothing to do with the book published under that title but which developed into Cocteau's ballet *Les Mariés de la Tour Eiffel.* And there was the manuscript of an unpublished *Noce massacrée*, Part II, called "Le Rire de Goya."

There were hundreds of manuscript poems, variant versions of those published in *Vocabulaire* and elsewhere, and dozens totally unpublished; the corrected typescript of his novel *Les Enfants terribles;* many notebooks in which Cocteau had jotted down lines for future poems, thoughts for future books and articles; drafts of letters to Gide, André Breton, Radiguet, and others. There were letters to Cocteau from Ezra Pound, Eluard, Stravinsky, Misia Sert, Gertrude Stein, Serge Lifar; letters from Walter Berry which were the other side of the correspondence I had bought earlier from Janine Daragnès; a delightful correspondence from Marie Laurencin with sketches and watercolors; more than a hundred letters from Max Jacob, the wittiest writer of his time, showing him at his maliciously clever best. As I read them more thoroughly later on, they seemed close to being the most important single literary correspondence of that milieu at that period.

Then there were letters addressed to Raymond Radiguet, including some from the man-eating English poet and journalist Beatrice Hastings, who had been Modigliani's mistress but had become enthralled—like so many others, male and female—by Radiguet; there were photographs, by Man Ray and others, of Cocteau, Radiguet, the trapeze performer Barbette, Montparnasse model Kiki, Jean and Valentine Hugo.

The artwork was a collection all by itself: excellent drawings by Cocteau, from the World War I period, for the reviews *Schéhérazade* and *Le Mot* and for *Le Potomak;* his illustrations for *Les Enfants terribles,* for *Les Parents terribles, Opium,* and *Orphée;* there were portraits by him of such friends as Léon Bakst, Charlotte Lysès (Sacha Guitry's first wife), the painter Jacques-Emile Blanche, Jean Desbordes, Georges Auric, Berthe Bovy, who created the role of the cast-off mistress in *La Voix humaine* and, of course, Raymond Radiguet.

In one of the sketchbooks, Cocteau had filled page after page with his own name written in different styles and with imitations of the signatures of such writers as Lucien and Alphonse Daudet, Edmond de Goncourt, Robert de Montesquiou, and Stéphane Mallarmé. He could reproduce all of them convincingly. The rest of that large folio notebook was filled with drawings, executed with incredible fluidity, of political and society figures treated in the most obscene terms.

There were many drawings in various media by other artists. Christian Bérard's were interpretations of some of Cocteau's plays and films. Among a number by Raoul Dufy, the best was a large and perceptive portrait of Cocteau in pen-and-ink, wash, and gouache, inscribed by Dufy to Cocteau's mother; there were two excellent portraits by Picabia, one of Cocteau and one of Erik Satie, *"le bon maître."* There were drawings by Picasso, including one, dated Rome 1917, of Cocteau and Marie Shabelska, who danced the role of the American girl in *Parade.* The finest of all the drawings was a portrait of Cocteau by Diego Rivera, done in 1918. To the extent that any drawing eighteen inches by twelve can be called monumental, that is the term for this one.

But one thing puzzled me. There was so much more here than just "a few . . . drawings and manuscripts"—Lefebvre's term for what Cocteau had authorized his friends to sell—that it was obvious Cocteau could have got back no more than a small fraction of the things he *hadn't* intended to sell. That just didn't make sense to me as I thought back to the account Lefebvre had given me of his dealings with Sachs and delle Donne and, finally, with Cocteau himself. Then I came across a pink file folder labeled in Lefebvre's hand *Affaire Cocteau.* In it was a letter to Lefebvre in which Cocteau stated that his intention had been "to sell certain manuscripts and drawings (of mine), *no portraits,* and some books with presentation inscriptions from people now dead. Anything else was [sold] without my knowledge (letters, de luxe editions of my books, photographs, maquettes by Bérard, etc.)." In another letter,

Cocteau defined Lefebvre's purchase as "inscribed books and one or two little manuscripts." And there was the telegram urgently requesting the return of "all intimate documents"—which could only have meant letters. Every one of the other papers in that pink file folder—Cocteau's letters to Lefebvre, copies of Lefebvre's to Cocteau, delle Donne's receipt to Lefebvre for the things he had taken back—included the word "letters." But there were letters by the hundreds remaining in the collection. And then I remembered that Lefebvre had mentioned to me, in speaking of letters that Cocteau was frantically asking to have returned to him, the names of Proust and François Mauriac. Cocteau and Proust—well, no surprises there. But Cocteau and François Mauriac would seem, on the surface, an odd couple to have given rise to "intimate documents": Mauriac, the family man, the devout Catholic, whose obsession with sin throughout a lifetime of fiction writing makes him the Catholic novelist *par excellence.* On the other hand, for years there had been gossip about his early friendship with Cocteau, and Roger Peyrefitte had written about their relations in more than merely suggestive terms. So it looked as though Cocteau's deep concern was limited to *those* letters, because there were all kinds of ordinary "personal" letters still remaining in Lefebvre's hands, the sale of which must not have troubled Cocteau at all, in the end, since he left them there.

As for the portraits of him—*"no portraits"* were to be sold, he had written in his second letter to Lefebvre—their loss must not have troubled him unduly, either. Why? In a letter sent five days after "all intimate documents" had been returned, Cocteau wrote Lefebvre that Marcel Khill, now back in Villefranche from his trip to Paris, had told him of Lefebvre's "extreme kindness in this affair which was blown up out of all proportion, it seems to me, by Parisian malice." It was true, Cocteau said, that Khill hadn't found, among the things bought back by delle Donne, everything that Jean Desbordes had listed as missing but Cocteau was sure that Lefebvre had seen to it that they were "removed from the danger of a sale." He had decided that Robert delle Donne was more lightweight than criminal and full of remorse for what he had done. And he did detest these little melodramas. Friends had been urging him to go up to Paris and hale Sachs into court, but why? It was all his own fault, he said. He'd been victimized by his own blind confidence.

Undoubtedly it would have been very hard, with the money spent, for the lightweight delle Donne and the welterweight Sachs to have scraped up anything beyond that initial repayment. Cocteau certainly realized that. And Lefebvre would hardly have felt called upon to make a philanthropic gesture. Cocteau knew that, too. Beyond that, Cocteau's life was one long history of running off, like the headless horseman, in all directions. With the things he *really* wanted—"all intimate documents"—back in his hands, eventually he must have scrubbed the whole affair from his agenda. Having made out of the incident one of his more celebrated and frequently quoted *bons mots*, to the effect that he preferred crooks to cops any day, he was off in pursuit of something else, content to leave "the rest," as he wrote in his last letter to Lefebvre, "under the sign of the god who looks after poets—he's the one I have to thank for being in your hands. I couldn't wish for whiter ones." White-handed or otherwise, Lefebvre did hold onto the collection until long after Cocteau's death. Whatever his reason, we have to give the devil his due. Sachs, on the other hand, paid back Cocteau's forgiveness by writing a very harsh chapter about him in his memoir *Le Sabbat* (1946). The only other treatment of Cocteau as harsh as Sachs's came in a book published the year before, *Jean Cocteau ou la vérité du mensonge* by François Mauriac's son, Claude.

One more unsolved mystery surfaced during that transaction, well before I had occasion to pay Lefebvre's son his money and load the whole collection into a huge old Marne-like taxi for the ride back to Paris. The son was, as I have said, amiable, but at the same time he was very businesslike from the start. He told me, straight off, that his father had left notes concerning the collection and its sale price and my interest in it. He saw no reason, he said, to reduce that price—all the more so since time had elapsed and inflation had to be considered. But if I was agreeable, he was willing to go ahead on the basis of that figure, and he quoted it. It was exactly one-half the amount that had been quoted to me in the first instance. Had the price I was hearing now been Lefebvre's original basic price which, thinking I might drive a hard bargain, he had doubled to give himself plenty of room for negotiation? Or had he started with the higher figure but reconsidered after our conversations?

I decided I'd be better off not to try to find out. Lefebvre's son and I closed the deal—on his terms—very happy, both of us.

Chapter 10

What is "objective chance"? In *L'Amour fou*, André Breton defines it—*le hasard objectif*—as the form in which an external necessity manifests itself as it makes its way through the unconscious—or words to that effect. Perhaps it would be clearer put this way: Coincidences are not the simple events they sometimes seem. We have a need or a desire. It emerges at a precise moment as we encounter some sign in the world around us to which it corresponds. My extended experience in the matter of Maurice Ravel and his music for the ballet *Daphnis et Chloé* might serve as a textbook case history of that phenomenon.

Beginning in the fall of 1959, Ravel and *Daphnis et Chloé* were much on my mind. I had been helping Marc Chagall, a good friend and longtime neighbor of mine on the Ile Saint-Louis, to patch up an unsatisfactory English translation of his autobiography that a New York publisher wanted to bring out. After the job was completed, Chagall invited my wife and me to accompany him and his wife to a performance of the "new" *Daphnis* at the Paris Opéra. It was new in a number of ways, one of which involved costumes and décors by Chagall, resplendently replacing the archaicizing original ones by Léon Bakst. But the music was still Ravel's—simple, clear lines, triumphantly lyrical—and echoes of its themes were to wander in and out of my life and memory from that evening on.

One day when those echoes were particularly insistent, I was at the Hôtel Drouot, poking my nose into several rooms where unimportant and generally uncatalogued mixed sales were taking place. Suddenly I heard the name "Ravel" pronounced. The lot being sold filled a large basket and consisted of a great mass of documents concerning a Ravel festival—photographs, press cuttings, programs, posters, and miscellaneous letters (not by Ravel). I bought the contents of the basket. Before leaving the saleroom, I learned that five autograph letters by Ravel had been sold individually before I arrived.

When I got home and examined the papers I had bought, I saw that I had a nearly complete documentation—except for the five letters which had been sold separately—concerning one of the major celebratory occasions in Ravel's life. But I needed those five letters. I found out that they had been bought by three dealers, all within easy reach of one another, a stone's throw from Saint-Germain-des-Prés: Jacques Lambert, in the Rue Bonaparte; Marc Loliée, in the Rue des Saints-Pères, and Marc's son, Bernard, in the Rue de Seine. Marc I considered a good friend, and since I had bought many things from him over a long period of years, I didn't expect any problems there—if he had bought the letters for himself, that is, rather than on order for a client. His son, Bernard, I had known from his boyhood. He knew his business very well indeed but was sometimes a tougher nut to crack than his father. Lambert, everyone agreed, was a man for whom money talked, and some would add that he knew only one language. I decided I would start with him. He had bought two of the letters, it turned out, both for stock. I asked him what he wanted for them. He said he hadn't priced them yet. What had he paid for them? He looked up his cost and wrote it down for me. I added 25% and made the total. He bowled me over by accepting, after the briefest of hesitations. I then went to see Bernard Loliée. He had bought one letter, for stock. He complained he had paid too much for it. I agreed with him and in the end he seemed relieved to let me have it at his marked price less ten percent. His father, Marc, who had bought the other two letters, fortunately for stock, went out of his way to be obliging. So in less than an hour I had all five. Had I been at the sale earlier, when the letters came up, they would have cost me more then, given the competition. French dealers never like to see someone who is not a member of what they call *la corporation* buy at what they consider *their* source.

That afternoon's haul told a delightful story. In August, 1930, the little fishing village of Ciboure—Maurice Ravel's birthplace, just across the Nivelle river from Saint-Jean-de-Luz, close to the Spanish border— staged a Grand Festival in his honor. The moving force behind the celebration was a former Parisian named Charles Mapou, who had settled into an active retirement in the Basque country, where he was municipal councillor at Ciboure and president of the town's Commission on Festivals. He had saved every scrap of documentation covering what must have been the high point of his entrepreneurial career in Ciboure; and then, after his death, the archive found its way to the Hôtel Drouot. The five letters of Ravel, like the letters in the large basket, were addressed to Mapou and all the other papers were clearly from the same source. Mapou had enlisted great talent for his festival: first of all, Ravel himself; then, the violinist Jacques Thibaud, the pianist Robert Casadesus, the singer Madeleine Grey, and Lucienne Lamballe, *première danseuse* of the Paris Opéra.

At the outset Ravel agreed to accompany Thibaud for his Violin Sonata and Madeleine Grey for the *Chansons Madécasses* and other melodies; also, if it did not make the program too long, to play, in an arrangement for four hands with Casadesus, *Ma mère l'oye*. Then it was proposed that he accompany Mlle. Lamballe as she danced. He drew the line there. "I wouldn't know how," he said. Robert Casadesus didn't choose to be drawn into that role, either, and didn't know anyone who would. In the end, Mapou hired a local pianist for the purpose.

Ravel's next letter was the most interesting of them all. Strictly speaking, it wasn't a letter *from* Ravel; it was an eight-page typed letter from Mapou *to* Ravel, to which Ravel had replied by internal emendations and marginal commentary that answered all of Mapou's questions and set him straight wherever he needed it.

Mapou had problems with everything and everybody, even his spelling of names and titles. There the remedies were easy: Ravel simply corrected his texts and proofs and rearranged the order and billing. For more serious problems Mapou had frequent assists from an old friend in Paris (who had also been a friend of Proust), the impresario Gabriel Astruc, a seasoned hand at smoothing ruffled feathers. Astruc had been the first to bring Diaghilev's Ballets Russes to Paris and, beginning with Stravinsky's *Le Sacre du printemps*, he had made his Théâtre des Champs-Elysées the Paris showcase of great music. He had, in fact, been the original publisher of Ravel's *String Quartet in F* and of his *Schéhérazade* song cycle—just the kind of gray eminence Mapou needed.

Astruc fine-tuned the program so that it would neither drag nor seem choppy; he told Mapou who should be given gifts and who not; warned him about misspelled names on the poster and made sure Mapou sent him and Ravel a proof to check. Astruc wanted to have the bust of Ravel which his niece, Louise Ochsé, had made reproduced on the cover of the program. Ravel preferred the bust by Léon Leyritz: "We'll put both of them on the program," he wrote to Mapou. "That will satisfy everybody, even me."

There were problems about scheduling rehearsals and about lodging for Mlle. Grey, about union terms and getting the right piano. The mayor of Biarritz agreed to participate, then backed out. The commemorative medals couldn't be struck because of technical problems the jeweller didn't seem able to solve. Then there was a problem about Jacques Thibaud: his close relationship with the pianist Alfred Cortot made it awkward for him to be accompanied by Robert Casadesus in playing Ravel's Sonata. The only solution would be to have Ravel as his accompanist. Would Ravel be willing? If so, would that put Casadesus's nose out of joint? Nobody wanted to handle that so they left it to Ravel, who found a way to make everyone happy. But Mlle. Grey! Not a bad singer, Astruc conceded (in fact, she was one of Ravel's favorites), but the kind of woman who, as one of a number of participants in a two-hour concert, would like to sing for an hour and three-quarters. She had nearly ruined everything that way at a concert for the Japanese, Astruc recalled. Obviously, another delicate mission for Ravel, and Ravel, as usual, handled it deftly. Astruc and Mapou were reluctant to get involved with Ravel's *Mélodies Hébraïques:* they were afraid that *Kaddisch* and *L'Enigme éternelle* wouldn't be to everyone's taste. When Mapou tactfully suggested to Ravel a substitution, hinting at a possible anti-Semitic reaction, Ravel gave him the French equivalent of Farragut's "Damn the torpedoes!"

The local and regional press gave wholehearted support to the Festival, with one exception—one of the leading newspapers in the area. Its editor was enthusiastic but his boss, the publisher—a man who Mapou had feared might not be happy about the inclusion of the *Mélodies Hébraïques*—closed the columns of his newspaper to the event. Shades of Captain Dreyfus!

The highlight of the Festival was, of course, the concert, which was to take place on Sunday evening, August 24th, at 9:30 at the Hôtel du Palais in nearby Biarritz. But for Sunday morning they had scheduled the unveiling of a commemorative plaque on the façade of the house where Ravel was born. A high-principled maiden lady who was now living in that house wrote to the mayor of Ciboure to protest the fact that in a Catholic country a public ceremony which necessarily involved her and her sister should take place at an hour that conflicted with High

Mass. Monsieur Mapou wrote amiably that he and the mayor were respectful above all of everyone's ideas and that the hour had therefore been changed. But the posters were already up and Mlle. Suzanne Petit de Meurville protested again. This time Monsieur Mapou called on the lady and smoothed out the wrinkles. Little stickers were placed on all the posters, changing the time. In a few days, Mademoiselle rose to the charge again, starting from scratch with her accusations. By now Monsieur Mapou, a fierce-looking but benevolent bearded giant, who weighed close to 300 pounds, felt his honor impugned and wrote her a long and seething letter but still, given the graces of the French language for that kind of polemical purpose, a polite one. In further deference to Mademoiselle's sensitivities, he invited the parish priest to attend the ceremony in front of what until then had been No. 12, Rue du Quai but, because Ravel had been born there on the 7th of March 1875, was now to be known as 12, Quai Maurice Ravel. Mademoiselle was mollified and confessed she had forgotten all about Monsieur Mapou's peacemaking visit. But when Mapou wrote to Ravel about the unveiling, Ravel told him that under no condition would he be present at that ceremony. "I know that great musician Saint-Saëns wasn't afraid of covering himself with ridicule by being on hand for the unveiling of his statue [in Dieppe]," he wrote, "but he never passed up *any* opportunity to so cover himself."

By the time the Festival opened, flags were everywhere. On every street corner, swinging in the breeze, banners proclaimed *"Gloire à Maurice Ravel"* and *"Vive Maurice Ravel."* Baron Henri de Rothschild's yacht was moored just offshore. Crowds filled the windows, balconies, and rooftops of the houses bordering Ciboure's main square.

The Paris press and other European papers were well represented. *Le Temps*, the leading Paris daily at that time, assigned Henry Malherbe. The pianist Joaquin Nin was covering the Festival for the principal Spanish music reviews—*La Revista Musical Catalana* and *Música* in Barcelona, and *Ritmo* in Madrid—and brought greetings from Spain's leading symphony orchestras. Belgium and Holland sent correspondents. Emile Vuillermoz, the dean of French music critics and an old friend of Ravel's from their days as students of Gabriel Fauré and fellow-members of the artistic group *"Les Apaches,"* filed stories for *L'Illustration* and *Excelsior*. And being a very practical man, without repeating himself he filled columns in *Candide*, also, with his account of the Festival and "Maurice Ravel, the greatest French composer of our time whom I am honored to have loved and admired from his very beginnings and whom I have always supported and defended with the most affectionate fidelity."

Ravel was as good as his word: he stayed away from the unveiling ceremony but he was on hand, right down front, for the pelota match, which featured Léon Dongaïtz, "king of the *pelotaris.*" Beside him were Don Luis Fernando and the Infanta Doña Maria Luisa of the Spanish royal family. Mapou, a Gargantuan figure wearing a straw boater, towered above the short, bright-eyed, wiry figure of Ravel, with his ever-present cigarette and the sharp, neat features of a little mouse. The once-popular novelist Claude Farrère, with white beard and *béret basque,* was the *président d'honneur.* But before the match there was the oratory. First, straight from Central Casting, *Monsieur le maire* Duhau, doffing his derby, took the podium, and in his "weak and slightly trembling voice," paid tribute to Ravel, to Léon Dongaïtz, and others without exhausting the patience of anyone. He was followed by Monsieur Mapou. Silver-tongued? Silver-plated at least. He was tireless—and endless—in evoking by name and deed all those who, near and far, high and low, had contributed to the success of the occasion, not omitting the Petit de Meurville sisters, "who agreed, with the good grace of which women alone bear the secret, to allow us to place the plaque. . . ." Finally he came to the end, with a hearty Franco-Basque thank-you for everybody: *"A vous tous, milesker."*

The pelota match was a cliff-hanger, right up to the final point. But even then, did anyone relax? Apparently not, because it was time for the fandango competition. And in the Basque country no celebration is complete without the fandango.

The climactic concert fulfilled everyone's expectations—and then some. Madeleine Grey sang—not for an hour and three-quarters, but longer than anyone else played: first, the *Chansons Madécasses,* with Philippe Gaubert as flutist; then the *Mélodies Hébraïques;* Concepción's aria from *L'Heure espagnole,* and a portion of *L'Enfant et les sortilèges.* Everyone would have liked to hear more. Robert Casadesus played *Jeux d'eaux* and two fragments of the *Tombeau de Couperin* and was called back again and again. Lucienne Lamballe, who had been a pupil of Madame Egorova, danced to the *Alborada del gracioso* and a segment of the *Tombeau.* Jacques Thibaud, with Ravel at the piano, brought the concert to a close with what Emile Vuillermoz referred to as the "awesome" Violin Sonata, a work which Ravel considered one of his most significant. The finale was "dazzling," Vuillermoz conceded, but nonetheless, for him, Ravel remained the subtle composer of *Daphnis et Chloé*—as he did for me, for I was still hearing replayed in my mind strains from that revival performance of the ballet I had attended with Chagall at the Paris Opéra.

* * * * *

Chagall had made two trips to Greece in the 1950s as background for another *Daphnis et Chloé* project. Tériade, publisher of the deluxe art review *Verve*, had asked him to illustrate, in color lithography, the Longus text in its revised French version. Whenever Chagall and I talked about *Daphnis*, whether as ballet or book, I would talk about Ravel and Chagall would talk about Greece. But in either form, *Daphnis* would soon give way to Chagall's main preoccupation—his "Message Biblique," a series of monumental paintings based on his interpretation of the Bible stories—the Creation of man, the role of Moses, the Song of Songs, and so on—into which he had been pouring much of his energy for the previous ten or twelve years. He wanted the collection to be kept intact and housed in some kind of suitable structure in the south of France. The town of Vence, where he had his studio, had offered him land for the purpose and we talked often of ways of making his dream a reality.

In the world of mythology, Daphnis and Chloé will go on living and loving eternally, but for the rest of us, there comes a time when one must face up to his own mortality. Something happens which makes it clear that death is, indeed, the central fact of life, even though one may have kept that thought at bay until then. That, I'm sure, was the driving force behind Chagall's constant concern for his "Message Biblique." I, too, began to feel those intimations of mortality. I was spending the summer of 1959 in Cambridge, England, when my father, a man who looked at least ten years younger than his actual age and had never been ill in his life, suddenly died. I returned to the States to help put things in order. During the month or so I spent handling his papers and assorted artifacts, I began to think about the future of my sprawling collections. Some collectors, like the novelist Edmond de Goncourt, go on amassing till the end of their days, arranging for a series of posthumous auction sales to pass along to other collectors the pleasure they had drawn from the treasure hunt.

Because my own collecting had increasingly become involved with research in literature and the arts and had resulted in the accumulation of great quantities of unpublished correspondence and other manuscript material, I had a different point of view. I wanted my collections to be kept together in a place where they could be used by other writers and researchers whose interests corresponded to my own.

That idea preyed on my mind intermittently over the next decade—without, however, slowing me down. My apartment in Paris was full; the more precious pieces were stored in a large safe at the Morgan bank in the Place Vendôme; my house in Massachusetts was filled with books and papers; trunkloads of the overflow were stored in a room-sized walk-in vault at a Boston bank. Something had to be done.

Like everyone else with an abiding interest in rare books and manuscripts, I knew what Harry Ransom and his associates at the University of Texas had been achieving since the 1950s in establishing their preeminent collection of modern American and British literary research materials. The French field, central and basic to both, had barely been skirted. Yet Yeats had made the point long ago that ever since Chaucer's time "it is from France that nearly all the great influences in art and literature have come."

A very old friend of mine on the faculty at Austin—Hartley Grattan, who had been the first literary critic to take Scott Fitzgerald seriously—brought me together with Harry Ransom and his deputy, Warren Roberts, the D. H. Lawrence scholar and bibliographer. We met and talked and as a result, my collections began moving toward Austin. I was brought to the University first as a consultant in 1969. A few months later Chancellor Ransom offered me essentially the job I have today at the Humanities Research Center—"lifetime curator of these collections," as he put it. I felt honored, even a bit flattered, but as an Eastern snob—the worst kind of provincial!—and one who had spent most of his life in Boston, New York, and Paris, I found that the idea of settling in central Texas went down rather hard. In fact, it took me nearly five years to digest it. But while I was in Austin in 1974, I took a longer, closer look at the University and liked what I saw. And I agreed to mount an exhibition of my collection. Throughout its preparation—working alternately in Paris, Boston, and Austin—I saw how much energy and enthusiasm Texans can deploy in a good cause. I was hooked.

All during my early years in Austin, I was continuing to pick up lambent echoes of *Daphnis et Chloé*. In the winter of 1975, I saw a news

Grand Festival Maurice Ravel, 1930.
Corrected proof of the handbill for the
concert.

Marc Chagall talking about his "Message Biblique." Reims, 1962.

Maurice Ravel and the *pelotaris* at the Ravel festival in Ciboure in 1930.

Ravel's notes for the program of the concert at the Grand Festival Ravel, 1930.

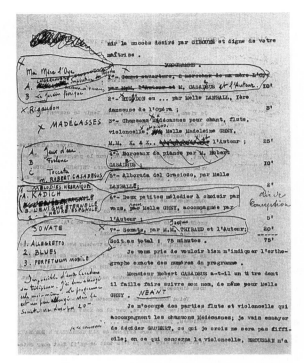

The final page of the autograph manuscript of Ravel's orchestral score for *Daphnis et Chloé,* signed and dated 5 April 1912.

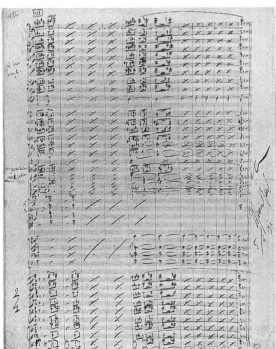

story in *The New York Times* about a New York musicologist's discovery of six works by Ravel that no one had been aware of, the earliest of them dating from 1893. The intrepid musicologist, then working on his dissertation, had gone to Saint-Jean-de-Luz to meet Ravel's heir, a man named Alexandre Taverne. In addition to the unknown early works, he had seen a number of other manuscripts of Ravel: corrected versions or different arrangements of known works.

In the spring of 1977, I was in Paris. The Pompidou Center had just opened and the Humanities Research Center was the principal lender to the literary exhibition put on for the occasion, titled "Paris—New York." While I was there, I wrote to Monsieur Taverne and told him I'd like to see his Ravel manuscripts. And I told him why. If I couldn't get there first, well, the race is not always to the swift (or so I hoped). Of course early works aren't often masterpieces, whether literary or musical, but whatever they may be, they do have research value and thus their own significance. I didn't have Monsieur Taverne's street address, but Saint-Jean-de-Luz isn't all that big a town, so I thought that even without it, a letter would reach him, one way or another. Two days later I had my letter back, marked "insufficient address." In America that would not have surprised me; in France it amazed me, and in the context it slowed me down. I didn't really have the time that summer to take a trip to Saint-Jean-de-Luz purely on speculation because other projects kept calling for attention; so I returned to Texas without meeting Monsieur Taverne.

A little later, a Debussy scholar and gifted interpreter, Roy Howat of Cambridge University, came to Austin to do some research in our Debussy collection. In the course of a conversation I was having with him about Ravel, in whose work he was equally interested, I mentioned the *New York Times* article about the cache of Ravel manuscripts and my frustrated attempt to get in touch with Alexandre Taverne. Taverne had died, Roy told me, and Madame Taverne, he said, had a reputation for being rather difficult. But Roy knew the intrepid musicologist who had discovered those early works of Ravel. "He's in Paris right now," he said. "I'll give you his address." And so I wrote and told him my Taverne story. I soon left for Paris and in the first package of mail forwarded from Austin, I received a note from the musicologist, inviting me to call him. When I did, I learned that Madame Taverne had moved to Switzerland—he didn't know exactly where—that she was indeed, if not downright reclusive, certainly not hospitable. The conversation then took another turn and soon I was learning about another collection which my informant had studied during his doctoral research, this one vastly more important than what Madame Taverne was guarding so zealously. He asked and I answered a number of questions concerning our interests, our collections, and our financial possibilities and procedures. In my turn I asked all the questions one would normally ask in the circumstances. I got cautious but suggestive answers; clear enough, in any case, for me to think—and say—that such a large and magnificent collection would never be allowed to leave France. But it's not in France, I was told. Real progress. We talked on. By the time the conversation ended, nearly an hour had passed and we had agreed that he would take the next steps and get back to me in Austin as soon as he had something to report. I still did not know the identity of the owner.

Two months later I had a call from New York. It looked as though the collection could be made available to us. The outlines became clearer: The collection consisted of about ninety autograph manuscripts, including eight by Paul Dukas, eleven by Gabriel Fauré, twenty-two by Maurice Ravel, and fifty by Albert Roussel—a total of more than 3,600 pages of music. "An extraordinary collection," the musicologist commented. An incredible collection, I thought. Nobody could have so many manuscripts by these great modern French composers. Next I received a short-title list, even more staggering than the numbers quoted. Dukas's manuscripts included the full orchestral scores of "The Sorcerer's Apprentice" and *La Péri*, and his monumental Beethovenesque Sonata for piano. Fauré's included the full score of *Masques et bergamasques* and the song cycle *Le Jardin clos*. Albert Roussel, an undervalued composer whom many would consider to belong in the company of Debussy and Ravel, was represented by the best of his entire *oeuvre:* his Second Symphony, the full orchestral scores of two of his three major ballets, *Le Festin de l'araignée* and *Aenéas*, as well as the piano version of the third—*Bacchus et Ariane;* and finally, the full score of his opera-ballet *Padmavati*.

The Ravel was a banquet: all six of his song cycles, including the *Histoires Naturelles, Don Quichotte à Dulcinée*, and the *Chansons Madécasses;* the *Rapsodie Espagnole*, with the perennial favorite, *Malagueña;* the orchestral score of his opera *L'Heure espagnole;* the *Introduction et allegro* for harp and chamber ensemble; the *Valses nobles et sentimentales;* the Sonata for violin and cello; the *Gaspard de la nuit* suite—*and* the orchestral score for *Daphnis et Chloé!* And more. In all, that represented about 8% of Fauré's total output, 40% of Ravel's, 50% of Dukas's, and more than 60% of Roussel's. The valuation was not far behind: nearly three million dollars. But we were talking about a collection so rich that none of the other collections one knows about of the work of these composers could even come close to matching it (with the sole exception of Fauré, most of whose manuscripts were left to the Paris Conservatoire, which he had headed for many years, but since have been transferred to the Bibliothèque Nationale).

There could be only one possible source for the collection—a family that had assembled and held these manuscripts through four generations—the French music publisher Durand. I put the question. The answer was yes. Finally, where were they now? In a vault in a northeastern state, I was told.

The quality was incomparable; the authenticity—sight unseen—impeccable, given the provenance; the sticking point, money. Research libraries, even the most generously endowed, can't usually come up with three million dollars from one day to the next. After looking in all the dusty corners of the budget and probing whatever other accessible sources we could think of, it seemed wiser to play a waiting game. If *we* couldn't hand over the three million, could anyone else? I felt relieved, rather than anxious, and I was sure we would be hearing more from our source.

Months passed. I heard that the Pierpont Morgan Library in New York badly wanted the Ravel, or at least a good part of it. The owner—wise man—refused to break up the collection. Finally I was approached again. The price began to soften. We tested each other. Another price was set by the owner's agent. We resisted. In time we made a counteroffer. There was a long silence. A new problem surfaced. A recheck of the inventory had revealed a few discrepancies: three of the Ravel manuscripts were missing, one of them *Daphnis et Chloé*. However, the news was not all bad. Two important Debussy manuscripts, not previously included, had been found and added, as well as three other Roussel manuscripts. But the *Daphnis et Chloé* was a low blow from fate. Another careful search was instituted for the three missing Ravel manuscripts. One—a short and minor work—was declared officially lost; the second proved to be a near-duplicate of something else in the collection; the third—*Daphnis*—suddenly reappeared. The agent proposed another price; I stood firm on our previous offer. In a week, a telephone call came through: "You've got yourself a deal."

The manuscripts were flown to Austin by special courier. A colleague and I spent three days examining them. The Ravel manuscripts, in particular, were extraordinary: worked over intensively, with many deletions; additions pasted down or pinned on—work for a whole army of musicologists for the rest of the century. Elsewhere there were a few problems: five of the manuscripts were not autograph, but were in the hands of copyists, presumably hired by the publisher to prepare them for the engraver. Most of the five were minor works and none was by Ravel. Our intermediary was shocked when I told him. He said he had carefully examined all of them. He asked me to return the questioned pieces to him. He would take them to Paris and submit them to the leading expert in music manuscripts for his authentication. He asked if I would abide by that decision.

I balked at that. Expert is as expert does. I have seen the "best" of them fall on their face and, in my younger (and more trusting) days, I had been taken more than once. I thought of a three-page letter by Hector Berlioz that I had bought from the catalogue of Michel Castaing, one of the more prominent Paris *experts en autographes.* It was an outstanding letter in which Berlioz defended himself vigorously against the accusation that he had been responsible for the "mutilations" inflicted on Carl Maria von Weber's opera *Der Freischütz* in a production at the Paris Opéra. Two years after I bought the letter I received a catalogue of a sale at the Hôtel Drouot which included a Berlioz letter that sounded very much like the one I had purchased from Castaing. It had the same date—7 January 1854—and the catalogue description covered the same ground in paraphrasing the contents. I attended the sale and bought the letter. Comparing the two afterward, I saw that the second one was the genuine original letter; the one I had bought earlier was a copy in a hand that was close to Berlioz's but was not his. I took the letters to Castaing. He studied them and was obliged to agree that his letter was only a copy, and not in the hand of Berlioz. He returned my money.

And so I told the musicologist that I had done my homework on the five suspect manuscripts very carefully. I had compared them with other, demonstrably authentic originals by Roussel, Dukas, and Fauré and with facsimiles of still others, also known to be authentic. There was no doubt whatever—in *my* mind—that the five in question were more than questionable; they were simply not originals. I told him I was satisfied with my decision but would send him the five pieces to do with as he saw fit. He took them to Paris and called me on his return to tell me the expert had agreed with me in all cases. He offered them to me free as useful historical documents without particular monetary value, we settled on an appropriate proportional deduction from the price of the collection, and he returned them to me that day.

Right now I am listening to a recording of *Daphnis et Chloé* by the Boston Symphony conducted by Charles Munch. One senses clearly Ravel's intention to compose a "vast musical fresco," less concerned with archaic Greece than with the Greece of his dreams as seen through the works of the late-eighteenth-century French painters. Before me is the 186-page autograph manuscript of Ravel's score of *Daphnis*. The orchestra plays; I listen and turn pages. The cycle of objective chance has run its course.

In this business there are good days and bad. This is one of the good ones.

Chapter 11

It would be hard to imagine any list of the three or four most distinguished Paris booksellers of recent decades that didn't include the name of the late Georges Blaizot. In a field where continuity is rare, the House of Blaizot is now in its third generation and still thriving, although Georges is undoubtedly a hard act to follow.

I came slowly, almost reluctantly, to appreciate Georges's qualities. From a distance he appeared haughty, on the verge of arrogance. He sent me his catalogues, I read them with pleasure and profit, but it was some time before I could overcome my disinclination to buy from him. Then one day I saw a number of things in his current catalogue that I felt I had to have—one of them being the original manuscript of *Tous les hommes sont mortels*, the novel Simone de Beauvoir had dedicated to Sartre. I decided to get my feet wet. My first hand-to-hand contact with Georges was not immediately reassuring, but I gradually came to see that his haughtiness was a kind of defensive dignity to protect him against the threat of importunate or invasive outsiders. If he was going to let down his guard, he wanted to be sure he was letting it down to someone worthwhile, by his rather patrician standards. But once he had relaxed, I found him not merely possible but even likable. He was exceedingly knowledgeable, had excellent taste and none of the Oriental-bazaar mannerisms that characterized certain of his colleagues. In time he took to writing me—telephoning would have been a bit too hucksterish for him—whenever he had something he thought would be of particular interest to me, and it was in response to one such letter that I found myself seated opposite him one Friday morning in the late 1960s in his small Art-Deco-style office at the back of the Librairie Auguste Blaizot, in the Faubourg Saint-Honoré.

Blaizot had dark, aquiline, not-quite-jaded good looks, a thin mustache, and he often played with an unlighted cigarette, as he was doing then. He habitually talked little and slowly; that morning he seemed even more restrained, perhaps because I hadn't taken him up on his offer. I was getting ready to leave when the phone rang. He answered it. "Oh, good, bring it in," he said. Someone knocked. It was his clerk, with a large registered package. Suddenly Blaizot was full of life. *"Enfin,"* he said with a good deal more enthusiasm than he customarily displayed. "I've been waiting for weeks." He took a letter from his desk drawer, checked its date and then the postal stamping on the package. He shook his head. "Oh, well," he said, "it was worth the wait."

By now I was curious. I asked him, as tactfully as I could, what "it" was.

He paused reflectively. "Are you interested in Paul Valéry?" he asked.

Who isn't, I thought, but the only reasonable answer to a question like his, it seemed to me, was: Depends on what it is, and that's what I told him.

He leaned over his desk and smiled. "These are the most important Paul Valéry papers you—or I, who have been deeply interested in Valéry since 1926—have ever seen or heard of. This man"—he waved the letter in front of me—"has been holding them in secret since Valéry died, in 1945. He has been promising to sell them to me for God knows how long. He described them to me in detail in this letter and finally put a price on them. I accepted. Now here they are."

As he began to unwrap the package, he told me something of the story. Valéry, at sixty-six, had fallen in love with an attractive woman half his age. She had been married to a popular playwright, then divorced, was a good friend of Jean Giraudoux and Saint-John Perse, and had literary aspirations of her own. She took, as her *nom de plume*, the name Jean Voilier. Valéry came to look upon her as—potentially—a successor to Colette. He spent more and more time in her company and often wrote in the secluded little garden behind her house.

Their affair continued through the war years, brightening Valéry's life and stimulating his creative processes. Gradually it became the most significant element in the elaboration of what he hoped would prove to be his great achievement—a play based on the Faust legend. He had written three acts, with a fourth still in the planning stages when, on Easter Sunday 1944, the young woman announced to him that she had decided to marry. The man, close to her own age, was the publisher

Robert Denoël. She herself owned a publishing business inherited from her father, and she and Denoël planned to merge their firms. She told Valéry that she wanted *their* friendship to continue on the same basis as before. There was no change in her feeling for him, she said.

Valéry was stunned. He had never been in love to that extent before. He understood what her declaration meant, not only for the future but—alas—for the past. The sky fell in on him.

He tried to bear up under the shock. He filled pages and whole notebooks with letters—not sent—and poems in which he tried to make his peace with the situation. He tried to put it out of his mind and finish his work on *Mon Faust.* He never did. His health gave out and the following summer he died.

By now, Blaizot had the package open and was sorting through the sheets, checking them against the letter in front of him.

"It's all there," he said. "Nobody knows about this but you and me and the seller. I haven't even read them yet." He paused, then looked up at me. "Are you interested?"

I asked him the price. He thought a while, then gave me a figure. It was substantial. I probably pursed my lips.

"That's the price this morning," he said. "If you're not interested, I'll add 50% to that amount and put them in my next catalogue."

I looked through the pile as well as I could in the circumstances. I caught a line here, a sentence there that let me understand that the answer had to be yes. I asked him how he wanted to be paid.

"Dollars," he said. I took out a blank check. "I want half in banknotes," he said. I didn't have them in the necessary quantity so I wrote him a dollar check for half the amount and told him—this being Friday—I'd be back on Tuesday with the equivalent in bills.

"Fine," he said. "That will give me the chance I've been waiting for to read these papers. I'll turn them over to you on Tuesday." He accompanied me to the front door. It was past the lunch hour and the shop was empty. He unlocked the door, bowed, and shook my hand. "You're a very lucky man," he said.

When I returned to see Blaizot the following Tuesday, he had undergone a complete personality change. His eyes were pained. The suave, dignified, urbane mask had been removed; his anguish lay exposed.

"I'll never forgive myself," he said bitterly. "If I had read those papers, as I should have done before making the deal with you, I'd never have sold them. Not for that price; not for 50% more. For three times as much—maybe. But I'm not sure. What a disaster!" He continued his recital, ticking off the incredibly moving revelations that, after more than forty years as a *valéryen*, he had only now been made aware of by these papers. "And then to let them go. Just like that." He looked sick and I don't think he was acting. My heart went out to him. But I checked the sheets carefully, counted out the banknotes, and went on my way, trying not to look too unfeelingly cheerful.

As soon as I got home, I set the papers out on a large table. The previous owner had made things easy by numbering each sheet in sequence. And so it was possible to follow the story of Valéry's decline from onset to climax.

There were draft pages from the never-to-be-completed four-act *Mon Faust*. The role of Faust, quite clearly, was identified in Valéry's mind with himself. Faust's secretary—*"la demoiselle de cristal"*—to whom Valéry had given the name "Lust," probably from the German word for pleasure, joy, delight, rather than the corresponding English word, was obviously built around his inamorata. The relationship between the two—although never resolved and in the end somewhat ambiguous and confused—was based on Valéry's concept of his formative role in the development of Lust's flesh-and-blood prototype from a repository of unrealized virtualities to the perfect female expression of heart and mind which he had visualized.

But in the private journal, which ran parallel to and eventually replaced his work on *Mon Faust*, Valéry came to grips with the effects of his betrayal by Héra (as he referred to her) on his life and work. There were letters to himself and to her, and poems—some savage, some tender, all magnificent—in which he set down his appraisal of his present condition, human and creative. Each morning before daybreak he sat down at his table to write, just as he had done all his working life. But now, surveying the wreckage—thousands of hours given over to someone to whom all that meant nothing, except perhaps as a source of vanity—he is embittered to feel himself at the mercy of who knows what kind of demon. One of the avenging Furies? In expiation of what? The crime, perhaps, of having exalted with all his poetic powers to the peak of the absurd a monument of love which suddenly, without warning, had fallen over to crush him beneath it. He had felt that Héra stood between him and death. It was now clear that he apparently stood between her and life. And ever since that shattering Easter present—the announcement of her plans for the future—he is no longer alive. He hasn't slept two hours since then. He feels his way blindly through the ruins—*his* ruins.

His sanity is under siege, like a pier shaken by the tempest. He begins to write "Mes Mémoires," but doesn't get far beyond the title. Sometimes he loses his memory. When it returns, it brings with it dreams of childhood fantasies.

Throughout, there is the insistent need to finish *Mon Faust.* But he is at the end of his strength from unrelieved insomnia. He has new thoughts about Act IV that reinforce those vague ideas he had earlier. He analyzes the metaphysics of the problem in terms which are conceptually extraordinary but practically—for him, now—unrealizable.

In one ten-page letter, he traces the history of his hopes to model Héra into an incomparable being, a work, he now recognizes, that is as illusory as a certain fourth act—and so many other things. One of those other things was to have been a book called "Inferno." Its early notations and analyses are set down in a schoolboy's notebook. They relate in equal measure to the catastrophe and to *Mon Faust*—how one destroys oneself through not knowing how to destroy an image or its power.

At other moments, Valéry seemed rational, compassionate, and at times passionately lyrical. Occasionally he could write with a wry humor. But as his mood turned darker, he became jealous, vindictive, self-absorbed, and desperate. And some of these pages were as raw and intolerably painful as the wounds and spasms that produced them. And yet, in spite of this, time and again I could see the creative process advancing a step beyond the confession or the dramatization to a conditioned refinement of the facts. One day they would appear *so;* the next day, approaching from a different vantage point, he had metamorphosed them into a quite different result: from the local to the universal, from private pain to a near-serenity achieved through the ordering of art.

It is not too much to say that Valéry is one of the two or three greatest poets of the twentieth century. To see him here, literally bleeding to death, but "still giving light, dying," was one of the most moving experiences I had had in literature. I bled a little along with Valéry and in the process almost felt sorry for Blaizot.

The final sheet of the dossier was the one on which Valéry set down, on 25 May 1945, a last, clear-eyed statement of his role as a writer. Six days later he was confined to his bed and on 20 July he died. On the 24th his coffin was carried by uniformed guards, in a torchlight procession to the rhythm of muffled drums, from the Place Victor-Hugo to the Trocadéro. It was placed on a catafalque draped with the tricolor and set up between the two wings of the Palais de Chaillot, on whose façade are engraved four brief texts by Valéry. Across the Seine the Panthéon was illuminated. All the rest of Paris was in darkness. Throughout the night, students kept watch as crowds filed past the bier. In the morning General de Gaulle presided over the official ceremony that preceded the convoy's departure for the Mediterranean fishing port of Sète, Valéry's birthplace, where he was to be buried in the Saint-Charles cemetery—his "Cimetière Marin." The pomp and ceremony with which France paid its final respects to its most eminent man of letters underlined the pathos of the bitter epitaph he had written for himself:

> I finish this life in vulgarity, a ridiculous victim in my own eyes, after having believed I would finish it in a twilight of love absolute and incorruptible and of spiritual power recognized by all as rigorously and justly acquired.

*   *   *   *   *

I had a great curiosity to learn more about Héra. I wondered whether she knew about these papers. Some of the letters had been, technically speaking, addressed to her, but I sensed that they had really been written by Valéry to himself and in any case not sent. Obviously she must have other letters, Valéry being—like George Sand, like Proust, like Cocteau—a compulsive letter writer in certain circumstances. What else did she have? What did she plan to do with it? Was she even still alive? I spoke about her to Janine Daragnès, since Janine, too, had been a publisher. She knew—or had known—almost everybody, and it turned out she had known both Valéry and Héra. She remembered Héra chiefly for her legs—very solid, substantial ones, she said.

"She never did marry Denoël, you know," Janine told me. "He was killed, very mysteriously, on the Esplanade des Invalides, a few months after Valéry died. It was very odd. She and Denoël had gone to the theater one night and not far from the Invalides he got a flat tire. He started to change it and she left him to go to a police station nearby to call a taxi. When she got to the station, they had just received word of a shooting near the Invalides. She rode back with the squad car they dispatched to investigate, and when they reached Denoël's car, there he was, stretched out with a bullet in his back. There were no clues, aside from the bullet. They thought at first that it might have been a deserter from the American Army. But it wasn't a robbery; Denoël had plenty of money in his pocket when they found him. He was due to stand trial about a week later, on charges of collaboration with the Germans during the Occupation, but that angle didn't lead anywhere, either. Finally they closed out the inquest, without a solution.

"I heard that she had inherited his business, which is very strange, because I believe he had a wife and children. Anyway, she operated the business for nearly four years after he died. Eventually it was sold to Gallimard. But I feel sure she's still around."

Janine leafed through a large address book on a library table near the telephone stand. After a few minutes' search, talking to herself all the while, she found me Héra's address and telephone number. Later that afternoon I called Héra's house and a maid answered. Madame was not in Paris but was expected back the next day. I left my name and a message that I would call again in a day or two. Meanwhile perhaps I could try another tack—the Doucet Collection.

The Bibliothèque Littéraire Jacques Doucet, founded by the couturier whose name it bears, holds substantial quantities of letters, manuscripts, and books by most of the great modern French writers. Doucet was aided in putting together this collection—as always with his collections, whether Oriental art, eighteenth-century French art, modern painting, or the great fine-arts reference library now part of the Institut d'art et d'archéologie—by a number of knowledgeable and innovative writer friends and protégés: first, beginning in 1916, by the proud and disdainful André Suarès; then by Pierre Reverdy, Max Jacob, and Blaise Cendrars; later, and more effectively, by André Breton and Louis Aragon. After Doucet's death, the Literary Collection was administered by the City and the University of Paris.

Years ago, when Marie Dormoy, the good friend of the irascible drama critic, diarist, and cat-lover Paul Léautaud, was at the Doucet's helm, I had met there at regular intervals with the other members of a committee formed to look after the Collection's interests and future. The committee included Jean Schlumberger, the writer and co-founder of the *Nouvelle Revue Française;* the art binder Rose Adler, the novelist Renée Massip, the collector André Rodocanachi, and one or two others. Marie Dormoy was approaching retirement, and to take her place they had brought in as her understudy a scholarly young man named François Chapon who later became curator of the Collection, under a series of directors. Why not pay Chapon a visit and look over the "Valéryanum," their Valéry collection, which I knew only by reputation?

The Valéryanum had been assembled by a friend and admirer of Valéry, a businessman named Julien Monod. He lavished on its formation all the time and energy, the love and devotion that the passionate collector dedicates to such an enterprise. Madame Monod was rather less devoted to the cult of Paul Valéry than was her husband, who, as Valéry's *homme de confiance*, ran errands for the Great Man, accompanied him on trips, and served him in innumerable ways. In the course of one argument of the kind that occasionally erupts between a husband who is overzealous as a collector and—in his wife's eyes, at least—underzealous as a husband, Madame Monod let it be known—as the story reached me—that as soon as they carried Monod out of the house on his last journey, she would see to it that his collection followed promptly thereafter. That gave Monod quite a jolt. And it wasn't long after that discussion that he concluded an agreement with the Bollingen Foundation whereby Monod received a sum of money one can only call modest in view of the importance of his collection, and the Bibliothèque Littéraire Jacques Doucet received—thanks to Bollingen's generous gesture—a Valéry collection unmatched anywhere in the world at that time.

The Doucet Collection is housed in a building that faces the Bibliothèque Sainte-Geneviève in the Place du Panthéon. I went to the office there that serves as an outpost to the collections themselves and asked to see Chapon. After a telephone exchange between the doorkeeper and the inner sanctum, I was directed to the appropriate area of the building adjoining. There Chapon was waiting for me. He looked little changed from the time, fifteen years or so earlier, when I had had occasion to see him periodically: a bit small for his clothes, thinning brown hair, large, heavy eyeglasses, and just a whiff of the novice funeral director. He was effusive in his greeting, pressing on me catalogues of exhibitions he had mounted in recent years in connection with gifts made to the Doucet Collection—which has a minuscule budget—of material by François Mauriac, Paul Claudel, René Char, and one or two others. I thanked him. "Who deserves it more than you?" he asked, with rhetorical overkill. "They'll give you some idea of what we've been up to lately. Of course we don't get everything we'd like. You take all the good things away from us." He beamed in amiable resignation. I'm not sure why. I had never competed against him at an auction sale. Nor had I ever seen him bid at any sale I had attended.

"What brings you here today?" he asked. I told him I had heard so much about the Doucet's Valéry collection, I wanted to take a look at the catalogue for it. He took me to the card catalogue, ran through some of the classifications, and while I was looking more or less at random through the cards, he continued to chat. Soon he was called away. I looked, carefully now, through all the manuscript entries. Many of them appeared to represent things that Valéry had given to Monod for services rendered or that Monod had dutifully gathered together from publishing processes, talks Valéry had given, and so on. There was no trace of Héra. She might never have existed. Chapon still had not returned when I finished. I left a word of thanks with a library assistant working nearby and went on my way.

* * * * *

When I called Héra's house again, she was there. She had been in a terrible shipwreck, she said, when the yacht of some friends had burned in the Mediterranean. She had spent hours in the water, never expected to survive, but—here she was. She'd lost everything, including her jewels. But if I could overlook her appearance, she'd be glad to have me come by.

After lunch I drove to her house, in a quiet, elegant section of Auteuil, in the 16th *arrondissement.* It was a smallish house but very chic and admirably situated. A maid let me in and went upstairs to announce me. The décor was English in tone, but the pictures were wholeheartedly French, beginning with Degas and Berthe Morisot. I was ushered to an upstairs sitting room. Héra—consort of Zeus and queen of heaven, in Greek mythology—was telephoning, half-sitting, half-lying on a large expanse of daybed. She motioned me to a chair and continued her conversation, repeating in more detailed form the story of the shipwreck and the loss of her jewels. She was rather handsome in a large blond way, freshly coiffed, and exceedingly well preserved for the age she had to have. Her legs were covered, since she was wearing harem pants. Finally she hung up, told me more about the "horrible" experience, the lost jewels, the suit she was planning to bring against her friends for negligence, and so on. Another call came through—her lawyer, apparently—and after that we began to talk about Valéry.

She pointed to a bookcase against the wall to my right. "Those are my Valéry first editions, all inscribed to me, some with original drawings by him." The books had been bound in crimson calf bindings or half bindings, which gave them a rather uninspired uniformity.

"You know he wrote me hundreds of letters," she said. "And he gave me many manuscripts—including the notebook in which he set down the original drafts for *Charmes.*" I asked her if she had made any plans for her collection.

"I have," she said. "I want to see this house transformed into a Paul Valéry museum. And I have another house next to it, and a garage. The other house, which I keep empty, will be living quarters for the curator of the museum. Don't you think that's a lovely idea? Valéry spent *so* much time here, often worked outside in my garden. I call it 'the garden of *Mon Faust.*'"

I told her about the papers I had just acquired. I didn't tell her the harshest things Valéry had said about her but I quoted a number of passages which would give her a fair idea of the gamut of his feelings in those final, tortured months. She brushed it all aside. "I was the great love of his life," she said. "You should read some of the letters he wrote to me. Perhaps you will one day. Don't you know some American who would like to help me make this into a museum?"

Not offhand, I told her. I asked her how she planned to work it out.

"I would sell the property but retain a life interest," she said, "and go on living here for the rest of my days, and then it would become a museum. I would leave my Valéry papers to the museum, perhaps some of the other things, some of the drawings he liked to look at, for example."

I asked her how much it would cost to buy the property under those conditions.

"Oh, I don't know. Maybe a million." I asked whether that was dollars or francs. She looked at me in disbelief.

"Why, dollars—naturally. It's worth much more than that. The developers have been after me to sell for a long time. But I would never do that." I asked her what she would do with her Valéry papers if she didn't find her Maecenas.

"Oh, probably give them to the Bibliothèque Jacques Doucet," she said. "They have the Valéryanum, that wonderful collection formed by Monod."

I told her that the Doucet's Valéry collection hadn't a trace of her passage through Valéry's life.

She looked at me sharply. "Where did you get those papers, anyway? I have an idea about that, but why don't you tell me?" I told her I didn't think it would be proper to name names in this situation.

"Well," she said, "I want *my* papers to stay right here and I'm going to try to find someone who will help me see that they do."

I told her if I ran across some uncommitted, internationally minded, poetry-loving American, I'd get back to her. She, in turn, assured me of her pro-American sentiments, urged me to keep in touch, called in a maid to show me out and settled into another telephone session.

* * * * *

In Boston, where I had gone for the Christmas holidays, I received a letter from Héra. She had not been able to forget my visit, she wrote, but I had probably forgotten about her hope to see her house transformed into a Paul Valéry museum, administered by a curator happy to live in this last Parisian paradise. In any case, she concluded, I probably wouldn't find the wonderful Maecenas she was looking for. A friend of hers—a minor novelist whom she characterized as one of the greatest names in twentieth-century French literature—was thinking about selling his manuscripts. Would I be interested? I wasn't, but I answered her letter as tactfully as possible and wished her well in her museum aspirations.

When I returned to Paris that spring, I wrote to her, as she had asked me to do, and learned that she was leaving for her château in the center of France. She invited me to visit her there, but I had little time for traveling. Paris, as always, kept me very busy. She was back in a month or so and I had an engraved invitation to dine with her the following week. I was not happy to come down with the flu the day before the dinner but rather glad to have a legitimate excuse to stay away from her dinner party. After I came back to the land of the living, I kept busy, she soon left for her country house outside Paris, then returned to her château, and our paths did not cross that year.

The following year, too, I stayed away from the last Parisian paradise, but in the fall, the French press was full of articles celebrating Valéry's centenary. Héra sent me a clipping that spoke of her and quoted a few lines from poems Valéry had dedicated to her. When would I be back in France? she asked. She wanted to talk to me about her "voluminous" correspondence. I had the feeling that what she really wanted to talk about was money—and in large quantities.

A Paris friend sent me another clipping—a full page from *Le Figaro* devoted to Valéry and Jean Voilier, his "most faithful friend, an incomparable Egeria," with particular emphasis on her relics of the poet. Hagiography? P.R.? By any other name it was hype at its most naïvely transparent:

> Through delicacy, through discretion, Jeanne [*sic*] Voilier has always refused to show her treasures to any living soul. And yet Americans, Australians, Canadians . . . still come each year [trying] to buy the manuscripts, drawings and relics in her possession. She meets them invariably with a clear-cut refusal. It is at one and the same time touching and deplorable: these documents are absolutely necessary to a new understanding of the work of Valéry and to the discovery of an absolutely unknown [facet of his] personality . . . strange, prophetic, passionate, mystical, terrifying and tender all at once.

And every year the real-estate developers, the article continued, go on trying to buy her 45,000 square feet of land in one of the choicest sections of Paris. But she refuses. She had offered to sell the French government ownership without usufruct of her property in the Rue de l'Assomption as a basis for setting up a Valéry Foundation. The Minister of Cultural Affairs was examining the question. A curator from the National Archives had spent eight uninterrupted hours appraising the value of her books, drawings, and manuscripts. And if the Minister refused? Valéry's posthumous fate trembled in the balance. The article closed with lines by Valéry designed to show what life outside that sheltering Eden held for him:

> . . . distress, boredom, pain or lie,
> For all is black to me once that door is closed.

The page was illustrated with one photograph: Valéry, hat in hand, leaning against a low stone parapet on which sat a younger, slimmer Héra. She was wearing a skirt for the first time in my experience of her. Her long legs faced candidly into the camera—every bit as solid and substantial as Janine Daragnès had remembered them.

* * * * *

One day in Paris the autograph dealer Jacques Lambert offered me another voluminous Valéry correspondence—this one addressed to an earlier love, the sculptor Renée Vautier. There were about 150 letters. The price—$20,000—seemed a bit stiff, and as I read them over, I was struck, time and again, with the archness, the game-playing tenor of many of them. There was no real fire there. It was quite clear that Valéry had written such things before and, like that other unrepentant amatory recidivist, Bertrand Russell, would write them again. I decided not to buy the correspondence. As for Héra's letters, I knew that in her eyes, twenty-thousand dollars—or anything remotely approaching that figure—would be either an unfunny joke or an insult. I saw no point in getting back to her.

In 1975, at the Humanities Research Center, as I was preparing the exhibition of my collection that Warren Roberts had asked me to mount—it was called "Baudelaire to Beckett: A Century of French Art and Literature"—the question came up of including those papers covering Valéry's final years. A large wall case was devoted to Valéry and I saw to it that the Héra papers were arranged so as to be very visible but not too revealing. In describing them for the catalogue, I came across a number of points that called for clarification, so I wrote to Héra from Austin asking her to be a little more precise about some of the questions I had raised with her in our conversation at her house right after the shipwreck.

My letter, she wrote in answer, had followed her from Paris to her château to the south of France, where she had gone to commune with the spirit of Valéry over his grave in the little cemetery at Sète. Her plans for the museum had fallen through. Heartbroken, she had sold the property and moved to an apartment nearer the center of Paris. It had been an exhausting move, and though it represented a complete change in lifestyle, she was accepting it as an occasion for renewal.

But I was studying some Valéry documents? What documents? Where did they come from? What was I planning to do with my study? she wanted to know. She had recently given a radio interview about her first meeting with Valéry. She sent me a copy of her script, but warned me not to publish it; she was planning to do that herself. It was written in a breathless, schoolgirl style, and what it told was of little help to anyone looking for facts. She enclosed similar papers covering her first meetings with Jean Giraudoux and Saint-John Perse. One detail remained with me from her Valéry script: at twenty she had been the youngest woman lawyer before the Paris bar.

I wrote to ask her about some of the discrepancies between what she had said during my visit and the stories she told in the three scripts, and I gave her a fuller account of our exhibition and its catalogue. Most of the space devoted to Valéry, I told her, was given over to the papers I had discussed with her at our meeting. I had had to refer to her but I hadn't used her name.

Her next letter was written from a lakeside clinic in Switzerland where she had gone for rest and detoxication, as she put it—what we would call a fat farm, I judged. She had completely forgotten about any Valéry papers I had mentioned to her during my visit to her house. What were they all about? Couldn't she come to Texas to see them? When would she see the catalogue? When was I coming to Paris? In the meantime, there was no problem about her name. Use it, by all means. In France, Belgium, Italy, everyone knew what she was to him and he to her. She ticked off all the people who knew, all the events that had shown her to be the great and last love of his life, the one that brought him back to the cosmic questions. She tried to help me with the dates but they were troublesome—sometimes contradictory, sometimes missing. Actually, she had been seeing Valéry, Giraudoux, and Saint-John Perse all during the same period—nothing scandalous about that, she said. Giraudoux had been the first to die and that made her very unhappy. Valéry, her only confidant, understood that. As for Saint-John Perse, Valéry respected him but never liked him very much. In spite of the difference in their ages—hers and Valéry's—what held them together was stronger than all the rest, until the day when she told him she loved a man whom she was going to marry—Robert Denoël. She had only told him, she said, to be honest. She realized now she should have kept quiet, because Valéry died in July, 1945, and Denoël the following December. What a nightmare!

In my reply I told her once more, as I had told her when I first went to see her, about the papers I had acquired: the lyricism and the violence, the sadness and the anger, in Valéry's analysis of the woman who had meant so much to him and let him down so roughly. Her reply—eight pages—told me of her shock and handed *me* a shocker: Those papers had been sold to me, she was sure, by the Valéry family, probably Valéry's daughter, Agathe, or his son Claude, as a moneymaking operation—the only interest they had, from childhood on, in their glorious lineage, she said. She begged me to confirm what she was already convinced of. Decency would have dictated that the papers be offered first to her. She would have bought them whatever the price. The children's act was a betrayal of a man who wrote for himself alone. She wasn't concerned about posterity's judgment of her. The truth was already badly blurred; the rest would soon die with her. After her death, her letters from him would tell the true story; even before, should she decide to part with them sooner. Valéry hadn't been the only one to suffer. The sacrifices she had made for him had often torn her heart to shreds. It seemed to her now that she was already speaking to me from beyond the grave.

A month later, she was making plans for a visit to Texas to read through our Valéry papers, however agonizing an experience that might prove to be. There was to be a charity ball in New Orleans presided over by Madame Giscard d'Estaing. From there to Austin was a quick flight.

Her next letter, three months later, struck a different note. It sounded like the kind of speech a wily prosecutor would make in setting the stage for the denunciation. She referred to our first meeting so soon after that frightful shipwreck—which she had barely survived after losing precious property and blighting her health for the rest of her days. I had mentioned briefly something about documents relating to Valéry, she said. What could they be, she had wondered vaguely—a few letters, scraps of manuscript? Nothing that amounted to very much, certainly, since everyone was saying that the Valéry family had sold to the Bibliothèque Nationale everything they owned of their father's work for around $600,000, after having asked for $800,000 (and the vital core of it all—the notebooks—not even unpublished). As a result, she said, as far as she knew, there was nothing left available that was important or valuable except her own Valéry archive. Now, all these years later, I tell her that my documents are to be exhibited in a year, but still without saying a word—and this is the important point, she stressed (and underlined)—about the nature, the tone and the object of these documents. I had told her, she conceded, that I had referred to her without giving her name. Blithely unaware of the context in which that name would appear, she had given me her permission [i.e., urged me] to use her name. She had assumed she might have been mentioned in passing, in a phrase or two, perhaps a poem. No importance. How could she have known that these papers were made up for the most part, probably, of unpublished poems that she had inspired and of which, until now, she

The Paris bookseller Georges Blaizot early in his career, *c.* 1930.

Paul Valéry by Henri Martinie. Inscribed to Matilde Pomès.

Jean Voilier in the garden of her house in Auteuil—*"le jardin de 'Mon Faust'."*

Paul Valéry. Autograph manuscript of journal entry concerning Jean Voilier, c. 1944.

had believed she owned the only texts in existence. Suddenly, a month later, she learns *when* the documents were written, *what* they were all about—the violence, the anger, that flared up when she had told him about her intent to marry. Totally uncalled for, that anger; so unfair, it had made her ill. But now she must know in what context and what manner I had made use of her name. These were problems relating to her private life and she was insisting that I send her a copy of the text.

Rewriting history is a popular pursuit: The Stalinists, religious fanatics, politicians everywhere have been practicing it with varying degrees of success for aeons. Héra too, perhaps, but she needed more practice to do it well or convincingly. I wrote to set the record straight. If I had gone to see her in the first instance, it was with the explicit purpose of speaking with her very frankly about "the nature, the tone and the object" of those papers, for several reasons: (1) to find out whether she knew they existed; (2) to find out what papers she might have that were complementary to them, and (3) to try to learn what she planned to do with hers. And so I had told her exactly what they were all about. I had even quoted passages from them so she would understand their tone. She had found it all very interesting but hadn't seemed troubled by the words *or* the tone. Mostly she was concerned about where I had got them. And I hadn't, of course, told her *that*. She had spent a good part of the time talking about her shipwreck, her lost jewels, her lawsuit, her own Valéry papers, and the museum she wanted to establish for them, with help from a wealthy benefactor. If nothing came of it, she had told me, she would probably give them to the Doucet Library.

I told her also that when I left her at the end of that afternoon, I had gone home and written down our conversation, as I was in the habit of doing, so that years later, if I wanted to know who said what to whom, I wouldn't have to rely on a creaking or rebellious memory or a convenient latter-day reconstruction. As for her name, I had used it only because she seemed to prefer it that way, and I quoted the passage from the letter in which she had made that clear. The text, I told her, she would see when the catalogue was published. I promised to send her a copy.

* * * * *

The letters Valéry had written to the sculptor Renée Vautier, which had been offered to me by Jacques Lambert for $20,000, showed up in the catalogue of a sale of manuscript material scheduled by Sotheby's in London for May 25, 1976. They were bought by the Bibliothèque Nationale for the equivalent of a little under $7,000. A few days after the sale, Héra sent me a clipping from *Le Figaro*, which she had marked in red crayon. It included two significant passages:

> Mme. Renée Vautier, to whom these letters had been written, tried to block the sale. In vain. Not being the beneficiary of the sale and these letters having been put on sale by someone else, in accordance with English law she was unable to prevent the sale from taking place as scheduled.

> Nevertheless, Mme. Vautier maintains her protest, claiming it to be contrary to proper usage for intimate texts to be made public in the form of excerpts quoted in the catalogue. Unfortunately, these texts, in passing out of her possession, became documents that are part of the literary patrimony of all mankind.

Despite the court's ruling, Héra judged this matter to be "very grave." It had been giving her pause for thought. She was further troubled by not yet having received the catalogue of our exhibition.

When the catalogue finally did reach her, she was taking the cure at another fat farm, this one in Brittany and run by the French champion cyclist Louison Bobet. She was obviously relieved. She had read, in my last letter, my account of our original conversation about the Valéry papers that I had acquired shortly before coming to see her and she had come to the conclusion that she must have been unconscious, as though anesthetized, at the time. But my letter made everything very clear to her now. She had never had such a lapse before. The catalogue she characterized as marvelous and fascinating. I ought to write a book which would tell everything about the intelligent, sensitive, patient work involved in the gathering in of all those treasures, she said. On the other hand, if I had sent her my text in advance, she would have asked me not to use her name. She had heard about an article coming out in connection with our Valéry collection and had written to the author and the editor requesting that her name and two of the dates I had given in the catalogue not appear in their article. She was sure they would acquiesce. You mustn't forget I'm alive, she added, as if I needed reminding. She was again thinking of a trip to Texas, perhaps after taking a breather at her château. She had now decided to try to find some Maecenas who would buy her papers to give to the University of

Texas at Austin. Meanwhile she asked me to send copies of the catalogue to three friends of hers, one of them also a great friend of the State of Texas, she said.

The catalogue of the exhibition was beginning to circulate, even in Europe. Two months after the exhibition opened, I had a letter from Agathe Rouart-Valéry, Paul Valéry's daughter, asking me to send her a copy. I was in Massachusetts at the time because my house there had been broken into and a number of the things thieves usually look for had been stolen. Fortunately they had been interrupted in the midst of their work and most of what they had assembled in the first-floor central hall was still piled up there when the police arrived. But dealing with the problems raised by the loss of what they had made away with and the repairs and further security measures that were needed kept me from going to France that summer. I had brought a copy of the catalogue with me from Austin and I sent it to Valéry's daughter, along with a letter telling her about the success of the exhibition and the program of related events that would follow in the months to come.

A few weeks later, I had a letter, written in idiomatic English, from her brother Claude. His signature, I noticed, was very similar to his father's. He had seen the copy of the catalogue I had sent to his sister and asked me to send one to him too. He said that as Valéry's elder son, he was "rather shocked by the extremely intimate nature" of some of the papers referred to. Also, he was curious about their source. They were not the kind one normally finds in circulation, he said. He wanted to know how we happened to have them.

I was somewhat puzzled at his shock and I told him so. That episode in Valéry's life was widely known to all manner of people who were not even Valéry specialists, as I had learned in Paris over the years; well-known, too, to members of the Valéry family, I had been reliably informed.

I understood his curiosity about the source of the papers, but I told him, as I had told Héra, that if one were anything less than discreet in discussing sources, material that would otherwise become available might be withheld or—in some cases—even destroyed. And if that were to happen, then all of us, along with posterity and the entire scholarly, humanist tradition, would be the losers. I had no reply from Claude Valéry but his sister sent me a pained acknowledgment of the catalogue and told me of her distress at the thought of what her father's reaction to such revelations would have been.

Early in the New Year, Héra announced her arrival in Austin within the next ten days. A day before I was expecting to see her, she telephoned to say the health of her adopted daughter would not allow her to leave Paris. I felt relieved. Her letters all along had made it clear that she was expecting to be wined, dined, toured, chauffeured, and socially promenaded from one end of the Lone Star State to the other. At the beginning of May, I wrote to tell her I would be in Paris soon. When I got there, the usual pile of priority projects kept me from thinking of her. One morning in June, a delivery boy brought me a telegram from her. She had learned I was there and apologized for her silence, which was due to a "grave accident," she said. She asked me to have lunch with her the following Saturday at her new apartment.

I already knew that she had sold the property in Auteuil, where I had gone to see her the first time, to a real-estate developer. The price, I now heard, was $1,400,000. Her new address, in the 8th *arrondissement,* not far from the Avenue des Champs-Elysées, proved to be a pleasant apartment building of the early twentieth century, characteristic of the next thrust of expansion after the Baron Haussmann period. I was shown into the salon, which was lighter and fresher than the building's public areas, but somewhat overfurnished. The interior decorators had cut a wide swath through the place: even the walls were overdressed. I recognized some of the pictures I had seen in her house in Auteuil, but not much else looked familiar. After a long wait, Héra emerged, limping; the "grave accident" she had referred to in her telegram had involved an ankle. The intervening years and her periodic rest cures had been kind to her. Her legs were again shrouded from view. She sank into the down cushions, like a modern Récamier, on a divan covered by an immense stole of champagne-colored mink. She launched into what I could see was a standard monologue: her health, money problems, loss of jewelry, lawsuits in profusion, treachery on all sides. She was still complaining when the doors to the dining room were opened and we went in to lunch. We were served some very expensive food by an impeccably groomed butler wearing white gloves as she told me how hard up she was and how well off the French working class *really* was. Back in the salon, stretched out once again on the eight-foot mink-covered sofa, she finally got around to her Valéry papers. She was still classifying them. Did I understand that there were about 400 letters, 80 manuscript poems, and a notebook containing the early drafts of Valéry's book *Charmes?* And how did I like her apartment? I should have seen it when she bought it. A pigpen. Which is why it was such a steal—only $200,000. But she had had to gut it completely and put in another $200,000 to make it habitable. What did I *really* think of it?

A few days before I received Héra's telegram inviting me to lunch, I had had a note from a colleague in Austin. He had just heard from a woman in Houston, who was writing in behalf of a French lawyer friend of hers—I recognized his name as that of one of the three "friends" to whom Héra had asked me to send copies of the *Baudelaire to Beckett* catalogue. He wanted no commission, he said, but was hoping to "embellish Franco-American gallantry" by selling Héra's Valéry memorabilia to some appropriate American buyer, and he was soliciting the help of the Houston woman. She had enclosed a text which gave an account of Valéry's "romance with the lady lawyer . . . a great love story." The three lush folio pages of that text could have been written by the soapy French novelist Delly, by Barbara Cartland, or by Héra—but the typewriter was unmistakably Héra's. For the price and content of the collection my colleague was directed to the Paris address of the Houston woman's lawyer friend. So when Héra told me, before I left her apartment that Saturday, that her one desire was to have her papers given to our Valéry collection in Austin, I mentioned the efforts by the Paris lawyer and the Houston woman to sell them to anybody— including the University of Texas. She seemed embarrassed and said she knew nothing about all that; a misunderstanding on the part of well-meaning friends, she supposed.

About two weeks later Héra called me. She had just learned about the Houston maneuver from her lawyer friend. It was a misunderstanding, as she had supposed, and she asked me to have lunch with her again on Saturday because she had completed the inventory and wanted me to see the papers. I found an excuse not to break bread with her this time but told her I would drop by after lunch. When I got there, she introduced me to her adopted daughter, a dark, melancholy little woman of indeterminate age. They had laid the papers out for me on the dining-room table. The *Charmes* notebook, of about seventy pages, had all the appeal one would expect from that kind of document. It had been worked on between 1917 and 1920 and given to Héra in 1944. There was another, more miscellaneous, notebook, with notes and sketches. The "manuscript poems" included a bound volume entitled "Corona," made up, for the most part, of typed copies of poems. They had been typed by Valéry, she said, but the neatness and precision of the typing were a bit off-putting. From a scholarly point of view there is no real juice to a "manuscript" like that one. In a real manuscript one sees the mind of the writer at work; one follows the path he took to get to wherever he ended up. And it is often an exciting journey. This type-script was mildly decorative, but as a research document, a creative adventure—flat. Outside the bound volume was another group of poems of a minor sort: poems of circumstance largely, some handwritten, most of them typed.

The letters were photocopies and not very sharp or clear. I asked Héra if I could look at the originals. They were in a Swiss bank vault, she said. I'd have to make do with the copies. I looked through the material, making notes as I went along. The letters were the familiar mixture: Valéry, the head—Monsieur Teste—playing games with his heart, *Le Vert Galant.* Some were informative, some amusing, but none, as far as I could see, burned with the intensity of the pages he had written after Héra's crushing announcement to him on Easter Sunday 1944. After I had examined everything, I asked her what the next step was.

"It's all for sale," she said crisply. "Four hundred thousand dollars. It seems more natural for me to think in dollars." Her intentions were now quite clear but I was puzzled about the price. I asked her what she had based her valuation on.

"Nothing in particular," she said. "It just seemed a reasonable figure." Then I remembered that on my previous visit she had told me that the new apartment and its refurbishing had cost her $400,000. A coincidence, perhaps. I told her if she was thinking of the University as buyer rather than merely recipient, I could hardly encourage her. She asked me to put a valuation on the papers. I told her we didn't do that.

"Perhaps the Japanese will be interested," she said. "They're spend-ing a lot of money on things like that these days. Besides, there are more translations of Valéry in Japan than in any other country."

She tried once more to get me to put a figure on the archive. I suggested she get an official French-government-appointed *expert* to make an appraisal. She asked for a name. I recommended Michel Castaing of the firm of Charavay in the Rue de Furstenberg as the most experienced person in the manuscript field. She wrinkled her nose. She couldn't go to Castaing, she said; she was currently in litigation with a member of his family. And besides, she said, you probably know more about these things than any official *expert.* I told her she still ought to hear the facts from somebody else; in that way, she wouldn't think I was trying to influence the result.

She thought about it briefly. "If I do and the appraisal is too low," she said, "I'll keep the papers."

So be it, I said. That encounter took four and a quarter hours. By the time I extricated myself from the quicksand, I had come to the conclusion that I had seen enough of Héra and her papers.

Héra wasn't the only one who had heard I was in Paris. The word had reached Valéry's daughter, too, and a few days later I received a telephone call from a Valéry scholar I knew who had just seen her. She wanted to see me and he asked if I would call her. I did and we made an appointment. She lived in a new apartment building in the Paris suburb of Neuilly, not far from the American Hospital. She was cool—although courteous—at first, but thawed as the afternoon went on. To the extent that our diametrically opposed positions allowed, we got on well.

The Valéry family had sold to the Bibliothèque Nationale, in July, 1972, a major portion of Paul Valéry's archives. Ever since reading the *Baudelaire to Beckett* catalogue, the curator who had been put in charge of sorting and classifying the material at the B.N. had been pleading with me, by correspondence, to turn over a microfilm of our papers to them, offering in exchange an equivalent number of images related to Valéry's work on *Mon Faust.* There was no real incentive to accept such an exchange: their material was standard fare; ours, unique. I asked Agathe what she thought of the idea. She said she fervently hoped I would not accede to the request. I told her, also, that Valéry scholars from many countries—the United States, Canada, Belgium, France, Israel, among them—had been writing, telephoning, working through intermediaries, or just dropping in, in the hope of getting access to the papers. She urged me, again, not to make them available. By the time I left her apartment, I had agreed to restrict the material indefinitely. A few days later I had a very appreciative letter from her and an invitation to join the Paul Valéry Society, a group of scholars devoted to Valéry's work.

Apparently Agathe had spoken to the curator at the Bibliothèque Nationale about my visit because a few months later, in Austin, I received a letter from the young woman telling me it seemed to her that any negotiation in the direction in which she had been moving was, under present conditions, premature and perhaps even out of place.

I now wrote to all the clamoring scholars to let them know that, for the time being at least, the papers were off limits. All were disappointed, understandably, since no find of that importance had ever been made in the field of Valéry studies. But they all took it in good grace, knowing that for a Valéry scholar to cross Valéry's dedicated daughter—or even to take issue with her—would prove a serious professional handicap.

I was more than a little astonished—let's say flabbergasted—a few weeks later when I received from Agathe a letter in which, speaking for herself and her two brothers, Claude and François, she asked that I deposit photocopies of our papers in the Valéryanum at the Bibliothèque Jacques Doucet. She had urged me to refuse to do that for the Bibliothèque Nationale, France's national library, one of the world's three greatest. Why should she now want me to turn over photocopies of the papers to the Doucet? The idea seemed even stranger in light of the fact that the Valéry family had sold, for a substantial sum, the bulk of Paul Valéry's papers to the B.N. While I was meditating on these matters, I received a letter from Agathe's second brother, François, writing as French ambassador to UNESCO, underlining and supporting his sister's request. Obviously I didn't have *all* the facts at my disposal, but the ones I did have inclined me to turn down their request and I did so.

* * * * *

Héra, meanwhile, had been lunching at the Japanese Embassy in Paris; her lawyer friend also, according to a letter he wrote to the colleague of mine who had been approached earlier by the Houston woman. As Héra hadn't heard from me since the summer, the lawyer wanted to know if he should tell her that we were no longer interested. And so I wrote and told him what I had told Héra: that the price she had set on the papers went so far beyond the market history for such things, there was not much point in talking. That brought me two letters from Héra. In one, dated November 16, she explained that she had written the other one six weeks before but hadn't mailed it. It had been lying on her desk, unsigned, since then. The earlier letter said that she wanted only to see her papers come to Texas and had chosen an *expert* for her appraisal. He had come up with a figure a little lower than her own. Should she send it?

The more recent letter apologized for the lawyer's new inquiry. She had been vexed when she received a photocopy of his letter. He had written it on his own initiative. The weather had been bad and her health, too, and not being able to go to Texas, she just felt the need to lean on someone else, so not wanting to complicate things, she had decided not to send me the letter she had written. But now that she had seen my answer to the lawyer, she realized she should have sent it and here it was. As for the *expert*, did I realize they got 3% of the appraised value? she asked. And if she had to have a second one, that would be 6%. She wasn't sure she could survive that kind of gouging. I wrote and told her again we were not the customer she was looking for. She needed to look elsewhere for a solution.

Héra's letter said nothing about the Japanese, but another Valéry scholar who had talked with her told me she was still working on them and taking soundings for Iranian petrodollars, as well. And still another visitor reported that Héra had told him, in a voice choked with emotion, that she would *never* part with those papers, not even if faced with starvation.

At the end of the following March, I received from her a letter dated February 8. With it she enclosed one "expertise" and one "impression." The impression—dated 4 October 1977—was on the letterhead of a well-known French book dealer, most of whose activity revolved around auction sales, not of manuscript material, except in a minor, incidental way, but principally of books. He was of the opinion—he used the word "impression"—that Héra's archive was worth in the neighborhood of something like $300,000. I gathered that this must have been the "appraisal" she had referred to earlier as being a little lower than her own.

The other document was a rather different kind of "expertise." In France appraisal documents are customarily prepared by specialist dealers in day-to-day contact with the market. This one had been done by a professor at a Swiss university. It filled five folio pages. After a long, melodramatic introduction, Héra's Swiss professor concluded that the collection was "priceless." Nevertheless, if one *had* to set a figure on it, his judgment would be as follows: the notebook of early drafts for *Charmes*, $37,500; the second notebook, odds and ends of a more personal nature, $22,500; the bound volume of poems labeled "Corona," mostly typed by Valéry, $40,000; the larger group of similar material, unbound, $50,000; and, finally, the correspondence, 415 letters of which about two-thirds were handwritten, $275,000. Total for everything: $425,000.

I thought back to the group of letters Valéry had written to the sculptor

Renée Vautier, which had been offered to me by Jacques Lambert at $20,000 and, after I had turned it down, had been sold in open competition at Sotheby's, in London, for a little under $7,000. Héra had 415 letters as against Renée Vautier's 150, about 2.75 times as many. On the basis of the Sotheby price, that would bring the theoretical price of Héra's letters to a little under $20,000. If we were to take quite literally everything the Swiss professor had written about them and in a burst of generosity say that Héra's letters were twice as good as Renée Vautier's, we could push the price up to nearly $40,000. And if we factored in something for inflation in view of the passage of three years since the Sotheby sale, we could perhaps justify a price of $50,000, possibly a bit more. But $275,000! And if that were true of the letters, the same principle applied to the poems and notebooks.

I wrote to Héra that her February-8 letter and its enclosures had just arrived and I could only repeat what I had written to her four months earlier: that I appreciated her thinking of us as a home for her papers but I preferred to leave the field open for others.

She was glad to feel free to look elsewhere, she replied, but couldn't I tell her what I *would* have been willing to pay? She had made a more careful search of her storage areas and come up with a lot more material—shattering things. She was exhausted. I ignored her but she came back again insisting I name a price. I told her then what I had told her before: count us out.

All during the fall and winter I was bombarded with letters and telephone calls from people seeking to interest us in Héra's papers—all manner of people, each one more surprising than the last: Arthur King Peters, then president of the French-American Foundation, said his only interest was in finding a good home for the letters in the United States. One day I had a call from a man telephoning in behalf of Mrs. Paul Mellon. He told me about the collection and asked me if we would be interested in acquiring it. I asked him what the price was. A million dollars, he said. I told him we were aware of the situation, had been in touch with the owner for some time, but had no real interest in it when she was asking $400,000. Even less now. He asked me questions, to which I gave honest answers. Finally, he asked if I would be willing to talk to Mrs. Mellon about our experience. I told him I would. In a few minutes my phone rang and it was "Bunny Mellon." We chatted for a long time, exchanging questions and answers. She said she had distrusted the woman from the start. She had been introduced to her in

Paris by—she mentioned a woman whose family name is one of the oldest and most resonant in French history and literature. A familiar scenario. She was very grateful for my answers to her questions and asked me to be sure to let her know when I would next be in New York, so we could talk more.

The most prickly of the proddings we got came in the form of a letter from Monte Carlo addressed to one of our manuscript librarians, who had recently returned from a stay in New York City. There she had met someone who, after her return to Texas, had sent her name and academic coordinates to a friend of his in Monaco named Douglas Cooper: "the terrible-tempered Mr. Cooper," as he had been known for years in art circles. Cooper, whose family had accumulated money through Australian land speculation and other means, had become a collector of modern art, with a particular interest in Cubist painting. In the process, he had worked his way into the Picasso inner circle. One day in the spring of 1965, I was having lunch with an old English friend on Beacon Hill who had known Cooper for years. *Life with Picasso* had just been published in London and my host had received a long, spluttery letter from Cooper, which he read to me. In it Cooper described a party he had given, the climax of which involved the burning of a copy of *Life with Picasso*. Since the French Communist Party and Picasso's courtiers were doing everything they could, by protest and petition (and eventually by legal action), to discredit the book, Cooper had decided to go everyone else one better by staging his own auto-da-fé and thus demonstrate to Picasso his loyalty and especially his worthiness.

Cooper knew, as his letter to the librarian made clear, that the Humanities Research Center at the University of Texas at Austin had a world-renowned collection of modern French literary research materials. But his intelligence network hadn't caught up with the fact that I was responsible for that collection and at that moment was Acting Director of the Research Center. And so he wrote boldly to my young colleague about an unnamed friend of his, "a very old lady" who had been the mistress of Paul Valéry toward the end of his life. (I don't think Héra, who spent so much time and money at her various Fountains of Youth, would have been happy with that description.) Valéry had written her at least three letters a week in which he recorded his daily life, his thoughts, emotional crises, health, passions, literary projects— the many things that a lovelorn and solitary old man wishes to put on record. All these papers, he said, were marvelously classified in chronological order, with envelopes and dates, each in a separate transparent envelope, the whole bound into thirteen volumes of fine quality, of which one specimen was visible in Paris. He said the owner had to sell for financial reasons—a delightful turn of phrase, I thought. The only point he needed to make clear was—and he underlined the next nine words—*she absolutely refuses to have anything to do with* that appalling crook called Carlton LAKE.

Cooper's purpose in writing, he said, was to try to prevent the collection from being broken up, or to prevent it from being published badly by a fraud and ignoramus such as Lake—a parasite and poisonous snake. The supposed GILOT-PICASSO farrago of scandal and dishonesty was proof enough to make anyone beware of *him*. The owner had talked to Cooper, he said, on the basis of four million French francs—not far, at that time, from a million dollars. Daniel Sickles, an American collector long resident in Paris, had told him that was too much money. Perhaps it could be negotiated. In any case, since he knew about the richness in modern European literature of our library, he felt that this unique corpus of manuscripts with its full poetic flow of amorous inspiration would interest us.

Then the dealers began calling—a slew of them from the East Coast to the West. The million-dollar figure apparently fascinated them. They would sound almost reverential as they intoned it. As the months wore on, they began to suggest that the price was open to discussion and solicited an offer—any reasonable one would be studied.

Christmas was on the horizon and Héra sent me holiday greetings. Her health had been poor but she expected much better from the New Year. As for her papers, she had made a decision which she believed would bring her great tranquility of spirit. I sensed that having run through all the possibilities for a private sale, she had decided to go the auction route. She was hoping to see me soon again in Paris and asked me to keep her informed about my activities. That would give her great pleasure, she said, because, as I knew, she felt very warmly about me.

A month later, I received a large, glossy, color-illustrated catalogue of a book and manuscript sale scheduled for late February, 1979, at the Hôtel Drouot in Paris. It included three of the five elements of Héra's Valéry papers: the notebook of early drafts for *Charmes;* the notebook of thoughts and reflections of a more general nature, decorated with sketches; the bound volume of twenty-three poems, only seven of them autograph, entitled "Corona." The correspondence had been withheld from sale, as well as the group of poems of circumstance.

After the sale I learned that all three lots had been bought by a Swiss dealer for an unidentified client in Switzerland. He had previously been observed in the Paris saleroom on December 15th. That earlier sale had included a unique proof copy of a collection of Valéry's poems which was to have been called simply "Poésies." Publication had been aborted by Valéry just before its scheduled appearance in 1922. He had decorated the copy with thirty-seven drawings and given it to a friend. It had been handsomely bound by the leading binder of the mid-twentieth century, Paul Bonet. Knowledgeable buyers had been expecting it to go for no more than 100,000 francs. Bidding against the *expert* and the *commissaire-priseur*, the Swiss buyer had paid 500,000 francs for it.

Longtime observers of French auctions have often wondered just how closely the *expert*—the specialist dealer who prepares the catalogue and reads the description as each lot is offered—and the *commissaire-priseur*—the auctioneer—coordinate their efforts to make prices keep moving along. Absentee buyers who send in bids rarely expect to get an object for a penny less than their bid, although in theory such bids are to be used competitively. But since the *expert*'s estimate is the basis of the bidding, it just seems to work out that when some absent person or institution like, for example, the Tahiti Museum, bids on a manuscript of—say—Gauguin's *Noa Noa*, which the *expert* had estimated at 250,000 francs, they wind up paying 250,000 francs, as they did that Wednesday afternoon, February 28, 1979, in the same sale that included Héra's things. Curious how it happens to work out that way time after time. And even when the bidder is in the saleroom, bids often have a way of bouncing back and forth until they reach the desired level.

The Swiss buyer was hot for Valéry; that had already been proved on December 15th when he paid five times what anyone expected he'd have to pay in order to get the volume of "Poésies." When Héra's three Valéry lots came up, he bought them—one, two, three. The *Charmes* notebook—the first of the three—had been tagged at 180,000 francs. He paid 190,000. The second was the miscellaneous notebook, estimated at 100,000. For that he paid 90,000, evening out the overage on the previous lot. The final one, the bound volume called "Corona," made up mostly of typed copies of poems with a few drawings, carried a very high estimate: 200,000 francs. There he was let off the hook with a 10% discount at 180,000 francs: in all, about a 7% increase above the Swiss professor's rosy estimates. What it took to achieve that record, one can only guess, because them as knows don't talk—or rather, talk only to each other. One correspondent for a leading book-trade journal referred to ". . . some strange goings-on at Paris auctions recently. . . ." Of course, as unbelievably high as they were, those prices were less than half of their proportionate share of the million dollars Héra had been shooting for.

Ten days after the sale, Héra wrote me an ecstatic letter and sent me clippings. She told me of two other follies committed by the new Valéry buff with the bottomless purse. So you see, she said, you're going to be able to mark up your Valéry inventory in Austin. She hoped my work wasn't proving too burdensome and asked me to believe, dear friend, in her faithful remembrance.

It was inevitable that the two remaining elements of Héra's Valéry papers—the unbound group of typed poems, similar to the bound volume titled "Corona," and the letters the poet had addressed to her—should show up at auction sooner or later. And in October, 1982, they did, in—not inappropriately—Monte Carlo. The perceptive, pseudonymous Anatole Braun, covering for the *Antiquarian Book Monthly Review* this last gasp of an overexploited passion, referred to it as the "first auction of love letters sold by the recipient." Héra's maneuvers had become so widely known by now that the dealers stayed away from the sale and genuine collectors were few. One dealer quoted the old saying, *"Ça sent la macaque"*—It smells to high heaven. The correspondence had been broken up into small lots. Monsieur Braun, a seasoned observer of auction antics, had the feeling that many of the lots were being bought in by the *expert* (i.e., knocked down but not actually sold). About one-third of the way into the sale, the Bibliothèque Nationale, which had received a special allotment for the occasion, began to participate. (The earlier lots had not interested them.) In French auctions, State institutions are not allowed to bid; they wait until a lot is knocked down, then step in and exercise their right of pre-emption. And so from that point on, as the auctioneer's hammer fell, in favor of the triumphant bid of "Mr. X" or "Mrs. Y," as Monsieur Braun referred to these possibly spectral—and in any case, unfulfilled—buyers, the functionary representing the B.N. (or some other of the group of French cultural departments that had teamed up in accordance with a carefully orchestrated purchasing strategy) spoke the prescribed phrase and ownership was transferred to the State. For a few of the lots toward the end, the crossfire between "Mr. X" and "Mrs. Y" drove prices to astronomical levels before the hammer fell and the pre-emption ritual took place.

During the sale Madame Voilier was closeted in her hotel room. Was it discretion? Fear? A sprained ankle, I was told. Her adopted daughter, however, was in the saleroom, visibly crestfallen at the results, which had fallen far short of their ambitious projections.

A postscript to the *ABMR* article reported that the *Gazette de l'Hôtel Drouot*'s account of the sale's official results omitted from its tabulation approximately 35% of the lots, ". . . which seems to confirm a high percentage of buying-in" [i.e., unsold lots]. *Caveat emptor.*

*　*　*　*　*

Shortly before leaving on my next trip to Paris, I heard from another elderly lady, this one in the south of France, who introduced herself as "an old friend of Paul Valéry." She had letters, photographs, books, and other "precious documents," memorabilia of her relations with him during World War II. Valéry had honored by his presence one of her family's country houses and had written there portions of *Mon Faust.* Would I be interested in these documents and if so under what conditions (i.e., how much)? She sent me a few samples:

> . . . tired, without letup . . . nearly incapable of work. . . . If only I could still write poems. But alas! Everything works against it: man, age, circumstances, and that weariness of oneself that sums it all up at the end. . . .

By now I had had my fill of Valéry's lady-loves—and his *Weltschmerz.* I closed the door gently on that one and tiptoed quietly away.

*　*　*　*　*

ADDENDUM

In clearing out the folders of papers relating to my Valéry adventures, I came across several obituaries of Douglas Cooper, who died in a London hospital in 1984, on April Fool's Day. The gentlest reference to his temperament and personality came in John Russell's restrained notice in *The New York Times* of Thursday, April 5th:

> Mr. Cooper was often criticized for what his detractors called the brutality with which he conducted himself in controversy. . . .

And elsewhere.

Afterword

P rivate collecting has always seemed to me one of the more pardonable forms of self-indulgence. Collecting for the expanding needs of a great research library, however, needs no apology: Along with the usual satisfactions inherent in collecting, it brings a sense of helping to push back the frontiers of knowledge and—just possibly—the chance to "light a candle of understanding . . . which shall not be put out."

But when Harry Ransom, the founder of the Humanities Research Center at the University of Texas at Austin, first proposed that I exchange the private delights of private collecting for the broader concerns of institutional collecting, I had to take it on faith that the other kinds of satisfaction would follow. Twenty years later, I know that they have. Scholars, writers, researchers of all kinds have found their way to the (now renamed) Harry Ransom Humanities Research Center, and in steadily increasing numbers they have come to work with the French collections here. That long-awaited book on Toulouse-Lautrec is on its way. We have helped to publish lost or unknown works by Alfred Jarry and Jean Cocteau. We have become involved in a long-range publishing project based on the works of H.-P. Roché. Marcel Duchamp and Erik Satie are on our publishing horizon.

We have loaned our materials to major exhibitions all over the world: time and again to the Pompidou Center and other French museums; to Pontus Hulten's giant Futurism show at the Palazzo Grassi in Venice; to the Grolier Club in New York; to museums and libraries in Switzerland and Germany and elsewhere in Europe, and as close to home as the Menil Collection in Houston. We have presented Samuel Beckett—greatest of all mid-twentieth-century French writers, whatever his country of birth—in a more extensive exhibition and catalogue of his work than had ever been done before.

Musicologists by the hundreds have poured into Austin to study the manuscripts of Ravel, Debussy, Fauré, and others. We have brought to light and made available hitherto-unknown material by Jean-Paul Sartre and Picasso, André Gide and Mallarmé. Even Céline's old *bête noire*, François Mauriac, has moved into the pantheon of Gallimard's *Bibliothèque de la Pléïade* with an assist from Texas. Our collections of Man Ray, Jean Genet, Antonin Artaud, Louis Aragon, Colette, and the ultimate novelist, Marcel Proust, have drawn their devotees to Austin— they and ever so many others. The result? We have contributed to a wide variety of literary histories, biographies, critical analyses, bibliographies—scholarship at its best.

Today, the Texas French collections are even better known in France than they are in Texas. Does that beat collecting for oneself? You bet it does!

C. L.

Index